EUGENE ARAM

EUGENE ARAM

LITERARY HISTORY
and TYPOLOGY
of the SCHOLAR-CRIMINAL

Nancy Jane Tyson

Archon Books
1983

First published 1983 as an Archon Book,
as an imprint of The Shoe String Press, Inc.,
Hamden, Connecticut 06514

Printed in the United States of America

The paper in this book meets the
guidelines for permanence and durability
of the Committee of Production Guidelines for
Book Longevity of the Council on Library Resources.

Library of Congress Cataloging in Publication Data

Tyson, Nancy Jane.
  Eugene Aram : literary history and typology
of the scholar-criminal.
  Bibliography: p.
  Includes index.
  1. English literature—19th century—History and
criticism. 2. Aram, Eugene, 1704–1759, in fiction,
drama, poetry, etc. 3. Aram, Eugene, 1704–1759.
4. Crime and criminals in literature. 5. Crime and
criminals—England—Yorkshire—Biography. 6. Scholars
in literature. 7. Lytton, Edward Bulwer Lytton, Baron,
1803–1873. Eugene Aram. I. Title.
PR469.A65T9 1983   820'.9'351   83-8790
ISBN 0-208-01996-0

To
my father

CONTENTS

PLATES

ACKNOWLEDGMENTS

F OREMOST AMONG MANY contributors to the research and writing of this book is Richard D. Altick, Regents' Professor of English Emeritus at The Ohio State University, for whose advice and friendship I am most grateful. He was director of the dissertation from which this study originated, and his insightful criticism and scholarly interest have inspired every phase of the work.

Numerous other individuals have assisted in a variety of ways. They include Professors Richard Martin, Charles Babcock, and Mark Auburn of The Ohio State University; Miss E. Allen, Curator of the Hunterian Museum, Royal College of Surgeons, London; Martin Bailey, Scolar Press, London; Scott Bennett, Special Collections Consultant, University Library, University of Illinois at Urbana-Champaign; Professor John Clubbe, University of Kentucky; Miss Sybilla Jane Flower, London, England; Catherine Jestin, Librarian, The Lewis Walpole Library, Farmington, Connecticut; William R. Johnson, Department of Rare Books, Cornell University Library, Ithaca, New York; Mr. Arnold Kellett, Knaresborough, Yorkshire; Michael Slater, University of London; John Vazquez, Columbus, Ohio; and John Ragusa. To the Division of Special Collections and to the Interlibrary Loan Staff of The Ohio State University Library particular appreciation is due for their efficient response to my many requests for obscure books and other materials. I wish to thank as well James and Julie Felty for their sympathetic criticism and many helpful discoveries.

Finally, a special debt of gratitude is owed to my father, A. Mervin Tyson, to whom this book is dedicated and without whose patient encouragement it could never have been completed.

N.J.T.

INTRODUCTION

O N THE EIGHTH of February, 1745, Daniel Clark vanished from the town of Knaresborough, Yorkshire — leaving behind a new bride and a number of outraged creditors.[1] Clark, a shoemaker, had married into a fortune sizable for one of his station, on the strength of which he had recently borrowed or purchased on credit at least £150 worth of leather, jewelry, and various household goods. These having vanished along with the man, the local merchants at once suspected fraud. They advertised for Clark in the March 12 *York Courant* as "a thin, pale looking Pock-broke Man, about five Foot six or eight Inches high, aged about twenty-three Years, has a very great Impediment and Stammering in his Speech."[2] Despite the unflatteringly explicit description and a £15 reward offer, Clark was not seen or heard of again. Oddly, his horse, the obvious expedient for a man in flight and presumably burdened with material wealth, remained tethered in the stable.

Several weeks later, Knaresborough lost another citizen, its schoolmaster since 1734. Eugene Aram, a self-educated gardener's son and a formulator of unusually advanced linguistic theories, had earned from the community a respect beyond his inherited social position. The eccentric ways attributed to him — his secretiveness, his customary long cloak and slouch hat, his habit of wheeling around "at once bodily" rather than turning his head when approached from behind — were regarded as only the inscrutable demeanor of the scholar. Aram, though seventeen years older, had been a close acquaintance of Clark, along with a husky, broad-shouldered "linning-weaver" named Richard Houseman. These two, the last to have been seen with Clark late on the night he disappeared, were implicated in the affair but not formally prosecuted at the time. Under the weight of some suspicion, Aram left Knaresborough secretly in April, deserting his wife and children.

Anna Aram, by most accounts, had been treated during her married life as more a chattel than a wife. In the years that followed, she sometimes hinted that it was in her power to have her husband hanged should he ever reappear. Whatever may have been the tenor of village gossip, there were no further developments in the case until nearly fourteen years later. On August 1, 1758, lime diggers uncovered on nearby Thistle Hill a human skeleton, which rumor at once conjectured to be Clark's. At the resulting inquest, Houseman was required to handle the thighbone, in accord with the still prevalent belief that a dead body could by some sign identify its murderer. Ironically, something of the kind did happen. Houseman, nervous and incautious, blurted out with incriminating certainty, "This is no more Dan Clark's bone than it is mine!" Under more rigorous questioning, he led the authorities to a second skeleton, which he swore was Clark's, unearthed in St. Robert's Cave, just outside the town, in exactly the position he predicted. Further testimony by Anna Aram revealed that her husband had conspired with Houseman and Clark on the fatal night, and that the following day she had discovered fragments of charred clothing in the dust pile and traces of blood on a scarf worn by Houseman. In private, she had confronted her husband with misgivings, whereupon he had threatened to shoot her. Fear had kept her silent ever since. On the strength of these developments, Aram and Houseman were formally charged with murder.

Aram, then employed as usher of a grammar school at Lynn, Norfolk, was discovered by an odd coincidence, arrested on August 19, and confined for nearly a year in York Castle to await trial. Since Anna, as his wife, could not legally testify in court, the Crown lawyers faced a dilemma. They could effectively try *either* Houseman or Aram with the incriminating testimony of the other, but on evidence otherwise entirely circumstantial they could not convict both. Apparently they settled upon Aram as the mastermind and arranged for Houseman to turn king's evidence in exchange for his own acquittal. His testimony, implausible and obviously fabricated for self-preservation, was nonetheless the primary ground for Aram's conviction.

However just or unjust, Aram's sentence was death. The condemned man, who maintained his innocence to the last, was brought to the gallows on August 6, 1759, already half dead, having attempted suicide with a razor in the early morning hours. His body was left to hang in chains in Knaresborough Forest near the spot where the crime was allegedly committed.

The case roused considerable interest, which intensified with the passage of time. Well before Eugene Aram was executed, the booksellers were ready with the typical cheap pamphlet versions of his life, and for a century and a half thereafter he was chronicled among the cutthroats and footpads of the ever popular literature of true crime. At the time of Aram's death there were few who sympathized with him, and even fewer who believed him innocent. By the century's close, however, his example was serving the cause of liberal reformers opposed to capital punishment, and he had begun to be viewed as something of a martyr. Two novels of political doctrine, William Godwin's *Caleb Williams* (1794) and Thomas Holcroft's *Memoirs of Bryan Perdue* (1805), deplored his execution for its waste of human potential. Inspired by the unusual circumstances of Aram's case, they questioned the morality of executing a man for a crime committed years before.

In 1829, Thomas Hood's ballad "The Dream of Eugene Aram" recalled the ruinous outcome of Aram's life with dramatic rather than reformist intent. This somber work, the first literary production to which Aram's character is central, was immensely popular in its own day and remained in vogue as a recitation piece well into the latter part of the century. Though the poem did not absolve the man or excuse his crime, it ensured the survival of his memory for a considerable time to come.

If Aram's resurrection was brought on primarily by Hood, it was Edward Bulwer who made him a hero. Hood's Aram, for all his melancholy dignity, was still a guilt-tormented murderer, and his crime a weighty offense. But in Bulwer's novel *Eugene Aram*, published in 1832 and partly inspired by the poem, the hero is noble of soul and exalted in learning, far above the common order. Bulwer became the murderer's apologist, defending him on the grounds of redeeming intellect and motive without denying his guilt. Under the novelist's hand, those details which had tinged Aram's life and character with disrepute were mitigated or ignored, and those which had spared him complete infamy were heightened to near exoneration.

Aram was, in this new incarnation, even more widely known than in his own day. W.T. Moncrieff's *Eugene Aram; or, St. Robert's Cave* (1832), an adaptation of Bulwer's novel, was the first of several stage versions to capitalize on its success. Later in the century, William Gorman Wills's *Eugene Aram* (1873) provided the renowned actor Sir Henry Irving one of his most famous and successful roles. Queen Victoria knew Aram's story, as did most of her subjects, and called it "fearfully interesting."[3] In fact, the literary treatments of the nineteenth century had so effectively revived the memory of the case that as late as 1901 Maj. Arthur Griffiths, in his comprehensive, three-volume *Mysteries of Police and Crime*, considered it "too familiar to need more than a passing reference."[4] In 1904, a historian could still refer to "the famous Eugene Aram,"[5] and another in 1913 could open with the observation that he "was, as all the world knows, executed on the 6th of August, 1759."[6] Aram had met, in 1759, a shameful death. Now, a tragic hero, he would survive the nineteenth century by more than a decade.

It is the purpose of this book to trace the Aram theme through its various manifestations in history and fiction. Aram himself is the focal point, and for inherent interest he deserves to be. From this main purpose derive several corollary aims. One of these is to present an unusual case history of the fictional process through which man becomes myth. The Aram who became so familiar in poem, novel, and drama to so many generations was of course mostly imaginary and much grander than life — a composite only loosely drawn from the historical original. Therefore, to permit comparison, chapter 1 reconstructs the events of Aram's life from a variety of largely fugitive sources. (See Appendix.)

The sections which follow, chapters 2 through 5, relate the popular literary and dramatic history of the Aram theme from the late eighteenth into the early twentieth centuries. As much as possible, I have allowed Eugene to lead the way — into whatever forgotten passages he might. I have pursued him round many an unexpected turn and into the company of some marvelous eccentrics. A second adjunct purpose, then, is the unfolding of the rare period interest which the study affords, for Aram seems to have appealed remarkably to Victorian tastes and attitudes. He is everywhere in the Victorian cultural scene, and the more one looks for and finds him there, the more odd it seems that a figure once so much a part of the times should have been by now so nearly forgotten.

A final purpose in this book, the typological, informs it all but culminates in chapter 6, where I have ranked Aram among similar figures of note in both history and literature. The scholar-criminal, a type of which Aram is a classic and influential example, has inspired some of the world's greatest writers, among them Marlowe, Goethe, Byron, Dickens, Dostoyevsky. Aram himself was never immortalized by such as these, but he interested other authors who appeared great in the perspective of their own times. As they and the truer masters knew, there is an irresistable mystique about the man who, learned above the average, stoops to evil. It is that quality of ominous mystery and sinister paradox which lends so uncommon a fascination to the story of Aram.

1 "EQUAL TO EITHER FORTUNE"
The Life, Trial, and Execution
of Eugene Aram, 1704-1759

THE INCONGRUITY which seems always to lie at the heart of Aram's story begins even before his birth, affecting his social station, and perhaps, by heredity, his natural gifts. Intellectual, haughty and aloof by nature, he was born to a rank beneath his capacity, in a family that had once held considerable status. This fate, compounding the usual frustrations of the "poor scholar," may well have contributed to his antisocial and ultimately criminal bent. The brief autobiography he composed in York Castle on the eve of his execution describes his maternal ancestry somewhat vaguely as "substantial and reputable." On the paternal side, however, was a strong tradition of former prominence. Aram was, behind a veil of assumed modesty, immensely proud of it:

> My father's ancestors were of great antiquity and consideration in this county [Yorkshire], and originally British. Their surname is local; for they were formerly lords of the town of Haram, or Aram, on the southern banks of the Tees, and opposite to Sockburn, in Bishopric [i.e., the Bishopric of Durham]; and appear in the records of St. Mary's, at York, among many charitable names, early and considerable benefactors to that abbey. They, many centuries ago, removed from these parts, and were settled, under the fee of the lords Mowbray in Nottinghamshire, at Aram, or Aram-Park, in the neighbourhood of Newark-upon-Trent; where they were possessed of no less than three knights fees in the reign of Edward III. Their lands, I find not whether by purchase or marriage, came into the hands of the present Lord Lexington. While the name existed in this county, some of them were several times high sheriffs for this

county; and one was professor of divinity, if I remember right, at Oxford, and died at York. The last of the chief of this family, was Thomas Aram, Esq; sometime of Gray's-Inn, and one of the commissioners of the salt-office, under the late Queen Anne. He married one of the co-heiresses of Sir John Coningsby of North-Mims, in Hertfordshire. His seat, which was his own estate, was at the Wild, near Shenley, in Hertfordshire, where I saw him, and where he died, without issue.

Many more anecdotes are contained in my papers, which are not present; yet these perhaps may be thought more than enough, as they may be consider'd rather as ostentatious than pertinent; but the first was always far from me.[1]

There are sources which support Aram's claims of pedigree in a general way, although some details are unverifiable. His ancestral Yorkshire village of "Haram, or Aram, on the southern banks of the Tees" exists today as Eryholme, and at least one document from William Farrer's compendium of *Early Yorkshire Charters* corroborates his reference to religious grants.[2] The high sheriffs Aram mentions are represented, in the singular at least, by Sir William de Eryam, who held that office for Yorkshire in the fifth year of Richard II's reign, 1381–82.[3] The presence of the Aram family in Nottinghamshire after the migration there from Yorkshire is readily confirmed,[4] and, in times more recent, the existence of Thomas Aram, Esq., whom Aram says he met.[5]

It is certain that a relatively powerful family named Aram had a place in history—first in Yorkshire and afterward in Nottinghamshire. But that alone is not conclusive proof of Eugene Aram's descent from their line, and we can hardly rely on his word. He was ambitious and self-seeking. Habitually, when he found himself in new surroundings, he would insinuate his way into polite company and hide his questionable past. Yet for this very reason it is not difficult to imagine the meeting between Eugene—the young, poor relation—and Thomas, the aging last representative of his race. That Eugene's own father came from Nottinghamshire further authenticates their connection with the formerly great. Although Eugene himself is untrustworthy, the tradition of past eminence proceeded not only from him but from his more credible parent. And finally, there is the argument of heredity. Aram was proud, aloof, and intelligent. Some said he was sensitive by nature, as his love of books and botany would suggest. In build, physiognomy, bearing, and inclination he was the aristocrat *manqué*.

Despite his claims to illustrious ancestry, Aram's immediate family was of modest status. Aram himself is described in the court records as a "yeoman," rather than a "gentleman." Of his mother there is no record, but the father, Peter Aram, gained some modest recognition of his own. Peter, although originally of Nottinghamshire, was employed as gardener for Sir Edward Blackett, at Newby Hall near Ripon, Yorkshire, when Eugene was born in 1704. He had come to Sir Edward with no less a recommendation than that of Dr. Crompton, bishop of London. Local tradition in later years remembered the elder Aram as industrious, irreproachable in character, and learned to a degree remarkable for one who was necessarily self-taught. Peter was highly skilled in botany and served in his time several of the northern Yorkshire gentry. When Thomas Gent, a prominent Yorkshire printer, published a history of Ripon in 1733, the volume was "introduced by a Poem on the surprizing Beauties of Studeley Park, with a Description of the venerable Ruins of Fountains Abbey, written by Mr. Peter Aram."[6] By Eric Watson's estimate in allusion to Dr. Johnson, the piece is "'like a dog walking on his hinder legs; it is not well done, but you are surprised to find it done at all.'"[7]

During his youth Eugene, like his father, was fortunate in the patronage of the Blackett family. Much of his early childhood and adolescence was spent at Newby Hall, which had been designed for Sir Edward Blackett by Sir Christopher Wren, who had personally selected its site. Little besides the barest facts is known of Eugene's upbringing. Beginning with his sixth year, he was taken away from the grand setting of the manor to the nearby village of Bondgate for schooling. For seven years thereafter, he lived about ten miles removed from his family, yet his father's influence is evident in the son's tastes for gardening and intellectual pursuits, as well as in his self-conscious pride in family heritage. At thirteen, Eugene ended his formal education, and his father's small library at Newby was opened to him. Eugene was employed during this time as attendant to Sir Edward, who encouraged the boy's studies, now primarily in mathematics. It was, no doubt, Aram's interest and ability in that field which led Sir Edward's fourth son, Christopher, to offer him at sixteen a clerkship in his London "accompting house." Perhaps it was on his journey southward that Eugene called on his wealthy elderly relation, Thomas Aram, in Hertfordshire.

Eugene's first employment in London, Dickensian in the images it evokes, could hardly have been pleasant and was certainly brief. Within a few months, he contracted smallpox. He returned home without regret to convalesce and to renew his studies — having shifted his interests to the humanities and, particularly, the classical languages.

Despite this one bout with illness, Aram appears never to have been sickly or disfigured. He grew into a sound and comely manhood and said in later years that as a youth he could throw any opponent in wrestling. At maturity he stood about five feet eight inches, tall for that time, and was commonly described as "'remarkably straight limbed, and well made.'"[8] He bore a gentlemanly demeanor, was very clean and careful in his dress, and usually wore, it is said, a blue coat lined with white, or a black coat. He was regularly seen in the coldest of weather pursuing his habitual secluded walks in a "horseman's great coat" and a "flapped" or "slouched" hat. The standard descriptions of Aram's physiognomy coincide well with the few portraits of him that have survived. He was, unlike Bulwer's dark hero, fair-haired, with cold blue eyes, a high, broad forehead, high cheekbones, and a bold aquiline nose—features most consonant with his proud bearing and aristocratic lineage.

The exact chronology of Aram's early maturity is nowhere recorded, but some time prior to 1731 he had become established at Gouthwaite Hall, the home of Dr. Craven, a clergyman, near Ramsgill. There he began what was to become his vocation, instructing the sons of respectable and prosperous farmers in the district. By his own account, what time he did not devote to his teaching duties he spent teaching himself Greek and Latin grammar. Yet he seems not to have slighted his pupils, for all his studious application to the midnight parsing and tedious memorization he describes. Nearly all the recorded reminiscences of his students at Ramsgill and later at Knaresborough and Lynn are favorable. One of his Ramsgill charges, in after years, described him as "'a somewhat rigid disciplinarian, but a famous scholar.'"[9] Other reports suggest that his discipline was more commonly effected by sarcasm than by physical punishment. A favorite tactic of his, when he had married and had children of his own, was to invite his daughter Sally to class, shaming the boys with her superior recitation. Several of his former students transcended such embarrassment to attain positions of eminence—among them William Craven (son of the Dr. Craven at Gouthwaite Hall), who became well known as a philanthropist and as professor of Arabic at St. John's College, Cambridge; and James Burney (brother of the novelist), who accompanied Captain Cook on his historic voyages and later won the admiralty. The awed respect which Aram's hauteur and fervid scholarship evoked from his students seems not to have diminished their devotion to him. Some time after his execution, two of them, now Oxford scholars, came up to Knaresborough to vandalize the shop and threaten the life of Houseman, whose testimony had convicted Aram.

Eugene Aram. From an engraving belonging to E. R. Watson, reproduced in
Eugene Aram: His Life and Trial (1913). Said by a contemporary of Aram's to have
been an authentic likeness.

The single brief return to a program of supervised tuition which Aram mentions in his autobiography was his one month of classical study under the guidance of the Reverend John Adcock of Burnsall. It seems to have taken place while Eugene was employed at Ramsgill, perhaps during an interval in the school year. The experience is interesting largely for the personality of his tutor, whose reputation as a true eccentric contrasts markedly with what we know of his taciturn and solemn disciple. It is told of Mr. Adcock that once upon ascending to the pulpit and discovering his sermon to have been misplaced, he announced that he would instead "read a passage of Holy Scripture worth ten of it." On a later occasion, some unknown prankster, no doubt inspired by the former incident, had shuffled the pages of Adcock's sermon out of sequence and bound them firmly—whereupon the minister proceeded to read it straight through, leaving the burden of sense with his congregation. Once, at a wedding, the bride being reluctant to vow obedience, Mr. Adcock softly concurred "that it was a rather awkward clause and they would skip on to the next."[10] This man, in his own day and after, was a local legend— that and his classical erudition being, it seems, the only traits he shared with his sometime pupil.

Not long after his tutorial with Mr. Adcock, Eugene, then twenty-eight years of age, took a bride. His choice proved disastrous to both parties, not least in the matter of obedience. Anna Spence was part Jewish in descent, described as a "tidy little body," a "weak, 'soft' kind of woman" of about middle size with dark brown eyes and a prominent nose.[11] She was, except for the prominent nose, the near antithesis of her husband. It is clear that from the start he was cruel to her. She later told a friend, almost charitably, that Eugene was "a very high, proud man, who made her an indifferent husband."[12] He believed himself so far above her that he refused to acknowledge her in public and, if obliged to accompany her, insisted that she walk several paces behind him. The story is also told that to spite her he once dressed a "shapely boy" in women's attire and paraded the streets with his arm around the "girl's" waist. Years later, Anna Aram would precipitate her husband's arrest and conviction (not, one suspects, without satisfaction). He, in turn, would go to the gallows accusing her of infidelity, of which there was no evidence and (more tellingly) not the least suspicion in village gossip.

Eugene and Anna, despite their differences and his consuming devotion to scholarship, had at least eight children—five girls and three boys. Two of the girls died young. Another, Sally, was like her father in disposition, intellect, and appearance. She was a "'LONELY girl,' [who] cared nothing about 'dress,' and 'finery,' and 'sweethearts,' but a great deal about '*books*,' which she carried out into the fields, and which were '*always Greek or Latin*.'"[13] There is some suggestion that Sally Aram followed her father to Lynn when eventually he deserted his wife and family. Even after his ultimate disgrace, she remained loyal to him. The other two girls, Jane and Betty, were entirely different—from Sally and from each other. Jane was dull and rather plain, Betty a "'miraculous,' wild, and giddy girl" who ran off with a "tramp currier."[14] One of the sons was demented and subject to fits. Of the other two boys, one became a saddler. His son, of the same trade, emigrated to America early in the nineteenth century.

All but three of the children were born after Eugene left his first teaching position at Ramsgill. In 1734, interrupting his professional duties and scholarship, Aram accepted an invitation from his "good friend, William Norton, Esquire" to come to Knaresborough as his steward. It was a move that would prove fateful. Shortly after his arrival, Aram brought his young family to join him and traded the role of steward for that of village schoolmaster. He now took up the study of Hebrew with the same diligent application he had given to Greek and Latin.

At this point, Aram's autobiography makes an abrupt leap of ten years, dismissing the period most crucial to our study with the vague assurance that at Knaresborough he was "well accepted and esteemed." The statement appears to have been true, though it conceals the supreme irony that his acceptance and esteem were probably undeserved. Even the most condemnatory of his early biographies tells us that

> ...through the general estimation and opinion, gentlemen had of his uncommon abilities and extensive learning, he was always looked upon and treated in a more genteel and respectable manner than people of his station, and in his way of life generally are. His way of living and outward deportment, were most remarkably unblameable for many years. He was most upright and fair, in all dealings and transactions he had with other people, of great outward tenderness and humanity.[15]

Aram's intellect and refinement so dazzled the villagers, it seems, that they were blind to the symptoms of a crueler nature. One wonders, for instance, how they interpreted his treatment of Anna. The story was told of him, and adopted by Bulwer, that in his kindness he would stoop and set aside the worm from the garden path lest it be trod upon. But another tale widely accepted, even by Norrisson Scatcherd, Aram's most partial biographer, shows him less respectful of life. Aram became so enraged with the neighborhood cats for uprooting his garden, the story goes, that he implanted a row of sharpened spikes just within the garden wall. When several of the cats leaped the forbidden barrier and were impaled, he "laughed heartily" at their fate. The "fairness" of his "dealings" is challenged by the tradition that Aram, together with Dan Clark, the young village shoemaker, would raid their neighbors' gardens in the night and steal their bulbs.

Aram's association with Clark and other low companions in the vicinity is yet another stain on his conduct, explained away by Scatcherd with only the greatest difficulty. Scatcherd is no doubt correct in attributing Aram's choice of friends in part to their close residence. The thatched cottage in which the schoolmaster lived and taught his students was just across the way from the house of Philip Coates, gentleman and attorney-at-law, the prosperous brother-in-law of Daniel Clark. (Coates was married to Clark's wife's sister.) Since Aram aspired to superior connections, it is likely that he made acquaintance first with Coates and met Clark there. Since Clark shared in a small way Aram's love of books and gardening, it also seems likely that the schoolmaster, flattered by Clark's regard, took him in tow and dominated the younger and weaker man.

Richard Houseman, usually regarded as the most reprehensible of the companions, also lived and had his weaver's shop in the same small courtyard — next door, in fact, to Aram's cottage. There is some suggestion that Houseman was a cousin of Aram's, but if so, the resemblance was slight. As described in most of the contemporary accounts, Houseman was crude and roughhewn — a stocky, surly, "dark ill-looking fellow" with a shaven head and a brown wig, "the real picture of a murderer."[16] Houseman ranked among his acquaintance one Henry Terry, publican and gamekeeper for a local baronet; and Francis Iles, a prominent Knaresborough citizen, ostensibly a printer and publisher but with a reputation as a receiver of stolen goods. Both Terry and Iles were, it seems, centrally involved in the conspiracies of which Aram soon became a part, although both, by their clout and cleverness, escaped justice. The latter is yet respectably commemorated in the name of a Knaresborough side street, Iles Lane.

The ever partisan Scatcherd explains Aram's connection with these men as an unfortunate result of circumstances. He implies without confirmation that Aram, a struggling family man, was forced to borrow money from his disreputable neighbor, the prosperous bachelor weaver. He further implies that these infamous acquaintances were foisted upon the schoolmaster by the vulgar tastes and associations of his lowbred wife. It is true that one or more of the marginal figures in the underhanded dealings which took place just before Clark's disappearance were described as "Jews." One of them was almost certainly Anna's brother,

Abraham Spence. Yet Eugene Aram does not impress us as the type of man who could be inveigled into questionable company and ill deeds against his better judgment—especially by the meek and simple wife whom he scorned and dominated.

It was more than ten years after Aram's establishment in Knaresborough that the scheme leading to Clark's disappearance originated. Clark was a shoemaker, successful in his trade and well-to-do since his marriage in January of 1745. His young wife's dowry of £300 was a considerable fortune at that time for a man of his position. He lived with his widowed mother, to whose home he brought his new bride. The wife and mother did not agree, and consequently the wife soon removed to family or friends at nearby Newell Hall. She and her husband nonetheless remained, it was said, on cordial terms. The wife was pregnant at the time, but it is not clear for how long she had been so. Such was the situation when Clark, for reasons which can only be speculated, apparently conspired with Aram, Houseman, and their associates to defraud his neighbors and decamp with the spoils.

Saying that he was now well off and intended to live in accord with his improved condition, and that he would first celebrate with an extravagant feast, Clark began to order on credit or borrow from friends, neighbors, and local merchants large quantities of goods in ludicrous array. The trial accounts provide a precise inventory. From one man he borrowed cloth of velvet and cambric, and fifteen guineas. Another, a saddler, lent him whips and leather; and his own servant, Peter Moor, forwarded him £38. His miscellaneous acquisitions also included gold plate, silver tankards, quart and pint measures, stockings, two snuff boxes, a pepper box, a silver milk pot, eight watches, nine gold and diamond rings, Pope's Homer and Chambers's Dictionary, some blankets, and a supply of bed and table linen. By one report, "he even descended so low, as to become a customer...for a tea-kettle."[17]

These strange borrowings continued for several weeks, yet however much of a nuisance Clark may have become he does not seem to have aroused suspicion. The credulous generosity of Knaresborough's citizenry must attest to his previously sound credit. About nine o'clock on the evening of February 7, 1745, however, Clark took leave of his mother, purportedly to visit his wife. He never arrived at Newell Hall, but he did call on a man named Tuton whom he aroused from bed at twelve o'clock and again at two a.m.—still trying to borrow tankards. As Tuton spoke with Clark through the window on the later occasion, he saw Aram and Houseman lurking at a distance in the shadowy moonlight. They drew back at his notice, but Tuton observed as Clark joined the two men and left in their company. Tuton was the last person, besides Houseman and Aram, who was known to have seen Clark alive.

Clark was discovered missing on the following morning by his brother-in-law, Coates, who had an appointment with him at nine o'clock. Coates searched the house to find that his sister-in-law's dowry was gone, along with all the other money and possessions Clark had gathered. The creditors were of course vastly resentful at the news. Within a few hours, Clark's former reputation was forgotten and he became generally regarded as a knave and scoundrel. No one seems to have considered the possibility that he himself had been a victim of crime — despite the odd circumstance that he had left his horse behind in his presumed flight. (Two days later the stableman sold the animal to pay for its keep.) Messengers were sent to search for Clark, and he was advertised for in the *York Courant* of March 12, but no word of him was heard. For the next thirteen years, his wife and mother shared with most of the community the belief that he was living somewhere in hiding, enjoying the spoils of fraud. Philip Coates acted on that belief by suing his absent brother-in-law, as a result of which suit Clark was outlawed on October 20, 1746. The mechanism of the law, with blind pertinacity, continued to tax Clark's lands, so that by 1832, when fiscal reforms curtailed the registry of such tallies, £638 6s. in arrears was charged to his name.

Since Clark obviously could not have taken with him all his awkward collection of valuables, it was reasoned upon his disappearance that he must have had accomplices in the fraud and that some of the missing goods might still be in the vicinity. Aram's house was therefore searched, as was Houseman's — not, as yet, under suspicion of murder but only of collusion. Some of the borrowed leather was indeed found at Houseman's, and the blankets and teakettle at Aram's. Some of the cloth was found buried in the schoolmaster's garden, along with a pickax (later assumed to have been the murder weapon) which had disappeared mysteriously from Tuton's yard the night of Clark's last visit. Henry Terry, the publican and gamekeeper, was found in possession of two saltcellars and a tankard which, though their owner recognized them, could not be positively identified since the engraving had been effaced.

An interesting postcript to this recovery operation is the conspicuous participation of Francis Iles, Knaresborough's bookseller/fence. Though Iles apparently had lost to Clark only the few blankets found at Aram's, he was one of six who offered the £15 reward advertised in the *Courant*. He was, moreover, "more than commonly diligent, and very instrumental in recovering as many of the goods &c. as he cou'd and dividing them amongst Clarke's creditors."[18] This behavior is strikingly at variance with the pretrial statement of Aram, who said that before Clark's disappearance Iles "by divers undue means and threatenings, possest himself of considerable effects belonging to Clark." Henry Terry's separate deposition—made, like Aram's, thirteen years after the events in question and with no possibility of the two having conferred—corroborates the charge that Iles "possest himself of such [goods, plate, or effects belonging to Clark] to a considerable amount."[19] These accusations were excluded from the trial and, until Watson unearthed the original documents in our own century, had never seen print, having been almost immediately suppressed under the influence of Iles. Their censorship, together with Iles's exaggerated public spirit, Watson notes, looks suspiciously like camouflaged guilt.

Despite the discovery of some of Clark's plunder at their houses, neither Houseman nor Aram was charged with complicity at the time. Though it is said that Houseman "increased in wealth surprisingly, and to some gave great suspicion,"[20] he escaped prosecution by claiming that the leather in his keeping had been given him by Clark as security for a £20 loan. Once, Anna Aram came to Houseman in a passion, demanding money she said was of right her husband's, but he turned her away, pretending ignorance of her meaning. Yet he had not forgotten the secret buried in the riverside cave a mile from town. Sometimes the Nidd would flood, and its rising waters would penetrate the deep recesses in its steep and rocky banks. Years afterwards it was recalled that on such occasions Houseman could be seen prowling the vicinity of St. Robert's Cave. Once an old woman saw him emerge from its entrance and wash his hands in the river. He was anxious, it was later assumed, lest nature and chance expose the remains concealed there.[21]

Shortly after Clark's disappearance, Aram was arrested for a debt owed to William Norton, the gentleman for whom he had briefly been steward. The intent, it seems, was merely to detain him until sufficient evidence permitted charging him with fraud in the present affair. But Aram frustrated that plan and surprised everyone by paying the debt at once with over a hundred guineas drawn from his breeches pocket. He had begun to feel, apparently, that Knaresborough was no longer a congenial place to live, for within weeks he too mysteriously disappeared, leaving his wife and children without support. No attempt was made to follow him, and except for vague rumor and speculation the incident went unrevived for more than thirteen years.

Little is known for certain of Aram's whereabouts from April, 1745 to December 1757. He later said that, after spending a few days with relations in Nottinghamshire, he went to London.[22] There, for over two years, he taught in Piccadilly, under the Reverend Mr. Painblanc, who helped him learn French. Aram's cursory mention of this interval in the capital city is amplified only by the mysterious York Pamphlet. The episode it relates is, for its singularity, worth repeating here:

> [In London, Aram] became the Gentleman, dressed well, and kept genteel company, to which he found easy admittance. . . . Having left his wife behind in the country, he began to think of having a fresh one. . . . For this purpose, he singled out a fair one, of a good share of beauty, genteel and who carried the outward marks of having a competent fortune. . . . Here, the wily, and in general penetrating Aram, . . . was however deceived: She, notwithstanding her outward deportment being no other than a lady of pleasure, and kept, by a gentleman of L— —ds, whose name, tho' we have it in our power, we chuse rather to omit, than here mention with such a villain.
>
> Enamour'd as he was, his profusion in dress, and in presents to the object of his flame, scarce knew any Bounds. . . . Being, as he daily was, one afternoon on a visit to drink tea with his virtuous fair at her lodgings; the gentleman, her keeper, chanced to drop in. He was not . . . wholly pleased at finding her so familiarly engaged. . . . Tea being just brought up, he however staid, behaving civil and complaisant to Mr. Aram during the time. Aram's face however, being not altogether a stranger to him he took his leave, with a resolution of returning the next morning, and knowing of his suspected Lais [a famous courtesan of antiquity], the reason of his being there.
>
> He, pursuant to this resolution, came, and interrogated her very sternly, as to who, and what the Gentleman was, he found her with the day before; whether she knew him; on what account he was there, and other such-like questions. To which, the innocent nymph, ingenuously replied, that she, indeed, knew not particularly who, or what he was; that his name was Aram, and she believed a gentleman, from the appearance he made, as well as from the quantity of money, which she thought to be about three hundred pounds, he one day counted over before her, saying he had just been and received it of his banker: As also from the many handsome presents he had made her, . . . adding further, that she supposed she shou'd in a small time be forced to leave him to the caresses of another mistress; for that Mr. Aram paid his addresses to her in an honourable way. . . . He answer'd

her that he shou'd be extremely glad to see her at any time well
provided for,. . .but, that with respect to the courtship of her
present admirer, he wou'd advise her to be very cautious. . .for
that he knew him well, and instead of the gentleman he
outwardly appeared to be, he was in fact, as errant a villain as was
upon the earth. . . . He told her, if she follow'd his advice and the
next time he came to visit her, ask'd him; what Countryman he
was? whether he had not lived at Knaresbrough in Yorkshire?
Whether he did not know one Daniel Clarke of the town, and
whether he was then in London, or if he knew what was become
of him? The answers. . .continued he, will convince you, of his
not being wholly unembarrass'd. . . .

Aram, came. . .to prosecute his suit: And. . .enquired, who
the gentleman, there the day before was? She told him he was
a cousin, and a very good friend of her's. She in her turn, begun,
by slightly asking in what part of England he resided; He
answer'd, he generally spent a month or two in London every
year, but that his estate and place of residence was in Essex. Did
you never live in Yorkshire, Sir, at a place called Knaresbrough?
she replied; At this, he seem'd a little confounded, and began
to hesitate, saying; No; he never lived there; that he had indeed
been at the place, sometimes, for a few days on business. She
here more plainly saw the confusion he was under, and still continued her interrogatories, by asking, whether he was not
acquainted with one Daniel Clarke, and what was become of
him; whether he was with him in London, or not? Here, his confusion and the visible consternation that seized his whole frame,
firmly convinc'd her, that her gentleman had some very cogent
reasons for setting her upon interrogating her lover in the
manner he had. To the last questions, Aram, replied in a most
fault'ring Manner; That he never knew any such man, at Knaresbrough, and consequently could give no account of his being in
town or not; he had, he thought, indeed seen some such a man
advertised in the papers, but who, or what he was, he knew not;
and why shou'd she enquire of him about so low a creature as a
shoemaker? Here he immediately found he had overshot himself, and quickly recovering his blunder, continued,—A shoemaker, I think he was described to be in the papers. She carelessly replied, she had no great reasons, for such her enquiries, but
was desired, by the gentleman that was there the day before. He
desire you, madam! replied the still more confounded lover; Pray

what countryman is he? One of L— —ds, said she, and he thought he was not unacquainted with your person; but since it proved a mistake, there can be no great matter in it.

The mistake, if however, of little consequence to her, was not so to the conscious Aram....He, therefore, much sooner than common, took his leave of his fair one, under a faithful assurance of visiting her the next day....which, on hearing, made [her patron] resolve to meet Aram there in the afternoon, and have some further discourse with him. But this, the crafty Aram was aware of, for he never visited or came nigh his beloved again, nor cou'd the gentleman, tho' he made the most diligent enquiry, ever find, or discover the least tidings of, our sham Essex gentleman.[23]

The factuality of this private intrigue cannot of course be established, and it has all the earmarks of a conventional *chronique scandaleuse*. The author of the York Pamphlet is, like the gentleman of Leeds, anonymous. Yet his pamphlet, though crude and ill-written, bears in several respects the appearance of firsthand information. He seems, for example, to have interviewed or perhaps known Houseman and Coates, as the following passage suggests: "The deceased [Clark] was indebted to the unhappy Houseman in the sum of 20 *l*...for which he [Houseman] had, *and now has* [italics mine], in his custody, a note of hand in Clarke's own writing." The writer goes on to add that Coates could testify to the authenticity of that document and would do so willingly if called upon. The York Pamphlet is, in fact, so unusually sympathetic to Houseman, placing the criminal blame entirely upon Aram, that one wonders whether its author was not a friend of Houseman. The weaver, it reports, had "lived in... Knaresbrough, for the space of 40 years, in the greatest credit and esteem, with all his neighbours....He was particularly remarkable for his open, free, and inoffensive disposition, his sobriety of life, the most honest and disinterested manner of dealing, and was always looked upon as a most peaceable, quiet man, and one of the utmost humanity and tenderness."[24]

Biased as the pamphleteer is against Aram, he does not appear to have altered the facts of the case in any verifiable particulars. Watson, although ordinarily inclined to skepticism, finds evidence of the "Lais" story's authenticity in one significant detail: the gentleman of Leeds' suspicion that Clark as well as Aram might be in London ("Whether he did not know one Daniel Clarke of the town, and whether he was then in London, or if he knew what was become of him?"). When the York Pamphlet was published, in 1759, no one doubted that Clark had been murdered, but at the time of the narration, fourteen years earlier, he was indeed presumed alive. Had the account been fabricated in the aftermath of the trial, Watson suggests, a production so ingenuous would hardly have interwoven so subtle a point.

Upon Aram's departure from London, according to the autobiography, he went next to Hayes, in Middlesex, to serve as usher and tutor. There he lived for a time with the Reverend Anthony Hinton who, as they walked in company, was so much impressed with Aram's gesture in setting aside the worm from the garden path. Mr. Hinton later attributed the act to a guilty conscience seeking atonement for having sinned against the sanctity of life. It was Bulwer who saw in it, still more idealistically, an informing benevolence incompatible with the soul of a murderer. After this sojourn Aram traveled to "several other places in the south of England," of which nothing more is known. For a time, back in London, he found employment transcribing the Acts of Parliament into the official record, before settling in December, 1757, at Lynn, Norfolk, as usher in the grammar school.

In the midst of his wanderings, Aram says, he studied the Chaldaic, Arabic, and Celtic languages, as well as the French, and developed his knowledge of heraldry and botany. Aram's introduction to the Celtic dialects led him to formulate the linguistic theory on which estimates of his scholarship largely depend. Later, during the long months he spent in prison awaiting trial, knowing that he would very likely never finish the massive work he proposed, Aram summarized his views in the "Essay Towards a Lexicon upon an Entirely New Plan," which was commonly appended to pamphlet accounts of his life. Its hypothesis was based on his perception of etymological similarities linking the Celtic with the English, Hebrew, Phoenician, Greek, and Latin languages. He is said to have left behind notes comprising the detailed derivations of about 3,000 words which he considered these languages to hold in common. Other scholars, he admits, had previously noted such connections but had attributed them, if they considered the reasons at all, to superficial intercultural exchanges occasioned by trade or colonization in ancient times. Aram refuted that assumption. "Commerce," he wrote,

> has made, and always will make, continual additions to any language, by the introduction of exotic words: yet words of this kind, and at that time, would hardly extend a great way; they would only affect the maritime parts, and those places frequented by traders, and that but feebly, and would be very far

from acting or making any considerable impression upon the whole body of any language.

The similarities Aram perceived were, on the contrary, too numerous, ancient, and pervasive to be so lightly explained:

> It is not to be thought of...that the multitude of words among us, which are certainly Latin, Greek, and Phoenician, are all the relics of the Roman settlements in Britain, or the effects of Greek or Phoenician commerce here; no, this resemblance was coeval with the primary inhabitants of this island; and the accession of other colonies did not obliterate, but confirm this resemblance.

The true explanation, Aram believed, lay in the ancient history of the Celtic peoples. They were, he affirms, in ancient times the "*Scythians* or *Tatars*," descendants of Noah's grandson Gomer and therefore called in their own tongue *Cimmeri* or *Cimbri* (Cimmerians), from whence came the word "Cumberland." Since their origin was unknown, the ancient Greeks whom they conquered gave them the designation *Celtæ* or *Keletes* (meaning "light horsemen"), referring to their principal means of mobile warfare. Aram also associates them with the *Titanes* or *Gigantes* (meaning "sprung from the earth"), holding that Saturn and his son Jupiter were of their number and only later assimilated into the fabric of myth. Aram relates at length, drawing upon ancient historical references, their massive conquest of "parts of Asia, and thence into Europe and back again, like a retiring tide." Eventually, over many centuries, "there was absolute coalition in many nations of this people and their language, with those they conquered,... and all of them, a while after this incorporation, are found in history under the common name of *Celtæ*." From Greece, their principal settlement,

> ...colony peopled colony still farther and farther, till they with the language they brought along with them from the east and Greece, &c., arrived in and about Britain; and whither else we can fix no bounds; as waves departing from one centre swell with a wider and wider circumference, wave impelling wave, till at last these circles disappear.

Thus, the Celts were, "in Gaul, Britain, Greece and all the western parts of Europe,... if not the aborigines, at least their successors and masters." For that reason,

...their language, however obsolete, however mutilated, is at this day discernible in all those places which that victorious people conquered and retained; ...it has extended itself far and wide, visibly appearing in the ancient Greek, Latin, and English, of all of which it included a very considerable part; ...it emerges in the names of springs, torrents, rivers, woods, hills, plains, lakes, seas, mountains, towns, cities, and innumerable other local appellations of very remote antiquity. ...Much of it is still extant in the works of our earlier poets and historians; and much is yet living upon the tongues of multitudes (*inter Rura Brigantum*) in Cumberland, &c., unknown and unobserved, ...the same Celtic, which, polished by Greece and refined by Rome, only with dialectic variation, flowed from the lips of Virgil, and thundered from the mouth of Homer.[25]

The fervency of this essay bears witness to Aram's scholarly devotion — far more than any of his protestations to that effect, or those of his apologists. His theory placing Celtic in crucial relationship to the other developing languages of Europe and Asia Minor does not completely coincide with the views of modern linguists, but it was in the vanguard of new developments which were only beginning to revolutionize language study. Before Aram's time linguistics had been a haphazard pursuit. The foremost scholars, if they admitted any notion of derivation between languages, perceived it as a linear descent through time. Thus, Latin had borrowed from Greek, and the modern tongues from Latin. A few further pursued the retrogressive theory to entertain belief in a universal parent language. Some seized upon Hebrew as the source, for reasons biblical, while others chose Latin, for reasons classical. The seventeenth century saw publication of a treatise by John Webb, curiously entitled *An Historical Essay Endeavoring a Probability that the Language of the Empire of China is the Primitive Language* (1669). Such conclusions were formed, however, without benefit of systematic inductive reasoning. Aram's work was, then, progressive not only in his inductive approach — based upon notes and observations made over a period of years — but also in his recognition that contemporaneous languages may have reciprocal relationships.

Aram himself was not the first to perceive the influence of Celtic upon the ancient tongues of Europe and Asia Minor. The idea seems originally to have appeared in the work of Paul-Yves Pezron, a Cistercian monk of Brittany, who published in 1703 *L'Antiquité de la Nation et de la Langue des Celtes*, translated (and amplified to stress the Welsh connections) by D. Jones in 1706 as *The Antiquities of Nations; More Particularly of the* Celtae *or* Gauls, *Taken to be Originally the Same People as our Ancient* Britains. Aram may well have drawn from this treatise, since the connections he makes with biblical and mythical personages (Gomer and Japheth, Saturn and Jupiter) are identical with arguments set forth by the Breton monk. (Aram himself, accused by his detractors of atheism, was hardly a biblical literalist.) To Pezron's theories, however, if he did know of them, he brought the weight of empirical evidence.

Thus, Aram's Celtic theories were more advanced than those of any scholar prior to his time. He fell short of the twentieth-century linguist's perspective only in failing to infer the existence of the lost parent language, now termed Indo-European, from which the ancient Celtic, Greek, Latin, and their sister languages are said to have common descent. Modern linguistic histories confirm Aram's view of Celtic prominence in the post–Indo-European period and especially his insistence on the evidence of place and geographical names with common Celtic origins as far east as the Black Sea. Of his role in the progress of linguistic science, one fairly recent commentator notes: "What linguists now regard as the true nature of the relation between the various groups of languages in Europe was first perceived by the unfortunate Eugene Aram."[26] This tribute is, however, the exception rather than the rule. The standard works of historical linguistics make no such reference. Aram's name is forgotten in their pages. He took his place instead, with consuming irony, in a different volume of recorded history.

In December of 1757, as has been said, Eugene Aram packed his notes and left the south of England, establishing himself again in the north at over a hundred miles' remove from, yet still in dangerous proximity to, the scene of his earlier adventures. His engagement at Lynn Grammar School, in Norfolk, was to begin at the close of the holiday recess. The ushership at Lynn, though brief, seems to have brought Aram the same respect he had earned in his early years at Knaresborough. One local clergyman, a Dr. Weatherhead, made an observation similar to Mr. Hinton's regarding Aram's humanity to worms: "'Dr. Weatherhead said he could not help observing that Aram, in turning up the ground, carefully put aside the worms that he might not injure them, and he was astonished to find a man of so much humanity charged with murder.'"[27] In his spare hours, Aram associated with prominent gentlemen of the community and gave private lessons to children of affluent families. One of his pupils, a Miss Lidderdale, described in the effusive language of the times as "'an amiable and accomplished lady,'" was the daughter of a clergyman, himself "'a man of uncommon acquirements and extensive learning.'"[28] Between Aram and Miss Lidderdale, at eighteen, was rumored an incipient romance, which may point to her as the prototype for Bulwer's Madeline Lester. A second connection with Bulwer belongs also to this period. According to family tradition, Aram was briefly hired by "Justice" Bulwer (the novelist's paternal grandfather), at nearby Heydon Hall, as holiday tutor to his two daughters. The author's preface to the 1840 edition of *Eugene Aram* partially attributes to that association his motivation to write the novel.

Despite these signs of community acceptance and trust, Aram's character while at Lynn was afterwards questioned in two repects. One concerned a tale, inconsistent through many retellings, that Aram had been discovered lurking in the master's chamber, or the hallway outside it, late one night during Christmas vacation at the grammar school. The master having awakened and challenged him, Aram replied that he was (depending on the version) sleepwalking or indisposed. It was only later assumed that he had had designs upon the school fees collected the day before and deposited in the master's strongbox. The story, attributed to the headmaster himself, actually seems little more credible than the boys' reports of Aram's ghost, said to haunt the school corridors. Watson, furthermore, has suggested that Aram was not yet in residence there during the time in question.[29]

The second allegation was that Aram kept at Lynn and often visited a young woman whom he called his niece, a claim that was only later disputed. It is, in fact, highly probable that the young woman was really his daughter Sally, then aged about twenty-seven. One source, the derogatory York Pamphlet, always eager to cast odium upon its subject, combined the two possibilities. Aram was, it charged, guilty of "the dreadful and most shockingly unnatural crime of Incest...having had, by his daughter, issue of his loins, once, if not offener."[30] Watson, who translates the passage into decorous Latin, admits at least its possibility. Scatcherd, himself infatuated with the mysterious Sally, completely represses it in favor of encomiums to her filial devotion. He repeats with tender feeling a passage heard only by report but reputedly written by Sally to "a female friend" after her father's death: "'As to my dear father, I once believed that I never could have survived him long, but time softens down our sorrows, and I now CONSOLE MYSELF in the persuasion that he is *traversing* the Elysian fields, *associated* with the KINDRED *shades* of his beloved Homer and Virgil.'" Scatcherd concludes his "Gleanings" with an affecting poem composed by himself "To The Memory of 'Sally Aram'" who "Bloom'd, 'til she sunk,— the victim of despair."

That Aram would introduce Sally as his niece is understandable, for she was said to favor him in looks, and posing as a bachelor he could hardly publicize her true identity. What he did not conceal, and no doubt should have, was his own name. In June of 1758, a traveling horse-dealer, passing through Lynn with a stallion for sale, thought he recognized Aram as the former schoolmaster of Knaresborough and stopped to ask a townsman who he was. In this trivial happening began a coincidence to rank with Hardy's best. A few weeks later, in Knaresborough, the fatal convergence was completed. On August 1, a workman digging for lime uncovered a human skeleton on Thistle Hill, just across the river from St. Robert's Cave. The remains were at once assumed to be Clark's, and the scandal of thirteen years revived. An inquest was summoned, at which Richard Houseman in his nervous indiscretion so emphatically denied these were Clark's bones that he thereby revealed his knowledge of their actual resting place. After days of prevarication, he not only directed the authorities to search St. Robert's Cave but also forecast the exact position in which, on the seventeenth, what was presumed to be Clark's skeleton was unearthed in the turn to the inside right of the cave entranceway. At the several inquests held over the two skeletons, the repeated testimony of various witnesses, particularly that of Anna Aram, gave evidence of Aram's involvement in suspicious dealings with Houseman and Clark in the days preceding the latter's disappearance. Houseman was in custody, but the authorities had no inkling where to search for Aram. It was then that the horse-dealer, happening through town and hearing of the excitement, stepped forward. He had, he said, seen the schoolmaster at Lynn in Norfolk, "'but he was too proud to speak to me.'"[31]

At once constables were dispatched the one hundred twenty miles to Lynn. Instructed to call along the way at every post office for letters directed to Aram, they confiscated one anonymous missive dramatically inscribed, "Fly for your life, you are pursued." They made their arrest on August 19, 1758, in the Lynn Grammar School withdrawing room. Initially, Aram pretended never to have heard of Knaresborough or Clark, but on being confronted with one of the constables who knew him personally, he was forced to drop this pose. It was the first in a series of prevarications and altered statements which, together, trapped him in the semblance of guilt.

Aram's public arrival at Knaresborough in a post-chaise, according to one of Scatcherd's octogenarian informants, caused great excitement:

> "The streets were so choked with people that they could scarcely get down to the Bell Inn,[32] where they alighted, and were

received by the Vicar, Collins, and the Rev. _____ Brotheric;
...Aram was dressed in a very genteel suit of clothes, with
beautiful frills to his shirt wrists, and had every appearance of
a gentleman; ...Aram was quite composed and collected among
the many Knaresborough gentlemen in the room, talked much,
and said he could clear himself of the crime imputed to him."[33]

As it developed, Aram talked not well and too much. His repeated
affirmations of innocence were hardly convincing. At his first examination
before the local magistrate, he admitted acquaintance with Clark but
thoroughly denied any involvement in swindle or murder. When asked
to confirm or deny any detail, he pleaded forgetfulness. Thus, in the
record, he "does not recollect" having been in company with Houseman
and Clark "at that unseasonable time in the morning" of February 8,
1745, "nor does remember anything of a mason's tool being found in his
house, when he was arrested." Aram declined signing this deposition lest
"anything might be omitted or slip his memory. . .which may hereafter
occur to him."

The performance seems not to have impressed the court, for Aram
was at once remanded to York Castle, York being the nearest assize town.
On the road, however, his memory improved, and he asked to be returned
before the magistrate. The chaise retraced its journey and, despite a warn-
ing not to commit himself too hastily, Aram made a second statement,
the manuscript of which, by Watson's observation, "is crammed with
erasures, and the critical part—what happened at the cave—has been
written over and erased so often that it is only with the greatest difficulty
that it can be made out at all."[34] In this document, signed and later produced as evidence against him at the trial, Aram admitted helping Clark
and Houseman, on the night of February 7, thirteen years before, to carry
stolen plate to St. Robert's Cave, where they beat it flat for export from
the neighborhood. Clark, he said, was to hide in the cave and flee the
next evening. On that next evening, February 8, Aram continued, he went
to the cave with Houseman and Terry, who entered while Aram kept
watch outside at a distance. After a time, the two returned with the
beaten plate, for which they said they had paid Clark, who was now fled.
Whether this was so, or whether Clark was indeed murdered, Aram had
no inkling.

In York Castle, Aram spent nearly a year awaiting trial as the Crown
lawyers prepared their case, an effort hampered by the unusual lapse of
time since the events in question occurred. Houseman and Terry (the
latter having been arrested on the strength of Aram's second examina-

tion) also were confined there. Several letters written from prison show Aram appealing to friends for money and books to offset the deprivations and tedium of confinement. Acting as his own lawyer, a capacity for which he showed little talent, he researched and composed his lengthy defense speech during these months and wrote letters soliciting friends and former patrons, including the Blacketts, to appear in his behalf as character witnesses. None responded to his pleas. In a further attempt to raise money and support, Aram negotiated with booksellers and publishers for the sale of several poems later appended to various pamphlet editions of his life and trial. At last, by June of 1759, Aram was aware of the main strategy contemplated by the prosecution. In a letter to the publisher Etherington, dated the second of that month, he inquires "whether Houseman,...in custody, and commitment upon a charge of murder, can possibly be admitted evidence for the King, against me, as he says his counsel tells him he may...?"

The proceedings took place on Friday, August 3, 1759, with each of the three defendants pleading not guilty. First, Houseman received the summary acquittal requested by the prosecution. Yet, as Watson explains, his safety was not thereby assured under British law. Although acquitted as a principal, he might still be charged by the Crown as an accessory— especially if he did not meet expectations in his role as witness for the prosecution. Or he might well be "appealed of the murder" by Clark's heir-at-law, if during his testimony he let slip any implication of his own involvement in the murder. His only escape from this precarious position was a judicious balance of disclosure and concealment that must have seemed an ominous prospect to a man of no great cleverness, whose previous rashness had placed him in this jeopardy.

Houseman's consciousness of the dilemma was evident in his deportment as the lead witness in Aram's case. Delivering his testimony, he spoke so softly and with such diffident restraint that the judge several times asked him to repeat portions that were imperfectly heard. His account, ineptly improbable as it may have been, was nonetheless injurious. All that the Crown required at this stage was to confirm Aram's presence at the scene of the crime and in the company of such a rascal. On the morning of February 8, about two or three A.M., Houseman said, Clark and Aram asked him to take a walk with them. The three proceeded to the vicinity of St. Robert's Cave, where Clark and Aram crossed a hedge while he himself lingered behind. From that distance, he observed them quarreling. He saw Aram strike Clark down, but whether it was with a weapon or his hand Houseman could not tell. This occurrence so horrified him that he ran home at once. The next day Aram visited him, told him he had killed Clark and buried him in the cave, and with threats enjoined him to silence. In cross-examination Aram inquired why Houseman had stayed behind, whereupon Houseman threw himself upon the protection of the court. Since no one in the courtroom believed Houseman's story in the first place, Aram gained nothing by this move save making all the more apparent his own involvement in some intrigue.

There followed a series of lesser witnesses. Several reported having seen Houseman, Aram, and Clark in company on the night in question and having later discovered certain of the missing goods at Aram's house. The skull of the victim was next displayed and affirmed by a surgeon to have been fractured by a blow from the back with a rather blunt instrument. Whether the trial testimony included information regarding the age and sex of the skeleton is not known, but it is certain that, owing to the condition of the remains and the limitations of medical science, positive identification of the victim was not then feasible. Watson, in 1912, had the skull examined by a specialist, who judged it to be indeed that of a male about thirty years of age. The position of the wound at the back of the skull, of course, discredits Houseman's version of the murder as having ensued from an argument.

John Barker, the constable who had taken Aram into custody at Lynn, was the next to take the stand. In a statement that would never be admissible in a modern court, he told of an incident upon whose Gothic overtones Bulwer, the novelist, would later capitalize. En route to Knaresborough after the arrest, Barker said, the chaise had passed a crossroads where the remains of some lately executed felons hung in chains. The constable, having perceived Aram to shudder at this sight, attributed his reaction to qualms of guilt.

The evidence being thus arrayed against him, Aram proceeded to his own defense. After a brief statement as to the impossibility of gathering, after so long a time, witnesses who might have aided him, he began to read the address so laboriously prepared during his months of confinement. This document, quoted in abridged form near the close of Bulwer's novel and included in nearly every published account of Aram's life and trial, has been repeatedly praised out of all reason for its eloquence and penetration. In practical terms, it did little to advance its author's cause. His failure to refute directly any of the evidence brought forth against him, or even to straightforwardly deny the charges, on the contrary did him great damage. The theologian William Paley, who as a boy of sixteen attended Aram's trial, later remarked that with the speech Aram had "got himself hanged by his own cleverness."[35]

The argument for the defense fell into three main divisions. First, in a general way, Aram vindicated his own nature, since no one would come forward to do so for him. In humble tones, he represented himself as a man of long-standing integrity and sobriety to whom all thought of wrongdoing was foreign: "I concerted not schemes of fraud, projected no violence, injured no man's person or property. My days were honestly laborious, my nights intensely studious."[36] No man of established character, he added, could be suddenly transformed into a felon: "Mankind is never corrupted at once—villainy is always progressive."

This insubstantial argument gave way to a second, an alibi of sorts. At the time of the alleged murder, Aram held, he had barely emerged from an illness which had left him "so macerated, so enfeebled, that I was reduced to crutches," and "so far from being well...that I never to this day recovered." The difficulty of this defense was that Aram offered no proof of the claim. In all the wealth of traditionary material that has been handed down concerning him, there is nothing to corroborate it. He is universally described as sound of body and strong of frame. The point is in fact contradicted by Aram's own pretrial testimony that for two successive nights he accompanied Houseman, Terry, and Clark, with their load of valuables, back and forth to St. Robert's Cave, nearly a mile from his home.

The third and lengthiest portion of his defense was also the strongest. It was a legally substantial argument on the fallibility of circumstantial evidence, especially in a case such as this where the remains of the victim defied positive identification. Aram cited instances of such disappearances when the supposed victim returned alive after innocent persons had been executed for his murder. He reminded the court of the many historic battles fought in the vicinity of Knaresborough in which countless soldiers were slain, "and where they fell, were buried." The remains alleged to be Clark's, he suggested, might as well be attributed to such a death, or to that of some pious recluse who made the cave his cell, and was buried there.[37] Aram closed with dignified restraint, recommending himself to judge and jury: "I, last, after a year's confinement, equal to either fortune, put myself upon the candour, the justice, the humanity of your lordship, and upon yours, my countrymen, gentlemen of the jury."

This rhetoric seems not to have been received uniformly by all its auditors, or by its readers in after years. Paley, at sixteen, was convinced by it despite his later reference to Aram's excessive "cleverness." A "most respectable and very intelligent old gentleman" present at the trial as a youth is said to have recalled that on the strength of the speech, "it was the general belief a verdict of acquittal would be returned."[38] His statement is, however, unconfirmed by any other source and clearly contradicted by many. Some sixty years afterwards, in the 1820s, William Hazlitt listed Aram as one of several historical personages whom he would most like to conjure up and meet. For its "coolness, subtlety, and circumspection," he termed the defense "as masterly a legal document as there is upon record."[39] Leigh Hunt, speaking for many of his contemporaries in 1832, also gave it the highest praise. "Had Johnson been about him," he wrote, "the world would have attributed the defence to Johnson."[40] Others have been less moved. Even Bulwer, who puts the composition almost verbatim into the mouth of his hero, felt obligated to qualify its effect. Because (in the view of one literary historian) the speech "is such a patent example of sophistry," Bulwer, having quoted it, makes another character comment that he had "'expected a more earnest, though, perhaps, a less ingenious and artful defence.'"[41]

What the historian did not notice is that Bulwer had actually rephrased into kinder terms the opinion expressed by the real Aram's presiding judge. Justice William Noel, before recapitulating the evidence for the jury, reportedly called the defense "a most learned, subtle, and eloquent composition...but he thought it partook little of real feeling— that it strongly resembled, in style, the pleading of a practised rhetorician, who had no interest in the transaction, but took up the case solely for the purpose of displaying his own ingenuity."[42] For thus attempting to sway the jury, Justice Noel received much censure from Aram's sympathizers in later years.

The jury, to be sure, arrived at its decision with dispatch. By some accounts, its members never so much as left the box to deliberate. It is certain they required only a brief time to return their verdict of guilty. So strongly did they condemn the prisoner, in fact, that on hearing that Noel had ordered his body dissected after execution, as was customary, they returned to court and petitioned that he receive instead the more public indignity of hanging in chains, to which Noel afterwards consented. By way of contrast, Henry Terry, the gamekeeper, whose case followed Aram's, was acquitted for lack of evidence and rode promptly out of town, sporting in his hat a defiant blue cockade. Throughout his ordeal, Aram is said to have borne himself with unassailable modesty and decorum. According to one contemporary account, "He heard the verdict, and received his sentence, with the most profound composure, and even left the bar with a smile upon his countenance."[43] The smile, of course, is appropriately enigmatic, attributable equally to remorseless guilt or philosophic resignation. Whatever the truth may have been, Aram never made public confession. His proud and restrained nature would hardly

lend itself to the "last dying speech" of Tyburn fame. To the moral conscience of the times may be attributed the one existing report to the
contrary: a "confession" appearing first and only in the Newgate
Calendars. It is certainly spurious. Written in the manner and tone of the
most vulgar broadsides, it purports to have been found in Aram's cell
after his departure for execution but is entirely unconsonant with his
character and prose style.

Aram may, however, have admitted his guilt in private. An account
to that effect published in the *Annual Register* is accepted by some later
commentators. According to the *Register*, Aram,

> the morning after he was condemned,...confessed the justice
> of [his sentence] to two clergymen, (who had a licence from the
> judge to attend him) by declaring that he murdered Clark.
> Being asked by one of them, What his motive was for doing that
> abominable action? he told them, "He suspected Clark of
> having unlawful commerce with his wife; that he was per-
> suaded, at the time he committed the murder he did right; but
> since he has thought it wrong."
>
> After this, *Pray*, says Aram, *what became of Clark's body, if
> Houseman went home (as he said upon my trial) immediately
> on seeing him fall?* One of the clergymen replied, *I'll tell you
> what became of it; you and Houseman dragged it into the cave,
> and stripped and buried it there, brought away his cloaths, and
> burnt them at your house*: to which he assented.
>
> ...as he had promised to make a more ample confession on
> the day he was executed, it was generally believed every thing
> previous to the murder would have been disclosed; but he pre-
> vented any further discovery, by a horrid attempt upon his own
> life.[44]

One of these two clergymen, if the report is true, was almost certainly
the Reverend Thomas Collins, vicar of Knaresborough from 1735 to 1788.
Collins, who never publicly denied the *Annual Register's* account, attended Aram frequently during his confinement, raised a small sum in his
behalf to ease the hardships of prison, and administered the last rites
prior to his execution. It was also Collins who requested and received, in
letter form, the autobiography written by the condemned man in the few
hours remaining to him. The vicar perhaps expected it to contain the
promised confession. Indeed the original letter, now lost, may have done
so. The printed version, quoted in post-trial pamphlets, was admittedly

censored by its eighteenth-century editors to exclude remarks critical of Justice Noel and some mysterious others, chief of whom, it now appears, was almost certainly Francis Iles, who had suppressed the pretrial depositions of Aram and Terry. The excised portions, according to the York Pamphlet, were considerable: "The whole, notwithstanding his [Aram's] great judgment and learning, was a piece so infamous and incoherent, that it was judged totally unfit for the Press, without being altered, and rendered different in almost every particular."[45] At one point Aram relates, "In April...1744 [a few weeks after Clark's disappearance] I went again to London. (The reasons shall follow)," yet no reasons are forthcoming. If, as this omission suggests, the accusations Aram's censors considered so offensive to "characters that stand unimpeach'd" or to "the integrity and candor of the Court"[46] were inextricably interwoven with confession, the confession may have been lost along with them. Even as it stands, the final paragraph of this document, which concerns the distribution of stolen goods, conveys implicit guilt, in conspiracy if not in murder: "As for me I had nothing at all. My wife knows that Terry had the large plate, and that Houseman himself took both that and the watches, at my house, from Clark's own hand, and if she will not give this in evidence for the town, she wrongs both that and her own conscience."

Earlier in the autobiography Aram had denounced his wife, in a passage that seems to confirm the confession reported in the *Annual Register*. "I married," he wrote, "unfortunately enough for me, for the misconduct of the wife...afforded me has procured me this place — this prosecution — this infamy — and this sentence." The imputation is without support. No other source in a community alive, for generations thereafter, with gossip and legend concerning every facet of Aram's life affirms it in the least. It is extremely difficult to imagine such an affair between the plain, simple, and subjugated Anna, whose life must surely have been complicated by eight rather inescapable children, and the pockmarked, stuttering swain some fifteen years her junior, with his newly married and pregnant bride. It is far easier to believe that the ruined man was retaliating, in the only way possible, for his wife's involvement in bringing him to justice — and at the same time providing for himself a motive which allowed the infatuated Scatcherd and two French compilers to excuse his action by a *circonstance extenuante*.[47]

Aram was sentenced on Friday to be hanged the following Monday. When the Reverend Mr. Collins arrived early on the morning of the execution to administer the last rites, he found the prisoner feeble and bleeding from two self-inflicted razor cuts on his left arm.[48] A surgeon being called in to staunch the wounds, Aram was partially revived for the short journey to the gallows. At his execution he was conscious but very weak. Asked whether he had anything further to say, he replied in the negative and was summarily hanged. He had left on the table in his cell the following message, afterwards much deplored for its supposed heretical tendencies:

> What am I better than my fathers? To die is natural and necessary. Perfectly sensible of this, I fear no more to die than I did to be born. But the manner of it is something which should, in my opinion, be decent and manly. I think I have regarded both these points. Certainly nobody has a better right to dispose of a man's life than himself—and he, not others, should determine how. As for any indignities offered to my body, or silly reflections on my faith and morals, they are (as they always were) things indifferent to me. I think, tho' contrary to the common way of thinking, I wrong no man by this, and hope it is not offensive to that Eternal Being that form'd me and the world; and as by this I injure no man, no man can be reasonably offended. I solicitously recommend myself to the eternal and almighty Being, the God of Nature, if I have done amiss. But perhaps I have not; and I hope this thing will never be imputed to me. Though I am now stained by malevolence, and suffer by prejudice, I hope to rise fair and unblemished. My life was not polluted—my morals irreproachable—and my opinions orthodox.
>
> I slept soundly till three o'clock, awak'd, and then writ these lines—
>
> > Come, pleasing rest—eternal slumber fall,
> > Seal mine, that once must seal the eyes of all;
> > Calm and compos'd, my soul her journey takes.
> > No guilt that troubles—and no heart that aches.
> > Adieu! thou sun, all bright like her arise;
> > Adieu! fair friends, and all that's good and wise.[49]

Aram's religious assumptions are here so radically deistic that, given the date of composition, one must question what he meant by "orthodox." Although his expression of innocence at the close of the first paragraph and in the poetic lines is highly ambiguous, many of his sympathizers in later years took this document as an outright denial of guilt in the Clark affair. Aram did not die as he had hoped, in the dignity of solitude, but he did manage to preserve forever his darkest secret.

Aram's body was returned to Knaresborough, left in irons overnight in the stable of the Angel Inn, and gibbeted the next day at the edge of Knaresborough Forest, not far from Thistle Hill. As her husband's remains fell from the gibbet, which, tradition has it, Anna Aram could see from her window, she had them gathered and interred. The skull, however, later of much interest to phrenologists, suffered a different fate. As an aged woman, Mrs. Pickard, told Scatcherd, "After the gibbet was taken down [in 1778, when the forest was enclosed], my husband put a pair of hinges on the scalp for Dr. Hutchinson."[50] The latter, a Knaresborough physician, had stolen the skull for his museum. The feat is described in the *Literary Gazette* in a pseudonymous letter of December 9, 1931, occasioned by the appearance of Bulwer's novel:

> Some years since...the doctor sallied forth...with a ladder on his shoulders and with the firm purpose of mounting the gibbet and detaching from the iron hoop, which bound it, the skull of Eugene Aram. The gibbet clung to its own property with wonderful tenacity, but the *ardor* of the Doctor became a *furor* and he succeeded in extricating another neck at the risk of his own.[51]

The determined force applied by the doctor had, unfortunately, broken off a part of the "right mastoid process...and sawn [the skull] in two along the median line"—hence the hinges. For the next hundred years, the skull—always identifiable by the marks of Dr. Hutchinson's grapplings—made the rounds of local museums, private collectors, and phrenologists, to repose at length in the Royal College of Surgeons Museum, in London, where it is still preserved.

In Knaresborough there were other ironic reminders of Aram's notoriety in the years after his death, and a few signs linger today though one must search for them. The White Horse Inn of Aram's day, across the courtyard from his house and school, was afterwards renamed the Eugene Aram, to capitalize on the association which lured visitors there for many years. The inn no longer exists, and the dwellings of Aram and Houseman were demolished early in the nineteenth century, but the small cobblestone court, then known as the White Horse Yard, survives as Park Place in modern Knaresborough—still with cobblestones. Several blocks away, down a narrow side street, a weatherbeaten wooden beam that purports to be Aram's "original gibbet" incongruously straddles the roof of an

Italian restaurant. Adjacent to Iles Lane just off the main street stands Fysche Hall, once Iles's imposing home, which now serves as a child welfare center. Iles, who died in 1776, lies honorably buried in the chancel of the parish church.

The histories of several others closely connected with Aram are also recorded. Aram's daughter Betty, the "giddy" one, lived until 1805 at the neighboring village of Northallerton, where "she was quite a celebrity, and was sought out by people from all parts."[52] Sally Aram's mock-romantic fate is earnestly reported by Scatcherd: "After some misfortunes, which I shall not mention," he writes, she "became the mistress of a gentleman in London. One day, while walking with another female, she was driven, by a shower of rain, up an entry for shelter. Here she met with a respectable man, who being captivated by the person, the manners, or wit of Sally, made overtures of marriage, and was accepted. They kept a public-house, (the Crown, if I remember) on the Surrey side of Westminster Bridge."[53] Anna Aram survived her husband until 1774, wringing out a sparse livelihood by selling pies from a small shop off Knaresborough's High Street. Clark's widow, whose child by him died in infancy, lived into her eighties well respected in the town. Like Anna, she did not remarry. Her spinning wheel, once a museum piece, lies forgotten and falling to pieces in a corner of the guardroom of Knaresborough Castle.

There remains one last postscript of interest to Aram's strange story: that of his Judas. Richard Houseman, while he escaped the gallows and outlived Aram by eighteen years, was not otherwise fortunate. His reception in Knaresborough after the trial was, to say the least, strained. A few of the town's principal citizens, attempting to avert trouble, came out to congratulate him publicly for his "acquittal," but the gesture miscarried. The gathering became a mob, at whose hands Houseman barely escaped lynching. His effigy was carried through the streets, knocked on the head with a pickax, then hanged and burnt. The significance of the pickax suggests that the mob's resentment was directed not so much against Houseman the betrayer of Aram as against Houseman the unpunished murderer of Clark. His house would have been set on fire also, were it not for the pleadings of a next-door neighbor who, fearing for his own property, appeased the rioters by opening his cellar and giving them all his liquor.

Though his presence in Knaresborough was clearly unwanted, Houseman remained there for the rest of his days, a reclusive and enigmatic figure who only rarely ventured out of doors in the daylight hours. All night he would work alone in his weaver's shop—sometimes, so the neighbors said, pacing to and fro in conversation with himself. Often, with downcast head, he would leave his work, passing the apple tree and the filled-in well in the yard behind his house, scaling the wall which enclosed it, to walk in the fields. He married a widow named Johnson, whose daughter Ann kept the shop during business hours. His only other companion was, it was said, a large, domesticated black raven that commonly perched on the top of his front steps. After her mother's death, Ann remained with her father-in-law and cut him down once or twice from the apple tree after he had tried to hang himself from its boughs. When he died at last, his body was taken away by cart clandestinely at night for burial in another village. There were those who, had they not been prevented, would have made him share Aram's fate even in death.

2 GODWIN, HOLCROFT, AND HOOD

"A N AUTHOR SADLY ENTERED into his sixties," wrote the musicologist and biographer Percy Scholes in 1948, "never knows what literature that was widely popular amongst his own generation has become totally unknown, or at any rate only vaguely known by name, to the bright young generations following, and so it is possible that some readers of the present book are unacquainted with both Lytton's novel, *Eugene Aram* (1832), and Hood's poem...."[1] Just fifty years earlier, at the dawn of the twentieth century, the once modish writer and dilettante scholar, Lafcadio Hearn, then styled "interpreter of the Western world to Japan," had assured his students at the University of Tokyo that Hood's "Dream of Eugene Aram" was one of "those few pieces which every English person knows by heart" and which "certainly...will never die."[2] Hearn no doubt exaggerated Aram's fame; Scholes was more accurate. Aram was, in fact, well remembered for nearly a century and a half following his execution, a duration considerably greater than that of his present obscurity.

Although he is now little known, Aram is closely associated with several significant developments in literary history. Some of these associations, by their very nature, may in fact have contributed to his recent neglect. The many unusual circumstances of his life and character made him, above all, an obvious subject for the romantic excesses of Gothicism, Byronism, and melodrama. The maudlin propensities of the Aram theme inspired an emotional poem which became one of the nineteenth century's best-loved dramatic recitation pieces, and a novel whose rash sympathy for an avowed murderer outraged Victorian moralists but fed the less restricted tastes of the melodramatic theater-going public for several generations. The post–World War I reaction against the romantic modes to which Aram's story was so easily adapted is one clear reason for

Aram's subsequent decline as a fictional hero. That the reaction has now run its course is perhaps an equally good reason to revive him here.

As this and later chapters will show, Aram was not merely a subject for romance. He also figured in the topical literature of the liberal philosophical and political reform movements of late eighteenth- and early nineteenth-century England. His part in Godwin's *Caleb Williams* (1794), and in Bulwer's *Eugene Aram*, is important in the history of the Newgate (crime-and-punishment) novel, that popular genre which once flourished in the climate of penal reformist fervor.

1

William Godwin's *Things as They Are; Or, the Adventures of Caleb Williams* (later and more commonly called *Caleb Williams*) is considered by recent students of the genre to have been the first true detective novel in the language: "the first work of English fiction to display a sustained interest in the theme of detection,"[3] and "probably the most interesting novel in the last decade of the eighteenth century" for its innovative treatment of the criminal theme.[4] In it, "the characteristic note of crime literature is first struck."[5] While *Eugene Aram* is not a character in *Caleb Williams* and is specifically alluded to only once in the novel, there is substantial internal and biographical evidence to suggest that Aram's story was an important source from which Godwin drew thematic inspiration as well as details of incident and characterization.

Caleb Williams followed by one year the publication of Godwin's best-known work, *An Enquiry Concerning the Principles of Political Justice* (1793), which had been, like Thomas Paine's *The Rights of Man* (1791), a refutation of Burke's *Reflections on the Revolution in France* (1790). In the midst of the repressive, politically charged atmosphere of the late eighteenth-century reaction to the Jacobin revolution, Godwin risked arrest and prosecution by here setting forth the principles of his ideal anarchism and his opposition to governmental restraints upon individual freedom. *Political Justice* attacks nearly all the institutions of the organized state, including the legal system and the privileged aristocracy, the two most criticized in *Caleb Williams*.

Like Godwin's five other attempts at novel-writing after the appearance of *Political Justice,* Caleb Williams is a fictional complement to his master work, written to illustrate the ways in which a society founded on inequality makes victims of all its members. By its publication Godwin hoped to impress his revolutionary thought upon a larger segment of the reading public than any philosophical treatise would be likely to reach. For his subject he chose the outlaw life, a theme perennially appealing and yet expressive of his premise that society, not human nature, is responsible for criminal wrongdoing. As the philosopher-turned-novelist set out to write this, his first mature imaginative venture, he strained to create the details of plot necessary for credibility and interest. For inspiration he read systematically through the *Newgate Calendar* and several lesser chronicles of crime, particularly immersing himself in accounts of escape, flight, and pursuit, the pattern which he hoped would best exemplify the predatory qualities of social and legal injustice and so fulfill the philosophical purpose of his narrative. One recent article notes the many details Godwin drew from the life and escapades of the notorious eighteenth-century criminal and escape artist, Jack Sheppard.[6] No one has yet observed, however, the more pervasive influence of Eugene Aram, whose story of flight and capture after a fourteen-year interval has special bearing on the themes most central to *Caleb Williams*.

From childhood, Godwin must certainly have known Aram's history well, for in 1760, when Godwin was four and Aram dead less than a year, the Godwins moved from Debenham, Suffolk, to Guestwick, Norfolk, twenty-five miles from Lynn, the scene of Aram's arrest. Godwin is known to have visited Lynn with his family at least once. It would have been impossible to grow up in the area, still abuzz with the recent scandal, and not have heard many times of the usher who was executed for murder.

Later, an association of Godwin's school years must once again have brought the Aram story strikingly to his notice. During the years 1773–1778, while attending the dissenters' Coward Academy, at Hoxton, Kent, Godwin studied under Dr. Andrew Kippis, a respected philologist and classical scholar. Kippis, recognizing Godwin's potential, extended both moral and practical support to the young philosopher, introducing him to London publishers and securing him literary employment. In 1777 Kippis accepted a commission to revise and expand the monumental *Biographia Britannica*, whose first edition had appeared thirty years earlier. His inclusion of the life of Eugene Aram in this work memorializing England's great was warmly criticized at the time. Certainly the young Godwin would have been well aware of the ensuing controversy involving the convicted schoolmaster and his own friend and mentor.

Things as They Are, the original title of *Caleb Williams*, appropriately emphasizes its philosophical intent. The title was partly a play, no doubt, on that of Robert Bage's philosophical novel, *Man as He Is* (1792), although it has also been interpreted as an ironic comment on earlier novels of social ascendancy such as *Tom Jones* and *Pamela*, whose protagonists, unlike Godwin's, successfully surmount class barriers.[7] Godwin's novel, by contrast, was designed to illustrate the ways in which man, born without innate tendencies but equally capable of great evil or great good, is universally corrupted and victimized by society. In the scheme of the novel, as in *Political Justice*, it is society in the abstract which receives the blame — not the oppressors themselves or those whom the rigors of the social order impel to crime. The oppressed and the privileged alike, as symbolized by Godwin's protagonist and antagonist, suffer irreparable moral damage from the inequity that divides them.

The human race, Godwin believed, is ultimately perfectible and its members essentially equal at birth. Most of the differences among them and most individual human failings are artificially induced by social institutions, particularly the English class system, which, as *Caleb Williams* demonstrates, grants the young aristocrat full opportunity, economic and otherwise, for intellectual growth yet poisons his mind with a false sense of superiority. The lower classes, on the other hand, can better themselves only by exceptional initiative and against almost insurmountable hardship. Godwin's ideal vision of human perfectibility demands, in contrast, that each individual enjoy every means for self-fulfillment, free from the debilitating afflictions of poverty and social degradation.

"My neighbor," wrote Godwin, "has just as much right to put an end to my existence with a dagger or poison as to deny me that pecuniary assistance without which my intellectual attainments or my moral exertions will be materially injured."[8] The observation applies equally as well to Eugene Aram, whose bitter reaction to scholarly poverty was said to have driven him to crime, as it does to Godwin's own creation, the first-person narrator, Caleb Williams. Like Eugene Aram, Caleb, although "born of humble parents, in a remote county of England,"[9] possessed from youth an unusual eagerness for knowledge and a love of books incompatible with his means. The section in Caleb's memoirs that describes his early self-guided struggle for education of a level "greater than my condition in life afforded room to expect" (p. 4) is reminiscent of Aram's own autobiographical account, which Godwin must surely have read in the *Newgate Calendar*.

Aram's lack of books was, however, offset by his father's position as a favored servant of the neighboring squire, another detail which is echoed in Caleb's history. As Aram had served the Blackett family as clerk, so Caleb, upon his father's death, is employed as personal secretary to Squire Falkland, the paragon ostensibly of cultured, beneficent English gentility but actually of aristocratic oppression. Caleb's ruling passion, insatiable curiosity, soon leads him to unearth a mortal secret lurking in his employer's past. Some years previously, Caleb learns, Falkland was involved in a feud with another squire, Tyrrel, who was as much the brute and reprobate as Falkland is the gentleman. Tyrrel, shortly after having publicly humiliated Falkland in a fight, was found murdered, whereupon two of Tyrrel's yeoman-tenants, a father and son named Hawkins, whose lives he had mercilessly plagued for some time, were hanged for the crime. Caleb discovers, however, through artful interrogation of his master, that Falkland was the true murderer, and confirms his discovery by breaking into a forbidden iron chest containing some deliberately unspecified evidence of Falkland's guilt.

Falkland, who was nurtured on the "poison of chivalry" and whose sense of honor and respectability has once led him to murder, is now similarly compelled to persecution. In order to prevent disclosure, he threatens Caleb with virtual imprisonment at the manor, but the young man escapes. To explain his pursuit, Falkland secretes jewelry among Caleb's effects and publicly charges him with theft. Dogged by Falkland's agents, Caleb passes through numerous adventures. Like a melodramatic Lord Jim, wherever he establishes himself he finds that the influence of his enemy follows, stirring the prejudices of his neighbors and forcing him to move on. Despite the reputation his own integrity has won, the mere accusation is enough to ruin him, just as the citizens of Lynn, who respected Aram before his arrest, readily accused him afterwards not only of attempted theft of school moneys but of promiscuity and even incest. Several times in the course of the narrative Caleb is captured, and each time he escapes the authorities, who, like everyone else, are automatically convinced of his guilt by the simple fact of his accuser's rank and reputation.

At last, in desperation, Caleb resolves to confront and expose his tormentor in public court. It is not, however, the court system which ultimately upholds the justice of Caleb's accusation, but Falkland himself, who, broken and dying, confesses. Yet the victory is hollow for Caleb, who now realizes that his master was as much a victim as himself:

> Falkland, I will think only of thee...! A nobler spirit lived not among the sons of men. Thy intellectual powers were truly sublime, and thy bosom burned with a godlike ambition. But of what use are talents and sentiments in the corrupt wilderness of human society? It is a rank and rotten soil, from which every finer shrub draws poison as it grows. (p. 325)

Godwin, in a preface dated May 12, 1794, termed his novel "a general review of the modes of domestic and unrecorded despotism, by which man becomes the destroyer of man" (p. 1). The anti-aristocratic implications of this and similar statements led the booksellers to omit the preface from the first edition, although it was printed intact in the second edition of 1796. The original suppression of Godwin's statement of intent seems almost gratuitous since the anti-aristocratic theme is so conspicuous in the novel itself. Falkland, its main exponent, is, like all of Godwin's heroes who exemplify his philosophy of human development, a victim of environment, but he also, in turn, victimizes others. His adherence to the poisonous ingrained aristocratic ideal impels him to murder, firsthand in the case of Tyrrel and indirect in his acquiescence to the hanging of the innocent father and son subsequently accused of the crime. Always it is his distorted sense of honor and not self-preservation which motivates his concealment of the crime. That motivation becomes an obsession when Caleb discovers his secret and Falkland, feeling that he must hide his guilt at any cost, moves to protect his reputation by blasting Caleb's. In so doing he brings both himself and his servant to destruction. The tragedies which beset the lives of every major character before the novel's end are, as Godwin stresses in many an authorial aside, indirectly owing to that social system whose law is "better adapted for a weapon of tyranny in the hands of the rich, than for a shield to protect the humbler part of the community against their usurpations" (p. 73). Thus Falkland represents not only the squirearchy but the entire social order of rank and class whose power over the individual is so absolute and so malign.

In the radical philosophy of the late eighteenth century, the circumstances of Eugene Aram's life appeared to exemplify the evils of this unequal social order. The deprivations of his social station, in conflict with his intelligence and his scholarly inclinations, are noted in nearly every account of his life, including those two sources which Godwin read — the *Newgate Calendar* and the *Annual Register*. Such hardship, especially in view of Aram's consciousness of ancestral heritage and the prestige and wealth his family had once enjoyed, was often pointed to, by his sympathizers, as a psychological motive for his crime. To have been brought up in an atmosphere of refinement at Newby Hall with the doors of Sir Edward Blackett's library open to him, and then to have found his ultimate fortunes, like those of his family through the centuries, so undeservedly reduced, would have galled many a man less cognizant of his own worth. Thus interpreted, the Aram case is a clear instance of Godwin's belief that the criminal is to be pitied as a victim of circumstance and environment — and of social inequity in particular. As such it must certainly have struck the philosopher.

The Godwinian philosophy is still more applicable to Aram's case in the issue of penal reform, and it is in this context that *Caleb Williams* alludes specifically to Eugene Aram. In *Political Justice*, Godwin had taken the radical stance of almost complete opposition to any form of punishment for crime. Since he believed that environmental inequality is the source of most crime, the criminal in Godwin's fatalistic world view is not responsible for his own act in that, given the circumstances, he could not have done otherwise. Therefore, coercion is never justifiable as retribution for past sins. The one admissible action against the criminal, according to Godwinian utilitarianism, is humane detainment—an acceptable course only if the person detained is a threat to the general well-being. A primary spokesman of these views in *Caleb Williams* is Raymond, outlaw leader of a gang of thieves who come to Caleb's aid on the road. They are, in the tradition of Gay's *Beggar's Opera*, "thieves without a license, . . . at open war with another set of thieves according to law" (p. 216). Raymond condemns the law especially for holding men guilty of crimes long past, even though they have since repented and reformed. The courts, he says,

> leave no room for amendment. . . . It signifies not what is the character of the individual at the hour of trial. How changed, how spotless, and how useful, avails him nothing. If they discover at the distance of fourteen [Here Godwin's note reads: "Eugene Aram. See Annual Register for 1759."] or of forty years an action for which the law ordains that his life shall be the forfeit, though the interval should have been spent with the purity of a saint and the devotedness of a patriot, they disdain to enquire into it. (pp. 227–228)

There was, among Godwin's loose papers catalogued and recorded by his first major biographer, C. Kegan Paul, further evidence that the author strongly associated with Aram his aversion to civil punishment. A page from the period 1828–1830, more than thirty years after the publication of *Caleb Williams*, is interpreted by Kegan Paul as a fragmentary plan for a novel on the subject of Eugene Aram. There, preceded by a terse chronology of the major events of Aram's history, appears the following notation:

> Let there be an Act of $P^{t.}$ that, after a lapse of ten years, whoever shall be found to have spent that period blamelessly, and in labours conducive to the welfare of mankind, shall be absolved.
>
> No man shall die respecting whom it can reasonably be concluded that if his life were spared, it would be spent blamelessly, honourably, and usefully. [10]

Godwin, who died in 1836, never wrote the story of Aram's life. That was a project anticipated instead in 1831 by his young devotee, Edward Bulwer.

If Godwin himself did not fulfill his designs for a book-length, explicit treatment of the Aram theme, his history of Caleb Williams recalls Aram's in other striking ways. At one point Godwin describes a prison scene in order to evoke sympathy for those within. To emphasize that punitive detention is an affront to human dignity and human rights he draws upon the incongruity of great potential consigned to languish in squalor and disease. The most affecting episode in this section is Caleb's account of Brightwel, his fellow-prisoner, a scholar-soldier who dies of jail fever just prior to his acquittal:

> The character of the prisoner was such as has seldom been equalled. He had been ardent in the pursuit of intellectual cultivation, and was accustomed to draw his favourite amusement from the works of Virgil and Horace. The humbleness of his situation, combined with his ardour for literature, only served to give an inexpressible heightening to the interestingness of his character. . . . he declined offers that had been made him to become a sergeant or a corporal, saying that in a new situation he should have less leisure for study. . . .This man died while I was in prison. I received his last breath. (pp. 179–180)

The historical Brightwell (the actual spelling), whose tragic career Godwin closely recreated, was, like Aram, a classical scholar. As Godwin penned this episode he almost certainly had in mind the lives of both men, which he had recently read in the *Newgate Calendar*, in whose annals accounts of scholarly persons are rare.[11]

Caleb's character, in its scholarly inclination, also noticeably reflects Aram's. Both men owe their downfall in part to an intellectual acquisitiveness irreconcilable with the poverty of their origins. Caleb admits early in his narrative that "curiosity" is his ruling passion, without which he would never have suspected his master's guilt and aroused his antagonism. Aram, in the romantic view of his character, resorted to crime either as a desperate means of financing his studies and buying books, or in a spirit of moral rage at the immobilizing poverty to which he was bound.

The kinship of mind as well as circumstance between Caleb Williams and Eugene Aram is pointedly evident in one particular passage of Godwin's novel. Here, Caleb, having temporarily escaped the cognizance of Falkland and his agents, retreats to a peaceful, remote Welsh village where the schoolmaster, he relates, "was willing to admit me as a partner in the task of civilizing the unpolished manners of the inhabitants" (p. 290). While thus established, he continues,

> I soon felt the desire of some additional and vigorous pursuit. In this state of mind, I met by accident, in a neglected corner of the house of one of my neighbours, with a general dictionary of four of the northern languages. This incident gave a direction to my thoughts....I determined to attempt, at least for my own use, an etymological analysis of the English language. I easily perceived, that...a small number of books, consulted with this view, would afford employment for a considerable time. I procured other dictionaries. In my incidental reading, I noted the manner in which words were used, and applied these remarks to the illustration of my general enquiry. I was unintermitted in my assiduity, and my collections promised to accumulate. Thus I was provided with sources both of industry and recreation, the more completely to divert my thoughts from the recollection of my past misfortunes. (pp. 294–295)

In vocation and avocation Godwin's hero is at this point identical with the usher and philologist of Lynn.[12] Also like Aram, however, he soon finds the trust of his neighbors and his newfound reputation shattered by an accusatory reverberation from the past. This similar injustice, as Godwin perceived it, was for both Eugene Aram and Caleb Williams the crux of their tragedy.

Finally, the tone of the opening section of Aram's celebrated defense speech, which Godwin would also have found in the *Calendar*, seems to echo in the affirmation of innocence which prefaces Caleb's retrospective narrative:

> My life has for several years been a theatre of calamity....My fairest prospects have been blasted....Every one, as far as my story has been known, has refused to assist me in my distress, and has execrated my name. I have not deserved this treatment. My own conscience witnesses in behalf of that innocence, my pretensions to which are regarded in the world as incredible. There is now, however, little hope that I shall escape from the toils that universally beset me. (p. 3)

Through both Aram's self-defense and Caleb's there runs the same solitary dignity, the same personal fortitude in defiance of societal hostility and almost certain destruction. Thus *Caleb Williams* marks the beginning of Aram's association with fictional literature, although he informs its pages in spirit rather than — with the exception of a single note — in name.

2

A lesser instance of Aram's relevance to the late eighteenth- and early nineteenth-century liberal reform movement appears in another Jacobin novel, by a different hand, which followed soon after the publication of *Caleb Williams*. *The Memoirs of Bryan Perdue* (1805) deserves brief mention here because, like its predecessor, it also invokes the name of Eugene Aram in the cause against capital punishment. *Bryan Perdue* was Thomas Holcroft's last novel, a product of the declining years of a once notorious leader of the English radical camp. Holcroft is best known to literary historians for his doctrinal novel *Hugh Trevor* (1794), which was similar to *Caleb Williams* in its espousal of revolutionary ideas, and also for a number of sentimental dramas, the most successful of which was *The Road to Ruin* (1792). *Bryan Perdue*, an ungainly melding of past trends in fiction, superimposes upon a picaresque framework the contrasting modes of sentiment and broad satire. In the latter quality is manifest Holcroft's deep bitterness toward the social system which had been so unreceptive to his ideals. The digressive, eccentric, almost egomaniacal narrative *persona* of the *Memoirs* is crudely imitative of Fielding and Sterne but tiresome in its discursiveness and overdrawn in its use of irony.

The primary thematic intent of *Bryan Perdue* is to attack the institution of capital punishment. It was Holcroft's belief, as it was Godwin's, that moral character derives from external circumstances. Thus, like Caleb Williams and, by extension, Eugene Aram, Bryan Perdue, as his name suggests, is lost — not because he is innately wicked but because of the unfavorable conditions and influences of his formative years.

Born of Irish parents living in England, Bryan at the age of six falls under the pernicious control of his father, a reprobate gambler, upon the death of his gentle "lady mother." Sent away to school as an adolescent, he begins to practice his father's profession, gulling a schoolmate, Maximilian Lord Froth, out of his term allowance. Shortly after, Bryan is orphaned when his father is killed in a brawl, and cast out when Maximilian exposes his vice to the school authorities. Despite the help and advice of his former tutor, who secures him a place in an accounting firm, Bryan sinks further into dissipation, gambling feverishly to maintain a fashionable London courtesan, the Nonpareil, whom he steals away from another gull, Maximilian's adult counterpart, Lord Loiter. Inevitably, Bryan is arrested for debt. As an expedient to secure his release, he falsely endorses a check belonging to his employer. Again he is arrested, but this time for forgery, a capital crime. By the intervention of right-thinking friends who have consistently deplored his weakness, he is acquitted, having at last realized the folly of his youth. Chagrined and conscience-stricken, he flees to Jamaica to begin a new life. There, as a plantation overseer, he works to benefit the Negro slave population, securing them more humane treatment, seeking to dispel the superstitious traumas of their pagan beliefs and bring them to the light of reason. As the ultimate gesture at the story's end, he marries Rachel Palmer, the modest daughter of a neighboring Quaker plantation owner.

It is, of course, Bryan's near brush with the death penalty which occasions most of the novel's concern with penal reform. The elderly authorial *persona* of the *Memoirs*, reflecting on his treacherous past, stresses "that it is the duty of men not to take away life, which cannot be restored, and thus indolently to rid themselves of a supposed evil; but determinedly to inquire how life, even in the most depraved, may still be made a thing of utility?"[13] It is in this connection that our author calls upon the memory of Eugene Aram, in company with another notorious felon of the age:

> Oh, that the guilty might be sent, like patients afflicted with dangerous disease, to hospitable mansions, that might be humanely constructed for their reception, and their reform!
>
> How many men of enterprise and high faculty would then be preserved! What might the mind of Jack Shepherd [*sic*] have achieved, had its powers been directed to their proper end! He was abandoned; he gloried in vice: alas! it was only because such was the stimulus that had been given him. Turn such miraculous powers to a different purpose, to the mighty ends of virtue, and what would they then have produced? How inestimable might have been the labors of Eugene Aram, that man of extraordinary attainments and stupendous faculties! Nay, how doubtful was his guilt! how doubtful even the crime for which he suffered! How easily are minds like these destroyed! but by whom shall they be restored? (III, 127–128)

Bryan is intended, like Eugene and Caleb before him, to represent a prodigious intellect whose potential is stunted and misshapen by adversity. For him, as for them, the blind workings of punitive societal justice pose a threat not only to the full play of intellect but to the sacred existence of the individual as well. Bryan resembles his predecessors in one further respect, which places him even more decidedly in kinship with them. He is, like many fictional voices before him, in the best eighteenth-century tradition, a "projector"—a formulator of grand schemes and designs for the improvement of the world. The following passages will serve to describe his particular affinity with Aram and Williams:

> I cannot let this opportunity escape of informing the world of the system which I mean to write. . .in which I shall make a full display and copious communication of the acute, the learned, and the profound discoveries that I have made, and the innumerable analogies, synonimes, etimologies, orthographic transformations, metaphoric changes; words simple and words copulative, that I have observed generating and degenerating by and among the Syriac, Chaldaic, Hebrew, Celtic, Arabic, Persian, Grecian, Gothic, Sclavonic, Teutonic, and all their bastard progeny; connecting them all with nations and tribes, antiquities, chronologies, histories, local customs, oral traditions, legends, Eastern mythologies, migrations from— (I, 120–121)

Here, for a space, the narrator checks his digression and resumes the story line, returning to his linguistic bent some chapters later in satiric flight:

> I have in view to write a treatise on the organs of utterance, and the powers of sound, its modulations, and various degrees of intelligence; the whole illustrated by examples, beginning with animals, such as the goose and the ass, and ending with actors, divines, parliamentary orators, and the best singers of the grand French opera. (I, 157)

The study of language was, during Aram's time, as well as Godwin's and Holcroft's, a common interest among antiquaries and scholars. The interest in Celtic studies especially had, by the turn of the eighteenth century, become so great that it has since been characterized as "Celtomania." That both Godwin and Holcroft attributed this pursuit to their protagonists may, therefore, simply reflect its prevalence at that date. Yet it is coincidentally significant that all three linguists, Aram and his fictional counterparts, express particular concern with the ancient affinities of the same sister languages, in a pattern whose true significance was not universally recognized until much later. As Caleb Williams and Bryan Perdue give voice to an observation which Eugene Aram was among the first to make, that connection could hardly have been far from the thoughts of either Godwin or Holcroft.

It is possible that Thomas Holcroft's mention of Aram in much the same manner as Godwin's a decade before was not purely accidental. As the radicals of the day met to trade opinions, the instance of Eugene

Aram would have been a convenient case in point for their views on the deplorable state of English justice. Holcroft and Godwin were particularly prone to such exchange. They were close in friendship as well as in ideology, Holcroft having been one of twelve leaders of the London reform societies who together were indicted for treason in 1794 and eventually acquitted as the direct result, many believed, of a pamphlet written by Godwin in their defense. When Holcroft's narrator speaks of his desperation as a prisoner on trial for his life, overwhelmed by the manifest injustice of the threat against it, he speaks from the depth of his creator's heart.

3

The next noteworthy appearance of Eugene Aram in his native literature was not politically oriented. It is, however, of pivotal significance to the history of the Aram theme. Not only was Thomas Hood's ballad "The Dream of Eugene Aram" (1829) the first fictional work centrally devoted to its subject; it also captured the popular imagination and thus stimulated the fresh burst of interest in the story which was to endure throughout the nineteenth and into the twentieth century. The piece ranks high in the body of Hood's non-humorous work. After a period of self-consciously imitative romanticism, it was the first sustained evidence of his own individual powers as a serious poet.

"The Dream of Eugene Aram" was immediately recognized as an achievement. The *Literary Gazette* gave it high praise, printing it in full in the course of a review of *The Gem*, the literary annual edited by Hood in which it first appeared. Sir John Bowring, like Hood a contributor to the *London Magazine*, assured the author, "I will put ['The Dream'] by the side of the very grandest productions of poetical conception." The Quaker poet Bernard Barton, another *London Magazine* contributor, wrote him, "Thy own Poem of 'Eugene Aram' is the gem of the 'Gem'; and alone worth the price of the book. I thank the *Gazette* critic for quoting that entire, as I shall cut it out and save it."[14] (Barton, who intended to clip rather than buy, was apparently unaware of the contradiction in his words.) The poem was so well received that in 1831 it was republished in separate form as *The Dream of Eugene Aram, The Murderer*, this time with engravings by Hood's friend William Harvey and a dedication to his friend and brother-in-law, John Hamilton Reynolds.

Hood's preface to the 1831 edition attributes the story line of his poem to a tradition received from the reminiscences of Adm. James Burney (1750–1821). Burney, son of Dr. Charles Burney, the pioneer music historian, and brother of Fanny Burney, the novelist, was best known for participating in the second and third of Capt. James Cook's historic voyages of exploration (1772–1774 and 1775–1779). As a young lieutenant he came home in command of the *Discovery* after Cook was murdered during a native insurrection in the Sandwich Islands. At eight years of age, Burney had been one of Eugene Aram's pupils in the grammar school at Lynn when the usher was arrested in 1758. In later life, the veteran was fond of relating the story—how the melancholy Aram, beloved by the children under his charge, would indulge his habit of "pacing the play-ground arm-in-arm with some one of the elder boys, and seeking relief from the unsuspected burthen of his conscience by talking of strange murders, and how he [Burney]...had shuddered at the hand- cuffs on his teacher's hands when taken away in the post-chaise to prison."[15] Although Eric Watson discredits the authenticity of Burney's story on the basis of his extreme youth at the time, its credibility is some- what enhanced by the fact that James, at eight, was no ordinary child. Described as "an unusually bright and manly lad, full of vivacity and high spirits,"[16] he was to enter the navy just two years later as a nominal midshipman (the general term for a boy in training as an officer candidate). Thus while it is possible that his memories were elaborated by traditions prevalent in afteryears, there is little reason to entirely discount his childhood perceptions.

Burney's account, it may be conjectured, reached Hood, who had not known the admiral personally, through the agency of Charles Lamb, who had been frequently in his company. According to the reminiscences of Sir Thomas Noon Talfourd, Lamb's friend and executor, "Admiral Burney...seemed to unite our society with the circle over which Dr. Johnson reigned;...the Admiral being himself the centre of a little circle which his sister...sometimes graced."[17] A passage in a letter of 1843, from Hood to his son-in-law, further points to the possibility of Lamb's connection with the origins of this poem: "Charles Lamb once said to me that the most knowing man in the world was one who had done a Murder, & had not been found out:—for example Eugene Aram, during the 14 years that he was unsuspected."[18]

It was Burney's reminiscence which inspired the central device of Hood's poem—the tortured outpouring of Aram's guilt enacted in dramatic monologue before the startlingly incongruous audience of a child-confessor. The irony of that situation distinguishes Hood's work from all other fictional renderings of the Aram theme. The first section (ll. 1–72) juxtaposes images of innocence and lightheartedness in a flock of children newly released from school against the labored guilt and despair of the lonely usher brooding at a distance. These two strains converge when Aram comes upon one boy reading apart form the rest in a secluded grove. The core of the poem (ll. 73–210) is Aram's emotional monologue, an agonized recounting of the murder and its aftermath presented to the boy as events in a dream. The ambivalence of the dream state is a favorite romantic motif, but here it serves a special psychological purpose: by this deception, Aram can ease his guilty soul in the first person without direct admission of the crime. Hood's post-cathartic final stanza creates a memorable image of Aram's arrest and a subdued restoration of the initial calm.

The poem in its entirety is a study in paradox and discord. Its protagonist is a gentle murderer beloved by children, a moral philosopher who has committed the most vile of crimes, a man of exquisite feeling at odds with the universe. Hood's ability to convey these disparities without sacrificing unity of theme and image is remarkable. At the outset he establishes contrasting patterns of imagery suggestive, although in a rather hackneyed way, of ascendance and decline, health and infirmity, joy and sorrow, tranquillity and turbulence, warmth and chill, light and dark. The first sixteen lines are ostensibly given to youth, joy, and vitality:

'Twas in the prime of summer time,
　　An evening calm and cool,
And four-and-twenty happy boys
　　Came bounding out of school:
There were some that ran and some that leapt,
　　Like troutlets in a pool.

Away they sped with gamesome minds,
　　And souls untouched by sin;
To a level mead they came, and there
　　They drave the wickets in:
Pleasantly shone the setting sun
　　Over the town of Lynn.

Like sportive deer they cours'd about,
　　And shouted as they ran,—
Turning to mirth all things of earth,
　　As only boyhood can;...[19]

For their burden of subtle portent, these stanzas have been compared to the opening of Gray's "Ode on a Distant Prospect of Eton College."[20] Already there are undertones of what is to follow. Summer is at its zenith: decline is imminent. It is evening and the sun is setting over the town of

Lynn, as it is soon to set over the life of Aram. Above all, the comment
that the boys' souls are as yet "untouched by sin" foreshadows the ensuing
contrast.

The next three stanzas parallel the first three. As the boys pursue
their cricket match, the melancholy usher, removed from their gaiety both
physically and spiritually, pores over a book which several details suggest
may be a Bible:

> His hat was off, his vest apart,
>   To catch heaven's blessed breeze;
> For a burning thought was in his brow,
>   And his bosom ill at ease:
> So he lean'd his head on his hands, and read
>   The book between his knees!
>
> Leaf after leaf he turn'd it o'er,
>   Nor ever glanc'd aside,
> For the peace of his soul he read that book
>   In the golden eventide:
> Much study had made him very lean,
>   And pale, and leaden-ey'd.
>
> At last he shut the ponderous tome,
>   With a fast and fervent grasp
> He strain'd the dusky covers close,
>   And fix'd the brazen hasp:
> "Oh, God! could I so close my mind,
>   And clasp it with a clasp!"

Here the poet plays upon images of calm and turmoil. The boys, despite
the excitement of the cricket match, enjoy an innocent tranquillity of
spirit. Aram, despite his quiet bearing, suffers profound spiritual unrest.
Their vitality contrasts with his pale ill health.

Hood's next move is the conjunction of the disparate elements introduced in the first six stanzas. Aram can hardly interrupt the cricket match
in order to bare his guilt. Rather, he gravitates toward a soul more akin
with his own. Introspective and solitary, the child is, like Aram, reading
when first we see him. His tastes, furthermore, incline to the morbid, for
he says he is reading a murder story, Salomon Gessner's *The Death of
Abel*.[21] At this point originates the Cain motif which reappears in a
number of lines later in the poem. Aram's first reaction is shock. He
instinctively recoils, moves away a few paces, but then returns, drawn

compulsively into instruction heavily laced with masochistic self-absorption:

> And down he sat beside the lad,
>   And talk'd with him of Cain;
>
> And, long since then, of bloody men,
>   Whose deeds tradition saves;
> Of lonely folk cut off unseen,
>   And hid in sudden graves;
> Of horrid stabs, in groves forlorn,
>   And murders done in caves;. . .

(ll. 53–60)

That Aram and the boy meet in shade and forest is significant, for much of the poem's natural imagery dwells upon pits, grottoes, and dank wooded recesses suggestive of the dark forbidden places in the human soul.

"The young boy gave an upward glance." Engraving by William Harvey, accompanying Hood's *The Dream of Eugene Aram, The Murderer* (1831).

Aram's general discourse on murder soon becomes intensely personal as he pours forth the melodramatic nightmare confession which occupies most of the poem's length:

> "...Methought, last night, I wrought
>   A murder, in a dream!..."
>
> (ll. 77–78)

The usher continues, becoming increasingly agonized in his utterance as he recounts his brutal murder of a feeble old man, his sense that afterwards the corpse was not truly dead, and his futile attempts to conceal the body, first by casting it in a deep river and again by covering it with mounds of leaves in a secluded forest. His narrative moves inexorably, broken at one point only, when he suddenly recovers himself and pauses:

> "My gentle Boy, remember this
>   Is nothing but a dream!"
>
> (ll. 125–126)

In the dramatic simplicity of Hood's language and his eerie mingling of reality with unreality in the context of dream, an indebtedness to Coleridge's *The Rime of the Ancient Mariner* (1798) has often been detected. Throughout Aram's monologue, in a manner reminiscent of the mariner's, images of joy that recall the opening stanzas are consumed and obliterated in the speaker's mind by the encompassing agony of his nightmare vision:

> "Anon I cleans'd my bloody hands,
>   And wash'd my forehead cool,
> And sat among the urchins young,
>   That evening in the school!
>
> "Oh, Heaven! to think of their white souls,
>   And mine so black and grim!
> I could not share in childish prayer,
>   Nor join in Evening Hymn:
> Like a Devil of the Pit I seem'd,
>   'Mid holy Cherubim!
>
> (ll. 129–138)

> . . . .

> "Merrily rose the lark, and shook
>   The dew-drop from its wing;

> But I never mark'd its morning flight,
>   I never heard it sing:
> For I was stooping once again
>   Under the horrid thing."
>
> (ll. 169–174)

The dominant colors in the piece are starkly dramatic: black and white shot through with red and gold. The volume from which Aram reads in the "golden eventide" (l. 28) is bound in "dusky covers" (l. 33). The murder, perpetrated for the sake of gold, occurs in the dark of night under a pale, clear moon. The water into which the body is cast is "'black as ink'" (l. 123). The souls of the children are white; Aram's is "'black and grim'" (l. 134). The crimson of blood and flames permeates his guilty consciousness.

Personification, which Hood had hitherto employed with lavish excess in romantically imitative work, here is relatively rare, and when it does occur it is more or less appropriate to the speaker's distracted state and his sense of a universe bent on vengeance. The "'frowning sky'" (l. 115) looks down upon the murderer as he stands over his victim's corpse. Perhaps the best example of the sort is the following conceit:

> "...Guilt was my grim Chamberlain
>   That lighted me to bed;
> And drew my midnight curtains round,
>   With fingers bloody red!"
>
> (ll. 141–144)

The agony of guilt and, above all, the inevitability of its discovery are the essential themes of Hood's poem. Our first vision of the tormented usher shows us how guilt has racked his frame, but physical infirmity, it soon becomes clear, is as nothing compared to his sickness of soul. His anguish at the point of murder is worse than what his victim suffers, for "'A dozen times I groan'd; the dead / Had never groan'd but twice!'" (ll. 113–114). Just as he is impelled to the crime by some unnameable quality in his soul, he cannot help but dwell upon and relive its consequences:

> "Stronger and stronger every pulse
>   Did that temptation crave,—
> Still urging me to go and see
>   The Dead Man in his grave!"
>
> (ll. 159–162)

. . . .

"Oh, God! that horrid, horrid dream
    Besets me now awake!
Again — again, with dizzy brain,
    The human life I take;
And my red right hand grows raging hot,
    Like Cranmer's at the stake.

"And still no peace for the restless clay,
    Will wave or mould allow;
The horrid thing pursues my soul,—
    It stands before me now!"

(ll. 199–208)

The God in the poem, despite the fact that at one point He speaks
directly from the heavens to this latter-day Cain—"'Thou guilty man! take
up thy dead / And hide it from my sight!'" (ll. 119–120)—remains aloof
and indefinite. Yet the fatal certainty that "murder will out" is ever
present, until it is confirmed in the restrained irony of the final stanza:

That very night, while gentle sleep
    The urchin eyelids kiss'd,
Two stern-faced men set out from Lynn,
    Through the cold and heavy mist;
And Eugene Aram walked between,
    With gyves upon his wrist.

(ll. 211–216)[22]

Hood, as "The Dream of Eugene Aram" clearly demonstrates, considered the historical Aram to have been guilty of the crime imputed to
him. Presumably Admiral Burney's memories of the usher's habitual dis-
courses on murder led the poet to conceive of Aram as a man driven by
remorse. This romantic view, however, is inconsistent with the prevailing
tradition. Aram's reported bearing at his trial on the contrary suggests
moral indifference. There is no evidence that Hood researched his subject
before writing "The Dream" or even that he considered historical accuracy
at all important. But in several other respects as well the poem departs
significantly from the historical tradition. The real Aram, for instance,
appears to have taken religion rather lightly. The few references in his
writings to matters spiritual are characterized by a cool, deistic rationalism, and Aram was in fact censured by the contemporary pamphleteers
for his unorthodoxy. Whatever anxiety concerning his fate he may have
suffered during the months he spent at Lynn, it is quite unlikely that the

"'fierce avenging Sprite'" was uppermost in his thoughts. Other discrepancies, initiated by Hood to preserve focus and enhance the nightmare quality, include the facts that Aram did not act alone and that his victim was neither old, feeble, nor harmless but, on the contrary, appears to have been involved in conspiracy along with the men who murdered him. The accurate incorporation of such details would clearly have detracted from Hood's emphasis on personal guilt and rendered the story unworkable in so compact a form.

That Hood's poem first appeared in the gift-annual format so much in vogue at the time suggests its popular tendency. Designed primarily as genteel gifts for the holiday season and typically housed in an ostentatious cover and slipcase, the former of silk, velvet, or embossed morocco, appliquéd perhaps with pictures of flowers or cherubs, or bestudded with semiprecious jewels, these publications appealed not to the mind so much as to the eye and heart. Their titles—*Friendship's Offering, Forget Me Not, The Keepsake, The Amulet, The Winter's Wreath, The Iris, The Bijou, The Aurora Borealis*—are suggestive of tender sentiment or exotic elegance. More often than not, the stories and verses within were commissioned to accompany the illustrative plates to which they were appended, although such was not the case with this particular poem of Hood's. As the concept of the gift annual was imported from Germany, so also was its characteristic content: preoccupied with tombs and sepulchers, infanticide and premature burial; and peopled with mysterious monks, fated lovers, and reclusive, tormented aristocrats in the gloomiest romantic mode. It was a gallery of types in which Hood's Aram does not seem out of place. *The Gem*, which Hood edited in the year his poem appeared, was a literary annual much superior to the ordinary fare yet sharing many of the same proclivities. Among its contributors were Keats, Scott, Lamb, Hartley Coleridge, and the poet John Hamilton Reynolds. At the time, nearly every writer of any repute and many with none were published in the annuals, although they often shared the opinion of Southey, who scorned such productions as "picture books for adult children."[23]

Two additional circumstances in the poem's later history—its translation into German and its prominence in Victorian England as a recitation piece—still more clearly attest to its impact on the nineteenth-century audience both at home and abroad. In Germany, "The Dream" had a special fascination, as might be expected from the many elements in its make-up which coincide with German romanticism: the introspective torment of the guilt-stricken protagonist, the sense of a grand universal fate bent on exposing the evil deed and its perpetrator's guilt, the morbid emphasis on death and decay which pervades the mood of the poem. Although the work has since appeared in many languages, the first such translation was the German *Eugen Aram, oder das Verbrechen als Gegenstand der Kunst* [Crime as an object of art], published in 1841 by Philip Von Franck and H. A. Rühe.

In 1835, Hood had fallen temporarily into debt and, like Scott before him, had chosen to repay the sum rather than take the easier course of bankruptcy. He therefore removed his family for several years to Coblenz in order to escape his creditors and earn, by his pen, the money he owed them. There he initiated his long friendship with Lt. Philip Von Franck (or De Franck), who was an anglophile by virtue of partly English parentage. Hood was delighted to learn that the colonel in charge of the young lieutenant's regiment was translating "The Dream of Eugene Aram" for his wife, although letters written at the time suggest that his pleasure was mitigated by the fact that the colonel had heard of it through Bulwer's novel. ("Bulwer...is a demi-god here," Hood wrote.) (Furthermore, he was apprehensive of the translator's success, since the poem "was in the most difficult style possible to translate into German; plain, almost Quaker-like; whereas the German poetical style is flowery almost to excess."[24]

It was after Hood had returned to England that Von Franck and his collaborator, H. A. Rühe, prepared and published their own translation. In a gesture of international consocation it was dedicated to Albert, the royal consort, to whom Hood forwarded a complimentary copy at the translators' request. The letter of acknowledgment Hood wrote Von Franck upon receipt of the presentation copies facetiously belies his approval of the venture:

> How can I express my delight...? Jane [Hood's wife]...looked as happy as if I had been transported instead of translated. But the next moment I was horrified, for I saw your name, 'Von Franck,' as one of the translators!...a lieutenant of the 19th Infanterie regiment! Oh! Jane! (here I fairly groaned to think of it), Oh! Jane! We know...what sort of work a *Prussian soldier* will make of poetry! Zounds! he will make him *march* up and down [cf. ll. 38–39: "Some moody turns he took,— / Now up the mead, then down the mead"] '*rechtsum und linksum*'....I actually cried *dry*, for I was too shocked to shed tears at the picture.
>
> But this comes, said I, of your young whiskered Sword-Blades that sigh so for war, and because it is peace, and no other

butchery stirring, they must go and murder Eugene Aram, as well as Daniel Clarke![25]

In England, for decades afterward, the poem enjoyed another kind of translation—from the written to the spoken word. A favorite amusement of the Victorian era was the dramatic recitation of selections drawn from literature. The practitioners of this art were often amateurs: the *paterfamilias* who rehearsed the latest installment of a current novel for an evening's presentation before the drawing room circle; or the schoolboy whose term program might require a nervous rendition of Felicia Hemans's "The Boy Stood on the Burning Deck" or Macaulay's "Horatius at the Bridge." Professional actors and authors as well—Dickens being the most prominent example of the latter—commonly augmented their income by staged readings in lecture halls and theaters, usually alone but sometimes to an organ or pantomime accompaniment. "The Dream of Eugene Aram," because of its emotional intensity and the horrific effect it could have upon a susceptible audience, was one title so frequently chosen for recitation that it became a stock piece almost emblematic of the practice. As a former schoolmate of Aubrey Beardsley's later recalled, the future illustrator once "gave a most impressive rendering of 'Eugene Aram'" at a Brighton Grammar School program in the 1880s.[26] Some years earlier, the actors and management of London's Pavilion Theatre at their communal suppers were often entertained with Hood's poem delivered by a nonprofessional whose love of the theater had made him one of their society. Although they could not know it at the time, they were being treated to a striking display of pre-Stanislavskian character identification, for their soliloquist was none other than Henry Wainwright, the London businessman apprehended in 1875 trying to dispose of the severed remains of his mistress, whom he had murdered nearly a year before.[27]

The one great professional interpreter of "The Dream" was the renowned actor Sir Henry Irving. Said to have been his favorite among the readings in his vast repertoire, and certainly the most familiar to his audiences, it was performed by him on countless occasions throughout his career from the late 1860s until after the century's close, either as an interlude between two brief plays on the same bill or in the course of a program of readings. Irving, as was common with such recitations, did far more than merely read the poem: he acted it with all the power of his great gift, recreating in gesture the action of murder and assuming the character of the guilt-stricken homicide. As with Dickens's dramatic readings, Irving's violent involvement in the performance became at length a serious threat to his health. Ellen Terry, the actress, once said that as he read, "'He did really almost die—he imagined death with such horrible intensity.'"[28]

The emotional authenticity of Irving's rendition could not fail to affect his audience as well. Often it caused the more impressionable to faint. Once, an archbishop was moved to observe that "he could not conceive that any man, however provoked, could possibly bring himself to perpetrate, in hot blood or cold, a murder after hearing Sir Henry Irving's awesome and agonising rendering."[29] A similar comment was made by Lady Pollock, like the archbishop naïvely unconscious of such black souls as Wainwright's, when she wrote: "Even imaginative and sensitive readers fail to find in silent study the passion which the actor develops in Thomas Hood's poem. The agony of a terrible remorse is struck deep into the heart of the listener; any one among the audience who held a guilty secret would surely give it up or die."[30]

The most vivid account of Irving's rendition is that of his friend Bram Stoker, the author of *Dracula*, who in 1876, as an audience of one, received a private performance of rare intensity:

> . . . here was incarnate power, incarnate passion, so close to one that one could meet it eye to eye, within touch of one's outstretched hand. The surroundings became non-existent; the dress ceased to be noticeable; recurring thoughts of self-existence were not at all. Here was indeed Eugene Aram as he was face to face with his Lord: his very soul aflame in the light of his abiding horror. Looking back now I can realise the perfection of art with which the mind was led and swept and swayed, hither and thither as the actor wished. How a change of tone or time denoted the personality of the "Blood-avenging Sprite"—and how the nervous, eloquent hands slowly moving, outspread fanlike, round the fixed face—set as doom, with eyes as inflexible as Fate—emphasised it till one instinctively quivered with pity. Then the awful horror on the murderer's face as the ghost in his brain seemed to take external shape before his eyes, and enforced on him that from his sin there was no refuge. After the climax of horror the Actor was able by art and habit to control himself to the narrative mood whilst he spoke the few concluding lines of the poem.
> Then he collapsed half fainting. . . .
> . . .That night for a brief time in which the rest of the world seemed to sit still, Irving's genius floated in blazing triumph

above the summit of art. There is something in the soul which lifts it above all that has its base in material things. If once only in a lifetime the soul of a man can take wings and sweep for an instant into mortal gaze, then that "once" for Irving was on that, to me, ever memorable night.

As to its effect I had no adequate words. I can only say that after a few seconds of stony silence following his collapse I burst into something like hysterics.[31]

Hood's poem has both retrospective and anticipatory links with several of the highest-ranking literary achievements of the English-speaking world. The similarity in style and tone between "The Dream of Eugene Aram" and Coleridge's *The Rime of the Ancient Mariner* has already been mentioned. In theme and content as well, these two extended studies in guilt and atonement are quite similar. In each, the narrator is driven by remorse to share his nightmarish experience with a captive, mesmerized audience of one. The innocence of the child in Hood's poem corresponds with the genial mission of the wedding guest in Coleridge's — both of which are incongruously interrupted by a tale of horror and damnation. Both poems are pervaded with an aura of inescapable doom symbolized by the image of the corpse that will not die. The closing lines of Coleridge's poem, "A sadder and a wiser man, / He rose the morrow morn," convey a sense of overpowering individual guilt duly absorbed in the forward march of worldly affairs that in effect is not unlike the parting image of Eugene Aram led away through the mist by "stern-faced men...from Lynn."

The connection with Coleridge was extended in the later years of the nineteenth century to include a third important poem of a similar mold: Wilde's "Ballad of Reading Gaol" (1898). Lord Alfred Douglas was the first to note the influence: "From the formal point of view [the "Ballad"] was modelled on Coleridge's *Ancient Mariner*, and it may also be said to have owed something to that fine poem of Thomas Hood's, *Eugene Aram*."[32] What Wilde's poem owes to Hood's goes beyond the obvious similarities of subject and meter. Both ballads recount the bringing to justice of a real-life murderer. As with Coleridge, the central figure is viewed in each case from the perspective of a significantly detached observer. But above all, what links Hood's poem and Wilde's is the sense of something universal in the murderer's personal suffering and the solitary dignity — almost the sanctity — with which he endures his guilt.

Hood has also been compared with Poe in his capacity for sounding the depths of the tormented, guilty mind and creating an almost palpable atmosphere of horror. But Philip Collins and J. C. Reid have detected a more direct influence of Hood's ballad in the works of Charles Dickens. Collins hypothesizes that this immensely popular poem helped shape the closing chapters of *Oliver Twist* (1837–1838), in which Bill Sikes is terrorized to distraction by haunting visions of the murdered Nancy. Collins suggests, further, that it was the great success of Hood's "Dream" in the productions of such recitalists as Irving which led Dickens to perceive in the Sikes and Nancy episode a similar dramatic potential and consequently to feature it in the repertoire for his farewell tour of readings in 1868 — with results (swooning ladies) much like Irving's.[33] Reid notes, in relation to Dickens's later works *Martin Chuzzlewit* (1843–44) and *Our Mutual Friend* (1864–1865) that the inward absorption of Hood's protagonist has a bearing on the "introspective self-dissection of murderers and dreamers" such as Jonas Chuzzlewit and Bradley Headstone.[34]

Also of importance, especially in light of the present study, is the connection between Hood's poem and Bulwer's novel on the same subject. *Eugene Aram* followed by a mere three years and was doubtless encouraged by the success of "The Dream." Its bearing on the nineteenth-century literary scene was, as succeeding chapters will show, far greater. Yet, in the ultimate course of literary history, Hood has outlasted Bulwer, whose novel offers a substantial period interest but little of enduring literary worth. While Bulwer's volumes languish in attics and are scarcely to be found on the shelves of secondhand dealers, "The Dream of Eugene Aram" has survived the last few decades in at least a fair number of anthologies.[35] The funeral monument which was raised by public subscription in Kensal Green Cemetery and dedicated in 1854 to Hood's memory bespeaks a relative estimate from which later criticism has not substantially diverged: it bears bas reliefs on three sides, each depicting a scene from one of his greatest serious works—"The Bridge of Sighs," "The Song of the Shirt," and "The Dream of Eugene Aram."

3 BULWER'S *EUGENE ARAM*

IN HIS OWN CENTURY and until recently in ours, Edward Bulwer[1] has often been dismissed as a superficial intellect who pandered to the whims of his contemporary audience. He wrote to please, it is true, prolifically and in a surprisingly wide variety of modes. Most of what he produced was at least moderately successful in the popular market, and some of it phenomenally so. Traditionally, his immense appeal during his lifetime has been attributed to unusual versatility combined with the capacity to gauge emerging popular trends so precisely that his commentators could never agree whether he was initiating the fashion or riding its crest. His *Pelham* (1828) was "the most important," as it was among the earliest, of the silver-fork novels, and his *Paul Clifford* (1830) was the first true Newgate novel.[2] The whole of his work, covering nearly half a century, has made him a valuable barometer for the subsequent historian of literature. However, his studied resplendence ("dandyism") of style and sentiment, cultivated to suit the times, now alienates him, more than any other feature of his writing, from the later generations he fervently hoped to reach. fervently hoped to reach.

Yet it is unfair to conclude, as many of his critics have done, that Bulwer had no real artistic merit. Indeed, renewed interest in his work has begun to challenge the negative attitudes which in past years assumed authority by mere repetition. Observance of the centenary of Bulwer's death may partially account for the appearance of excellent new editions of *Falkland* and *Pelham* as well as paperback versions of *Zanoni* and *The Coming Race*. The publicity afforded several years ago in Europe, the United States, and Canada by the "Pompeii A.D. 79" exhibition has also contributed to a modest revitalization of the novel *The Last Days of Pompeii*. The most important recent evaluation is Allan Christensen's full-length defense, *Edward Bulwer-Lytton: The Fiction of New Regions*

(Athens, Georgia, 1976), which schematizes Bulwer's fictional canon, arguing for its "aesthetic coherence and intellectual vigor." Behind the twenty-three works which Christensen treats, he sees not the shallow crowd-pleaser of traditional Bulwer criticism but rather a vibrant and boldly innovative experimenter intensely committed "to his very personal form of idealism."[3] Christensen's study is a much-needed antidote to generations of blind insistence that the elegant egotist who coined the phrase "the great unwashed" and who termed his public "that largest of all asses"[4] knowingly sacrificed his creative integrity for their idle enjoyment.

As Christensen concedes, however, it is equally unrealistic to assume, in the face of evidence, that Bulwer did not consider his public before undertaking a new literary venture. His decision, early in his career, to base a novel on the life of Eugene Aram appears to have been a mixture of professional shrewdness and genuine philosophical and artistic interest.

1

Bulwer nowhere suggests that Thomas Hood's poem had a bearing on his choice of subject matter for the new novel he contemplated following the success of *Paul Clifford*. In the end note to Book V, chapter 7, of the first edition of the novel, Bulwer "recommends" Hood's poem to his readers although he finds fault with its characterization of Aram. The poet would, he says, "have formed a conception more true to nature, if he had described the stoical and dark character of the man, as rather attempting now to refine away, now to bear up against, his guilt — than as yielding so entirely to remorse." This, Bulwer's own recorded acknowledgment of Hood's poem, was withdrawn from later editions of the novel. Yet no literary man at the time could have overlooked the wide acclaim which "The Dream of Eugene Aram" had elicited upon its appearance in 1829 and which its separate publication in 1831 renewed. The true connection in the novelist's mind between his work and the poem that preceded it can only be a matter of speculation, but it seems likely that his awareness of Hood's work gave definition to a collection of vague personal associations which had previously attracted Bulwer to the Aram story. Prior to writing *Paul Clifford*, which deals with the criminal underworld, Bulwer had followed Godwin's example and immersed himself for atmosphere in an intensive study of the *Newgate Calendar*, reading it from beginning to end and taking notes with the help of his wife. Although he, like most of his contemporaries, was already acquainted with the essentials of Aram's life, its appearance in the *Calendar* would have brought the story freshly to mind.

The 1849 preface to *Eugene Aram* records Bulwer's own account of the growth of the idea in his consciousness:

> The strange history of Eugene Aram had excited my interest and wonder long before the present work was composed or conceived. It so happened, that during Aram's residence at Lynn, his reputation for learning had attracted the notice of my grandfather. . . . Aram frequently visited at Heydon (my grandfather's house), and gave lessons. . .to the younger members of the family. This I chanced to hear when I was on a visit in Norfolk, some two years before the novel was published, and it tended to increase the interest with which I had previously speculated on the phenomena of a trial which, take it altogether, is perhaps the most remarkable in the register of English crime.

"Two years before this novel was published" would have been late in 1829 — the date of Hood's poem. Hence it is plausible that the poem itself, at the time a likely topic for drawing-room conversation, initiated Bulwer's discovery of the historic link between his aunts at Heydon Hall and the notorious scholar who was, for a few months at best, their tutor. Even so early in his career, Bulwer had a reputation as a literary opportunist, his sensitivity to which may account for his reluctance to acknowledge any debt to Hood's phenomenally successful poem.

Bulwer had learned from the reception of his *Paul Clifford* that crime does pay, at least for the novelist. He needed money just now, since in 1827 his mother had cut off the income from his estate upon his marrying against her wishes. Both he and his bride, Rosina Wheeler, were accustomed to luxury, and it took all the industry he could muster to support them by his writings. His continued reputation for lavish display attests to his apparent success. The impression of an American correspondent, Nathaniel Parker Willis, a few years after the publication of *Eugene Aram* is typical:

> The author of *Pelham* is a younger son and depends on his writings for a livelihood, and truly measuring works of fancy by what they will bring (not an unfair standard perhaps), a glance around his luxurious and elegant rooms is worth reams of puff in the quarterlies. He lives in the heart of the fashionable quarter of London, where rents are ruinously extravagant, entertains a great deal, and is expensive in all his habits, and for this pay Messrs. Clifford, Pelham, and Aram — (it would seem) most excellent good bankers.[5]

THE AUTHOR OF "PELHAM".

graved by Thomson from an Original Drawing by F. Say.

EL Bulwer

Edward Bulwer. From the *New Monthly Magazine*, May 2, 1831. Engraved from a drawing by F. Say.

Willis was not alone in assuming that finances were no problem for the author of *Eugene Aram*: "To Bulwer it was given never to write for daily bread," commented the sensation-novelist and Bulwer devotee Mrs. M. E. Braddon upon his death.[6] But Bulwer was not enjoying the sweet life as he appeared to be. He worked feverishly to meet his needs. In the years 1831–1833 alone, besides making numerous contributions to several periodicals, he was editor of the *New Monthly Magazine* and published three novels, *The Pilgrims of the Rhine*, *Godolphin*, and *Eugene Aram* (the latter two composed simultaneously), as well as his incisive treatise on contemporary life, *England and the English*, and a long satirical poem, *The Siamese Twins*. Years later, in a state of ill health brought on by his lifelong habit of overwork, Bulwer wrote describing this period: "To a constitution far from strong, I allowed no pause or respite. The wear and tear went on without intermission. . . . As long as I was always at work, it seemed that I had no leisure to be ill. Quiet was my hell."[7] The great pressure under which he labored during and for some years after the composition of *Eugene Aram* eventually led not only to his physical debilitation but also, more surely than any other factor, to the collapse of his ill-fated marriage in 1836. Michael Sadleir, his biographer, attributes to the author's anxious state the bombast and hyper-emotionalism which are characteristic of Bulwer's style, but especially noticeable in *Eugene Aram*. This novel Sadleir terms "an obvious product of overwrought nerves."[8]

At this stage in Bulwer's literary development, the influence of William Godwin, who had previously interested himself in the Aram theme, was waning. Bulwer's first novel, *Falkland* (1827), had reflected his ideological association with the author of *Caleb Williams* in the naming of its central figure and in a number of passages reflective of Godwinian philosophy. In his second work, *Pelham* (1828), Bulwer had extended the debt by incorporating a murder-mystery derived substantially from the plot of *Caleb Williams*, and by naming the victim Tyrrell lest the connection be overlooked. Bulwer had met Godwin in 1830, having been recommended to him by Lady Caroline Lamb, whose favorite the young Edward had become for a few months in 1824 following the death of Lord Byron, her latest lover. Edward, whom Lady Caroline described to Godwin as "a very young man and an enthusiast,"[9] made no secret of his appreciation for the elder philosopher. His reflective essays in the *New Monthly Magazine* during the late 1820s and early 30s are, like *Falkland*, clearly influenced by the strain of benevolent utilitarianism set forth in Godwin's writings, whereby the attainment of "the greatest good for the greatest number" is the only viable motive in a choice involving human action.[10] Godwin in return praised Bulwer's *Paul Clifford*,[11] which is also, as Keith

Hollingsworth has shown, thematically grounded in utilitarianism.[12] The personal as well as the professional relationship between the two authors was at this point quite cordial.

As we have seen, Godwin had once considered basing a novel on the life of Eugene Aram but had never realized the design. Bulwer, in the 1840 preface to *Eugene Aram*, four years after the philosopher's death, alludes to that abandoned project only briefly:

> ...the late Mr. Godwin (in conversing with me after the publication of this romance) observed that "he had always thought the story of Eugene Aram peculiarly adapted for fiction, and that he had more than once entertained the notion of making it the foundation of a novel." I can well conceive what depth and power that gloomy record would have taken from the dark and inquiring genius of the author of *Caleb Williams*.

Since this passage, the sole admission on Bulwer's part that Godwin had any connection with the Aram theme, implies no indebtedness to Godwin and dates the latter's remark *after* the appearance of *Eugene Aram*, it would seem to contradict the assumption initiated by Kegan Paul, and accepted by numerous literary historians after him, that Godwin had passed on "his subject and material to his younger and more vigorous friend."[13] Whatever the truth may be, when the younger friend did turn to the story of Eugene Aram, the product was very different from the work which Godwin must have envisaged.

For some time, Godwin's reputation had been fading, and by the 1830s the age had left him behind. Bulwer was the only one of the rising young intellectuals to pay homage to his former greatness. Just two years after *Paul Clifford*, when Bulwer was writing *Eugene Aram*, he was no longer so infatuated. This novel marks the ideological defection of Godwin's last admirer.

2

Bulwer's original intention was to treat the Eugene Aram story in dramatic form. He wrote, in fact, somewhat less than two acts of *Eugene Aram, A Tragedy*, in blank verse, before giving it over in favor of *Eugene Aram. A tale*. After completion of the novel, he published the fragmentary drama as a curiosity in the *New Monthly Magazine* for August, 1833, on the occasion of his leaving the editorship of that periodical. The dramatic sketch has been appended to almost every edition of *Eugene Aram* since then. As Bulwer's Advertisement to the play explains, "the construction of the tragedy differs, in some respects, materially from that of the tale."[14] It is true that the time scheme of the novel, which opens in Norfolk thirteen years after Aram's crime, departs from that of the play, which opens in Yorkshire on the eve of the murder. But the greater difference is in the character of Aram himself, and especially in the thematic framework of the drama as opposed to that of the novel.

The Aram who appears in the dramatic fragment does not readily evoke sympathy. As the curtain opens, he is surrounded by books and creditors. Not only is he unable to appease the latter, but he is so poor that he has not eaten since breakfast the day before. He is ripe for the temptation which Boteler, his neighbor, comes to offer. Monson, a simpleton, has inherited a fortune. Boteler's plan, served up to Aram with the dinner he provides, is to kill and rob him. Aram, with spineless rapidity, agrees, and justifies the deed by sophistries:

> 'Tis but a death in either case;— or mine
> Or that poor dotard's! ...
>
> (I.3.107–108)

> . . . .
>
> Tis [sic] a fool less on earth!—a clod—a grain
> From the o'er-rich creation;—be it so.
> But I, in one brief year, could give to men
> More solid, glorious, undecaying good
> Than his whole life could purchase. ...
>
> (I.[4].3–7)

Despite the vague altruism of that speech, Aram's motives, like those of a lesser Faust, seem more inclined to self-indulgence. His kinship with Goethe's hero is most evident as he contemplates the potential fruits of his projected crime:

> Would *I* were rich...
> Oh! what a glorious and time-hallow'd world
> Would I invoke around me: and wall in
> A haunted solitude with those bright souls,
> That, with a still and warning aspect, gaze
> Upon us from the hallowing shroud of books!
>
> . . . .
>
> I'd build me domes, too; from whose giddy height
> My soul would watch the night stars, and unsphere
> The destinies of man, or track the ways
> Of God from world to world

. . . .

Would—would my life might boast one year of wealth
Though death should bound it!

(I.3.38–43, 49–52, 58–59)

Monson is dispatched, as planned, with an almost embarrassing haste, and Bulwer's nervous protagonist cuts no very admirable figure:

> . . . ARAM *rushes from the Cavern.*
>
> *Aram.* 'Tis done!—'tis done—'tis done!—
> A life is gone
> Out of a crowded world! *I* struck no more!
> Oh, God!—I did not slay him!—'twas not *I*!
> > (*Enter* BOTELER *more slowly from the Cave,*
> > *and looking round.*)
> *Boteler.* Why didst thou leave me ere our task was o'er?
> *Aram.* Was he not dead, then?—Did he breathe again?
> Or cry, "Help, help?"—*I* did not strike the blow!
> *Boteler.* Dead!—and no witness, save the blinded bat!
> But the gold, Aram! thou didst leave the gold?
> *Aram.* The gold! I had forgot. *Thou* hast the gold.
> Come, let us share, and part—
> *Boteler.*   Not here; the spot
> Is open, and the rolling moon may light
> Some wanderer's footsteps hither. To the deeps
> Which the stars pierce not—of the inmost woods—
> We will withdraw and share—and weave our plans,
> So that the world may know not of this deed.
> *Aram.* Thou sayest well! I did not strike the blow!
> How red the moon looks! let us hide from her!

(I.[7])

It is difficult to accept as a tragic hero this craven and clumsy sinner whose only thought at the moment of his spiritual downfall is to split the take and, without repenting, absolve himself of the mortal guilt. The Aram of Act II must be altered considerably in the intervening ten years to merit the confidence manifested by Lambourn, father of his betrothed:

> Nay, . . . Madeline, . . . I know, in truth,
> No man to whom I would so freely give
> Thy hand as his—no man so full of wisdom,
> And yet so gentle in his bearing of it;

> No man so kindly in his thoughts of others —
> So rigid of all virtues in himself.
>
> (II.1.31–36)

The drama's cynical import is pointedly discernible in the single line of Boteler/Houseman: "Behold the devil at all hearts!" (I.3.114). All men, that is, have some secret iniquity at the base of their souls; hunger and want can make the best of us forget our strongest compunctions. Lambourn, who has not learned this truth, is mystified by the peculiar urgency of Aram's generosity:

> ...Do but speak of want,
> And lo! he winces, and his nether lip
> Quivers impatient, and he sighs, and frowns,
>
> . . . .
>
> Then will he pause — and pause — and come at last
> And put some petty monies in my hand,
> And cry, "Go, feed the wretch; he must not starve,
> Or he will sin. . . ."
>
> (2.1.118–120, 125–128)

Perhaps Bulwer, having come so far, judged this an ignoble theme for tragedy and perceived the character of his hero as unconvincing and unappealing. Perhaps he considered the larger market value that a novel might have. He left no indication why he began afresh in a new genre, but surely the novel, despite its many faults, is far superior. It retains the idea of the corruptibility of man but with less emphasis on the corrupting influence of poverty. Instead, the point is simply that in all men there is some evil. Bulwer muses, in an authorial aside, on the image of Eugene Aram walking the streets of London with a secret guilt at his heart:

> What an incalculable field of dread and sombre contemplation
> is opened to every man who, with his heart disengaged from him-
> self, and his eyes accustomed to the sharp observance of his tribe,
> walks through the streets of a great city! What a world of dark and
> troubled secrets in the breast of everyone who hurries by you!
> Göethe has said somewhere, that each of us, the best as the worst,
> hides within him something — some feeling, some remembrance
> that, if known, would make you hate him. (4.5)[15]

Two other themes of equal importance radiate from the central moral question of murder in Bulwer's novel. They concern, essentially, the impulse toward that crime, and its consequences. On the one hand, the murder of Daniel Clarke exemplifies the evil that man invites when he heeds his intellect alone and allows his natural benevolence to be over-powered by "the entanglements of human reasoning."[16] This dangerous reliance on cold logic, which has convinced Aram that crime can be philosophically justified, is his tragic flaw and the first germ of his destruction. On the other hand, the murder, once committed, precipitates a further chain of misfortune. It signifies the one fatal act which can shatter an otherwise noble existence and ruin as well the innocent others bound by blood or affection to share in the catastrophe. Thus *Eugene Aram* argues that the least deviation of mind from the way of instinctive human virtue can lead to evils unforeseen and finally to utter disaster for all concerned.

The story opens in the early summer of 1758 in Grassdale, the fictional equivalent of Lynn, scene of the real Aram's arrest. Aram's victim is long dead and his own discovery is imminent. Four of the novel's five books relate the events of a few months prior to that climactic point. Aram, when first we see him, exists in self-imposed solitude surrounded by his books and scientific instruments. His comfortable house, one of the largest in the vicinity, is surmounted by a dome-shaped study and observatory where, like Faust, in the midnight hours, he charts the heavens, uttering apostrophes to the stars and vague soliloquies on the human condition, the nature of good and evil, and the implications of his own sin. His closest neighbor, Squire Lester, a kind and congenial man, concerned at the scholar's unhealthy seclusion, eagerly solicits his acquaintance. Aram, nursing his secret guilt, resists Lester's overtures for some time. At last, when he does relent, he falls in love with Lester's daughter, Madeline, a striking and high-minded beauty, and with their engagement rejoins the human community.

This decisive first step from isolation sets in motion the chain of events which will entangle and destroy him. Madeline's cousin, Walter, a disappointed rival, rides away to the north of England to forget his unrequited passion. During his travels, Walter encounters news of his long-lost father, Geoffrey Lester, whose desertion has perplexed and troubled his son since childhood. In a saddler's shop, Walter happens upon a whip, left for repair and unclaimed for fourteen years, which bears Geoffrey Lester's initials and crest. Pursuing this link, he further learns that his father, under the alias Daniel Clarke, was a wastrel and black-guard murdered for a fortune he had himself stolen from a friend. Walter, whose life has seemed purposeless without Madeline, seizes with all the fervor of compensatory zeal the object of finding and bringing to justice his father's murderer. Still in Yorkshire, the scene of the crime, he meets a scoundrel, Houseman, who some weeks previously visited Grassdale to

Frontispiece to Bulwer's *Eugene Aram. A tale* (1832). By Hablôt K. Browne.

blackmail Aram. The scholar, having arranged on the promise of an annuity that the blackmailer retire to France for life, considers himself rid of this threat from his guilty past and free to marry Madeline. The fatal illness of Houseman's daughter, however, prevents Houseman's departure and forestalls Aram's hopes. Dazed with grief at her death, Houseman lets slip his secret knowledge of Clarke's murder, and then to save himself transfers the blame to Aram.

Walter, the avenging spirit, hastens back to arrest Aram, arriving on Aram's wedding day in the late autumn of 1758. The months of imprisonment pending the trial in August of the following year occupy a single transitional chapter. When the fatal time arrives, Aram, though he maintains his innocence, is convicted nonetheless, and Madeline dies, overcome with grief. Aram takes his own life in jail to avoid the ignominy of death on the gallows. Walter, who has learned too late that forgiveness is divine, inherits Aram's guilt. Finding himself to blame for Madeline's death as well as Aram's, and for the ruination of everyone's happiness, he seeks atonement in a self-imposed exile. Years later, he returns to marry Ellinor, Madeline's more prosaic but sweet-temperered sister.

In a battle of wills on the eve of Aram's death, Walter has wrested a private letter of confession from Aram, against the latter's determination to carry his secret to the grave. The lengthy document, incorporated in a crucial chapter near the end of the final book, is Bulwer's fictional adaptation of the autobiography which the real Aram wrote for his friend, the Reverend Mr. Collins. Whereas the entire preceding part of the novel involves discovery of the crime long after its commission, now, at last, Bulwer turns in flashback to the crime itself and to the circumstances from which it arose. This section, disproportionately brief as it is, constitutes the ideological core of the novel. With poetic and philosophical expansiveness, it traces the chain of thought and occurrence culminating in Aram's "lamentable fall."[17]

In Knaresborough as a young man, Aram says in the confession, he first became frustrated with the pointless acquisition of knowledge for its own sake and was "seized, possessed, haunted with the ambition of enlightening my race." That Bulwer is nowhere more specific about Aram's projected contribution to the welfare of mankind detracts from the credibility of Aram's characterization and weakens his motivation for the crime. Even in the revised edition of 1849, where several passages are added to emphasize Aram's benevolent impulse to crime, Bulwer's only concern is to assure his readers that Aram had a specific project in mind. We, and presumably Bulwer also, still have not the fuzziest insight into its nature:

> ...suddenly, as I pored over my scanty books, a gigantic dis-
> covery in science gleamed across me. I saw the means of effect-
> ing a vast benefit to truth and to man.... And in this discovery
> I was stopped by the total inadequacy of my means. The books
> and implements I required were not within my reach. (5.7)

This feeble explanation, remarkable for its naiveté, clearly substantiates
John Reed's point (in relation to the type of the poor scholar in
nineteenth-century literature) that "it is the *state* of impoverished
scholarship that is important rather than the nature of the learning
involved."[18]

Too poor to realize his vague dream and too proud to beg from the
"dull fools of wealth," Aram continues, he chafed at the bitter necessity
of teaching simple matters to schoolchildren: "While I was thus grinding
down my soul in order to satisfy the vile physical wants, what golden
hours, what glorious advantages, what openings into new heavens of
science, what chances of illumining mankind were for ever lost to me!"
In this state of mind, he was particularly vulnerable to the temptations
of Houseman, his distant relative and a professional thief, to join him and
"wrest from society, to which I [Aram] owed nothing, the means to be
wise and great."

Though an overweening personal ambition underlies Aram's pro-
fessed humanitarian motive, he is yet, in this fictional incarnation, a far
better man than his grasping, self-centered prototype in the drama. In
the novel, as in the play, he seeks to justify his crime by considering the
benefits which society may derive from the removal of Clarke and the
realization of his own potential. The difference is in his priorities. For the
Aram of the drama, the larger good which may result is a rationalization.
For the Aram of the novel, it is a rationale.

The central philosophical issue of the novel, important not only in
respect to Bulwer's ideological development but in the context of the
nineteenth-century history of ideas as well, is the famous principle of
utilitarian ethics, "the greatest good for the greatest number." Bulwer's
disenchantment with utilitarianism appeared for the first time in Eugene
Aram's ill-advised espousal of that precept. "Was it not better," he recalls
asking himself, "...better for mankind—that I should commit one bold
wrong, and by that wrong purchase the power of good?"

When Houseman introduces his intended victim, Clarke, and Aram
perceives the man's base depravity, his question becomes a resolve. This
Aram, unlike the Aram of the unfinished play, does not slide easily into

the acceptance of murder. Instead, he endures weeks and perhaps months of temptation. He sees, at every turn, Clarke's coarseness, and hears from Clarke's own lips the story of his past iniquities. Clarke publicly insults Aram for his poverty and lords it over him in the streets. At last, an incident occurs that must have strained even Bulwer's penchant for pathos. A working girl of Aram's acquaintance, "a quiet, patient-looking, gentle creature" who supports herself by making lace, is lured by Clarke to his house and brutally raped. In "the paroxysm of shame and despair" she kills herself a few days later, clinching Aram's determination. Even if Clarke were a worthy man, the scholar reasons, might not the world be better off sacrificing him for the good which Aram, provided with means, might do? When he is, instead, so evil, how can it be wrong to destroy him? Aram compares his situation, finally, with that of a soldier, who murders for pay "and sleeps sound, and men applaud."

Once his mind is made up, this Aram, unlike the Aram of the play, is firm and brave in the accomplishment of the crime, bolstered by what he conceives to be the sanctity of his mission: "I had wrapped myself above fear into a high and preternatural madness of mind. *I looked on the deed I was about to commit as a great and solemn sacrifice to Knowledge, whose Priest I was.*" When the time comes for action, he strikes surely, although his, he still affirms, was "not the *death*-blow."

From the point of the murder, Aram's fate is determined. A supreme irony convinces him of that and of the error of his utilitarian reasoning: three days later, he inherits a fortune from a distant relative. In the awareness that his moral sacrifice was completely unnecessary, he begins to see the futility of meddling with the dictates of fate or attempting to tip the balance of good and evil. He sets out, with his new financial security, on the wanderings that will lead him to Grassdale. In the shock of realization, he has lost all desire to be the world's benefactor, although he rejoices in acts of individual charity. With a past to guard, he finds that the world at large is his potential enemy, and isolation and obscurity are his only protection.

From the beginning of the novel, a powerful foreboding haunts Aram with the knowledge that his secret must one day be his downfall. Can we look upon the stars, he asks, "and not feel that we are indeed the poorest puppets of an all-pervading and resistless destiny? . . . Shall we think that our prayers can avert a doom woven with the skein of events?" (1.4). Although Bulwer took great pains to absolve the character of Aram, he never, in either the first edition or the revised editions after 1849, went so far as to condone his crime. However generous and noble Aram may be thought to be, we are left with the conviction that his action was wrong, and above all, that he was mistaken in imagining evil could ever further the ends of good.

Aram himself, however, goes to his grave without absolute contrition. About midway through his confession, before narrating his arrival at Grassdale, he reaffirms the inhuman nature of his victim and insists that as a murderer, "I did not feel what men call remorse!" He felt, he adds, "regret," but only for the danger and apprehension which a three-days' wait would have made unnecessary. Later, still without remorse, when he is forced to bribe Houseman in Grassdale, he adds (with italic emphasis for the shock value) that "*the humbling part of crime, its low calculations, its poor defence, its paltry trickery, its mean hypocrisy—made my chiefest penance!*" These passages, removed from the 1849 and later editions, were often cited to show the blackness of Aram's character and Bulwer's moral irresponsibility in siding with him.

Only later, when he learns that the victim of his crime was Madeline's uncle and perceives the effects of his sinful deed on Madeline and her family, does Aram admit remorse; even then it is for their sake and not his victim's. Here, in retrospect, is the novel's decisive argument against the utilitarian principle of the greatest good, that ethical question which "opens a labyrinth of reasonings in which the soul may walk and lose itself for ever." The principle is invalid, Bulwer concludes, through Aram, for the simple reason that man can never foresee all the ramifications of any given act:

> ...the general consequence I had overlooked till now, and now it flashed upon me.... How incalculable—how measure-less—how viewless the consequences of one crime, even when we think we have weighed them all with scales that would have turned with a hair's weight! Yes; before I had felt no remorse. I felt it now. I had acknowledged no crime, and now crime seemed the essence itself of my soul.

Aram dies hoping that God will forgive him as "one bewildered by his reason rather than yielding to his vices." The ultimate moral of the novel, which follows from its romantic distrust of the reasoning faculty, is that, given man's limited perspective, his only resource is submission to fate—and his best defense, "caution for himself and charity for others" (5.8). It is determinism, but not dark determinism, with which Bulwer leaves us, for in the closing sentiment of the novel we are reminded that virtue balances vice. Just as the good man is not all good, "even the criminal is not all evil; the angel within us is not easily expelled; it survives sin, ay, and many sins, and leaves us sometimes in amaze and marvel, at the good that lingers round the heart even of the hardiest offender" (5.8).

3

At the height of his career, Bulwer was the recognized leader of a school of historical-fiction writers who took pride in faithfully representing the facts of history. Whereas Sir Walter Scott had used history as a colorful mantle in which to drape romance, these writers believed that the romantic elements of such fiction should be subordinate to the factual. Partly because of the current emphasis on reading as a strictly serious pursuit for the attainment of "useful knowledge," the deliberate distortion of history was now considered unethical. In the prefaces to *Rienzi* (1835), *The Last of the Barons* (1843), and *Harold, the Last of the Saxon Kings*, (1848), Bulwer outlines a strict code which permits the author conjecture only as regards the inner thoughts and feelings of his historical characters; it is not, he says, the author's prerogative to alter, in spirit or detail, the findings of historical scholarship.

But *Eugene Aram*, written before Bulwer adopted these principles, is a curious mixture of fact and fictional embellishment. Although it was criticized upon its publication for the liberties its author took with the facts of Aram's life, Bulwer in the original preface makes light of the changes: "I have exercised the common and fair license of writers of fiction: it is chiefly the more homely parts of the real story that have been altered." The difference in these "homely parts" between the real and the fictional murderer is, however, so vast that, as Leigh Hunt complained, Bulwer "might as well tell us that the Duke of Wellington is also the Marquis of Anglesea."[19]

In the largely fabulous narrative which comprises the bulk of the novel, Bulwer substitutes for the demeaning or mundane aspects of Aram's history others more noble and romantic. The real Aram, for example, was encumbered with a wife and numerous children, whom he deserted shortly after the murder. This was hardly compatible with his role as a hero of romance, so Bulwer made him a bachelor and gave him a beautiful young woman to fall in love with and lose. The addition of Madeline would appeal to sentimental readers and render Aram's ultimate fate more calamitous. The Lester family was probably related in the author's mind to his ancestors, the Bulwers of Heydon Hall. Squire Lester parallels Bulwer's grandfather, "Justice" Bulwer, as he was known to his contemporaries; and Madeline and Ellinor, the traditional contrasting sisters of romance, may partly represent the two aunts whom Aram tutored. The Lesters were not in any sense "life portraits" of the Bulwers, yet it is easy to imagine the novelist fantasizing the possibility of a romantic liaison between the brooding Aram and one of the Misses Bulwer. Cousin Walter is an ingenious addition to the plot, since he fulfills at once the dual roles of the rival in love and the avenger of a father's murder.[20] At the end, he is there to partake of the lesson which Aram's death has taught and to provide, with the inevitable post-climactic marriage, the calm which follows catharsis.

Bulwer's Aram differs from his historical counterpart not only in his domestic situation but in his religious and intellectual tendencies as well. His musings, particularly the long confession at the novel's end, are filled with an awareness of and eventual submission to the divine will operating in the affairs of men. In this respect, as Hood had done before him, Bulwer departs from the original to suit the religious temper of the times. All that Aram wrote and all that was written about him, before these fictions, disputes the assumption that he was in any way devout. It is hardly necessary to add that Bulwer exaggerated the mental powers of his hero, transforming as he did a diligent country scholar into a demigod. The nature of Aram's studies, as far as they are described in the novel, represents a selective adaptation of fact. Bulwer drops the emphasis on linguistics, which is after all a rather prosaic pursuit not likely to fascinate and charm a Madeline. Instead he appeals to the spirit of his own time, when botany was a favorite diversion, and, fixing on Eugene's penchant for that science, pictures him with Madeline and her sister roaming the countryside as he delights them with herbal lore. Reference is also made, on occasion, to Aram's having used his knowledge of medicinal plants to help the ailing poor in the vicinity. The reader who cares to do so may thus infer that the great discovery with which Aram had planned to enlighten society has to do with the life-sustaining properties of herbs. That is more likely, at any rate, than his saving the world by means of linguistics, astronomy, or metaphysics.

Finally, in keeping with his own and his readers' partiality for silver-fork fiction, Bulwer elevates his hero's social sphere well above the real Aram's. Bulwer's creation was once, but is not at the time of the narrative, a schoolmaster. A humble usher, as the real Aram was at Lynn, is less appropriate to high romance than a solitary seer who is mysteriously and independently wealthy. The Aram of history was never well-to-do. He ranked gentlemen among his acquaintance, but it was they who condescended to him, not vice versa as seems to be the case at the start of the novel, when Squire Lester courts his neighbor's society. Bulwer, indeed, does not stop at making a squire his hero's companion. The neighboring "Earl of * * *" repeatedly importunes Aram to become his secretary and confidant. Aram resists because he fears the exposure which fame might give him, but through his acquaintance with the earl he is at one point in the novel introduced to "a prince of the blood royal" (2.4), an honor to which the real Aram could never have aspired.

The air of refinement and worth investing the fictional Aram is calculated to mitigate his sin and further his acceptance in the face of unavoidable paradox. The degree to which it succeeds is questionable. We would hardly expect to meet this Aram's type in the world of everyday occurrences, but he was not drawn for the sake of realism. The hero who can tamper with destiny, transcend the inviolable moral code, and yet sustain romantic admiration belongs to another sphere. Like Byron's noble protagonists, he must stand a head above his fellow men and breathe a rarer atmosphere.

As Aram's character is exalted to Bulwer's purposes, so is Clarke's vilified. The Daniel Clark who was murdered in 1745 for the valuables his friends had duped him into stealing from his neighbors appears not to have been very honest or very bright, but he was certainly not the vicious reprobate he becomes in the novel. The historical Clark was a young tradesman, newly wed. His fictional counterpart is a jaded, unprincipled petty aristocrat who has deserted his wife and small son, throwing them on the mercy of their relatives and precipitating her death by fever. The rest of his life he has spent carousing in the streets, robbing his benefactors, and raping virgins. To justify Aram, Bulwer paints his victim in the deepest black.

In contrast with Clarke, even Houseman, who instigates his murder, is made to seem relatively innocuous. As Aram recalls:

> There was that in...[Clarke's] vices which revolted me far more than the villainy of Houseman. The latter had possessed no advantages of education; he descended to no minutiae of sin, he was a plain, blunt, coarse wretch, and his sense threw something respectable around his vices.... Had Houseman money in his purse, he would have paid a debt and relieved a friend from mere indifference. (5.7)

At the close of the novel, Houseman still has redeeming qualities. His sense of honor suffers when he must testify against Aram, and the more vile aspects of his nature are poignantly countered by affection for his little daughter, whom he has placed with a kindly matron in a decent home. The actual Houseman was, of course, unmarried until after Aram's death and had no children. Bulwer added the episode involving his daughter to provide a reason for his failure to depart for France and also to support the thematic concept that "the angel within us survives sin." Thus the two accomplices in Clarke's murder present a neat contrast: one exemplifies the idea that no man is all good, the other that no man is all evil.

These, the central figures in *Eugene Aram*, are joined by several entirely fictional characters whose purpose is to provide humorous relief or philosophic asides. All of them are types. As Walter journeys through England, for example, he looks up two of his uncle's former companions from his university days. Having been recommended by Squire Lester to John Courtland, "a seductive dog to drink with," and Peter Hales, "a generous, open-hearted fellow as ever lived" (1.11), he finds, respectively, a ludicrous hypochondriac and an obnoxious miser. Their ironic contrast with the youthful blades of Squire Lester's memory represents the lighter side of the thematic focus on unforeseeable destiny. Added to these are Dame Darkmans, the conventional harridan — much like Meg Murdockson in *The Heart of Midlothian*, exulting at funerals and cursing young love — and Cpl. Jacob Bunting, the comic servant and *miles gloriosus* who attends Walter in his travels. Dame Darkmans, the deranged product of a tragic past, is useful primarily for the ominous prophetic insight she occasionally supplies. "I have noted ye walk in the dusk with your eyes down and your arms crossed," she tells Aram in the presence of the Lesters, "an' I have said, — that man I do not hate, somehow, for he has something dark at his heart like me!" (1.7). Jacob Bunting, although Leslie Stephen called him "irrelevant,"[21] does provide a kind of humorous foil to Aram. They are, in odd juxtaposition, the two bachelors of the community, but Jacob, unlike the ascetic scholar, has immersed himself in worldly life, from which experience he has formulated a collection of shrewd homely maxims for every situation. In a comic reversal of Aram's lofty ideals, he greets chicanery with acclaim and charity with contempt, yet is intended to remain cantankerously lovable. Sharing with Dame Darkmans the function of Chorus, he is, significantly, the first character in the novel to regard Aram with suspicion: "Free to confess," he tells Walter in his telegraphese style of speaking,

> that I don't quite like this larned man, as much as the rest of 'em — something queer about him — can't see to the bottom of him — don't think he's quite so meek and lamb-like as he seems: — once saw a calm dead pool in foren parts — peered down into it — by little and little, my eye got used to it — saw something dark at the bottom — stared and stared — by Jupiter — a

great big alligator!—walked off immediately—never liked quiet pools since—augh, no! (1.9)

Although there is no evidence that Bulwer ever went to Knaresborough or Lynn in pursuit of Aram's biography, it is clear from a careful comparison with the fictional account that his research was thorough. While the larger respects in which he altered the history are considerable, at the same time there is often evident, even in the changes themselves, a minute attention to detail which reflects his close application. Although the real Aram's wife and children were supplanted by the fictional Lesters, Anna Aram survives vestigially in the "old woman" with whom Bulwer's Aram lodged at the time of the murder. She, like Aram's wife, suspects foul play in the disappearance of Clarke and, voicing that suspicion privately, finds her own life threatened by Houseman. Fear silences her until Walter, gathering evidence with which to charge Aram, interviews her years later at Knaresborough. Her story echoes, to the most minute particular, the deposition taken from Anna Aram at the Thistle Hill inquest in 1758.[22]

The account of Aram's death further exemplifies Bulwer's manipulation of the facts. The historical Aram attempted suicide the morning of his execution by cutting the veins of his arm in two places with (according to most accounts) a razor concealed in his cell. He was revived by a surgeon, and when hanged was still alive but barely sensible. Bulwer's Aram, to enhance the dignity of his exit, is more successful. He expires at the last minute before the noose is caught, so that "the law's last indignity was wreaked upon a breathless corpse!" (5.7). In all other details, Bulwer's narrative of Aram's final hours is meticulously close to that of the histories. The real Aram's suicide note echoes in the last words of the ill-fated hero. "Certainly nobody has a better right to dispose of a man's life than himself," wrote the historical Aram, "and he, not others, should determine how. . . . I think. . . I wrong no man by this, and hope it is not offensive to that Eternal Being that form'd me and the world." "I am the thing of an Immortality," writes his fictional counterpart, "and the creature of a God!. . .The courses of my life I swayed with my own hand: from my own hand shall come the manner and moment of my death!" (5.7).

The tradition behind the Aram of the novel includes, of course, not only the matter of history, but the two important literary treatments which the history had already inspired and of which Bulwer could not have been unmindful. Some interesting comparisons can be instituted between his work and its predecessors. We have already seen how Bulwer was reacting against a utilitarian precept of his earlier mentor, William Godwin. If Godwin had written *Eugene Aram* in keeping with the notes he had made for that purpose, his message would have been that it was wrong to hang Eugene Aram. That is not at all the theme of Bulwer's work, yet there are similarities between it and *Caleb Williams*, the novel Godwin did write. Both explore the mental anguish of an undiscovered murderer (Falkland paralleling Aram in that respect), and both capitalize on the lapse of time between the murder and its solution. In both, the murderer is painted as a gentleman and his victim as a brute to gain sympathy for the former. And finally, although Bulwer's reforming touch is largely a matter of tone, and far lighter than Godwin's, whose whole purpose is reform, both novels deplore the harshness of the penal laws and demonstrate the oppressiveness of established society against the poor and untitled (Caleb figuring, in this sense, with Aram) regardless of their genius and potential.

Although Bulwer's interest in the Aram theme was probably owing at least in part to the success of Hood's poem, the thematic similarities of these two works are actually slight. Bulwer's is as gloomy as Hood's, despite the several episodes of comic relief. His Aram is, like Hood's, racked by his consciousness of the murderer's inevitable fate. But there the resemblance ends. Hood's protagonist was a fairly ordinary rural schoolmaster, although extraordinarily learned, who murdered purely for gold and who differed from the real Aram primarily in the spiritual agonies he afterwards suffered. Bulwer's hero, on the other hand, though he pours out his spiritual malaise to the starry heavens, is not contrite. He is a brother to Faust and Manfred, whose morbid preoccupation supposedly becomes him and whose crime is all but dismissed as the result of an irrepressible, hubristic craving for knowledge.

4

Allan Christensen's schematization of Bulwer's fiction does not grant pivotal significance to *Eugene Aram*, but Bulwer himself regarded it in retrospect, as an important turning point in his career and the first product of his maturity. This judgment occurs in the 1848 preface to *Paul Clifford*:

> With the completion of this work [i.e., *Paul Clifford*, published 1830], closed an era in the writer's self-education. From *Pelham* to *Paul Clifford* (four fictions all written at a very early age) the author rather observes than imagines—rather deals

with the ordinary surface of human life than attempts, however
humbly, to soar above it, or to dive beneath. Looking back at
this distance of years, I can see as clearly as if they were mapped
before me the paths which led me across the boundary of invention from *Paul Clifford* to *Eugene Aram*.

The 1840 preface to *Eugene Aram*, more specifically, labels that work
a novel of "metaphysical speculation and analysis," the term "metaphysical" signifying approximately what "psychological" means today. Yet in
comparison with later masters of psychological inquiry—Conrad or Hardy
or Dostoyevsky—Bulwer's attempt at penetrating the secret wellsprings of
character, however earnest, seems superficial and melodramatic. It certainly does not equal the grandeur of his stated intent—"to show how the
consciousness of the deed was to exclude whatever humanity of character
preceded and belied it from all active exercise;...how the knowledge of
the bar between the minds of others and his own deprived the criminal
of all motive to ambition, and blighted knowledge of all fruit."
Something of the sort, it is true, takes place in the penultimate chapter,
containing Aram's written confession. But it is too hasty and too late to
attain the consummate purpose its author had sought. All the preceding
text together affords very little insight into Aram's mind. His vague and
broken mutterings, spoken in the isolation of the scholar's chamber,
convey the angst of a soul at war with the universe, but they do not
genuinely admit us to his innermost thoughts and motives.

The reason for this failure lies in Bulwer's fascination with the trappings of romance and sensationalism. There is much justice in Leslie
Stephen's claim that the sentimental plot of *Eugene Aram* obscures its
purpose, that all the "ingenious byplay" of romantic intrigue and comic
relief "distracts our attention from the murderer."[23] But within Aram
himself is yet another distracting feature—a heavy infusion of Byronic
self-consciousness which stylizes his characterization, lends it a disturbing
moral ambiguity, and thwarts Bulwer's effort to transcend the prevailing
mode of sensational romance with something more universal and more
profound.

As a young man, Bulwer, like many of his generation, identified
intensely with the grand gloomy figure of Byron and patterned his life
and his art in that manner. His earliest writings clearly reflect the power
of Byron's influence. A sensuous poetic narrative, "O'Neill, or the Rebel"
(1827), does little more than echo the sentiments and rhythmic cadence
of "The Corsair." Falkland, in the novel of the same year, has been called
a "snap-shot" of Byron.[24] *Pelham*, which appeared in 1828, marked a

departure chiefly in the character of its dandiacal hero, an apparent popinjay with the manners of an aristocrat but the conscience of a popular reformer. The "foibles" of Pelham, Bulwer claimed, were at least "more manly and noble, than the conceit of a general detestation of mankind, or the vanity of storming our pity by lamentations over imaginary sorrows and sombre hints at the fatal burthen of inexpiable crimes."[25] Pelhamism captured the fancy of post-Regency youth and influenced the fashion for years to come, but it could not supplant Byronism any more than Bulwer, in his own work, could elude this force which impregnated the intellectual atmosphere of his time. Certainly, as *Eugene Aram* shows, he did not eschew all interest in "the fatal burthen of inexpiable crimes."

Bulwer in fact recognized Eugene Aram's potential as a Byronic hero and realized in the novel's central character many of the traits associated with the type: his impassioned search for knowledge, his self-inflicted isolation, his conscious superiority to the ordinary inhabitants of Grassdale, his mysterious brooding, and the dark stigma of his secret guilt. That Aram, who is a murderer, nonetheless remains a sympathetic figure to the end, is a clear instance of the Byronic tendency of attributing to the man of genius the right to transcend commonplace morality. A crucial chapter wherein Houseman returns to blackmail Aram calls to mind another such genius with its epigraph from *Manfred*: "The spirits I have raised abandon me; / The spells which I have studied baffle me" (3.10).[26] So central is Aram, in fact, to the history of the Byronic hero that Walter C. Phillips in his early and still useful survey of nineteenth-century sensation literature habitually refers to the type as "the Schedoni-Lara-Aram kind of hero."[27]

The Byronic strain in Bulwer's novel invites sentimental Gothic overtones as well, particularly in the settings with which Aram is most closely associated. The grim prospect of his house early in the novel suggests a vague foreboding of its tenant, as yet unintroduced. "In the middle of a broad plain" it stands, "a lonely grey house" topped distinctively with the observatory dome where Aram pursues his late-night studies (1.2). In its remoteness, its bleakness, and its mystery—even in the "brain" which surmounts it—it is a metaphor for the scholar himself. The landscapes through which he walks, as the following passage illustrates, are overwritten with eerie personification and images calculated to chill the spine:

> The evening had already deepened into night. Along the sere
> and melancholy wood, the autumnal winds crept, with a lowly,
> but gathering moan. Where the water held its course, a damp

and ghostly mist clogged the air, but the skies were calm, and chequered only by a few clouds, that swept in long, white, spectral streaks, over the solemn stars. Now and then, the bat wheeled swiftly round, almost touching the figure of the Student, as he walked musingly onward. And the owl that before the month waned many days, would be seen no more in that region, came heavily from the trees, like a guilty thought that deserts its shade. (3.10)[28]

The novel's Gothic impulse is pointedly evident after an important scene between Houseman and Aram. The two have met by firelight in a cavern at the base of a thundering cataract, to plot Houseman's departure to France. They emerge to find the rain descending in torrents:

> ...every instant the lightning...became more and more frequent, converting the black waters into billows of living fire, or wreathing itself in lurid spires around the huge crag that now rose in sight; and again,...the thunder rolled onward, darting its vain fury upon the rushing cataract, and the tortured breast of the gulf that raved below.

As if the effect were not complete, Aram passes, on his return home across the moor, a gibbet from which swings the skeleton of a parricide hanged in chains, "its ghastly tenant waving to and fro, as the winds rattled through the parched and arid bones [so described despite the inclement weather]; and the inexpressible grin of the skull fixed, as in mockery, upon his countenance" (3.15).[29]

Years later, after Madeline's death and Aram's suicide, Walter returns, still grieving, to pay his predictable, almost obligatory visit to the neglected churchyard by the Lester manor house. He stands "in undisturbed contemplation for some time." Then, as he looks up, the air of brooding mystery implicit in the novel's setting from the start is brought full circle, and the ghost of Aram seems silently invoked:

> ...his eye caught afar, embedded among the soft verdure of the spring, one lone and grey house, from whose chimney there rose no smoke—sad, inhospitable, dismantled as that beside which he now stood;—as if the curse which had fallen on the inmates of either mansion, still clung to either roof. (5.8)

Although Bulwer "fell into the deepest despondency" concerning the merits of *Eugene Aram* just after it was written,[30] its enduring popular appeal and some years' perspective seem to have revived him. For the 1849 preface to the novel, he wrote the following:

> In point of composition EUGENE ARAM is, I think, entitled to rank amongst the best of my fictions. It somewhat humiliates me to acknowledge, that neither practice nor study has enabled me to surpass a work written at a very early age, in the skillful construction and patient development of plot; and though I have since sought to call forth higher and more subtle passions, I doubt if I have ever excited the two elementary passions of tragedy, viz., pity and terror, to the same degree.

Much of Bulwer's confidence was feigned, for his unorthodox celebration of Aram as a figure removed from traditional morality had launched them both onto a rough sea of controversy that was only then subsiding.

4

A LION IN CURL-PAPERS
The Reaction to *Eugene Aram*

THROUGHOUT HIS LONG CAREER, Edward Bulwer, like many successful men, inspired enmity in his contemporaries as well as admiration. At the relatively early period with which we are concerned, he had already aroused considerable hostility in influential critical circles. *Eugene Aram* not only revived the artistic objections prompted by Bulwer's earlier work but also, because of the serious philosophical questions it raised, was the object of sustained criticism on moral grounds. So persistent, in fact, was the opposition to this particular novel that its author was forced to capitulate, seventeen years after its first appearance, by substantially revising the original version. The adverse reaction to Bulwer's literary fame as symbolized by *Eugene Aram*, although nourished by private antagonism and professional envy, had its origins in the shifting ground of nineteenth-century morality and fictional theory. Centrally involved were two legitimate issues crucial to the development of the English novel at the time: the didactic responsibility of the artist, and the ascendance of realism over outworn romanticism.

One quality of *Eugene Aram* which makes it nearly unreadable today also contributed to the unfavorable element of its initial reception. This, the unnaturally heightened romantic idealism that permeates the work, reflects the elaborate aesthetic system to whose principles Bulwer remained dedicated, contrary to the best thought of the rising generation's most progressive critical minds. The fullest expression of Bulwer's aesthetic would appear in his important essay of 1838, "On Art in Fiction."[1] The central purpose of the novel, as Bulwer here envisioned it, was not to copy nature but, in the tradition of Reynolds and Hazlitt, to intuit and capture its sublime potential. The order of his priorities is evident in his observation of 1840 that "it would be difficult to find any

subject more adapted [than Eugene Aram] for that metaphysical speculation and analysis, in order to indulge which, Fiction...seeks its materials
and grounds its lessons in the chronicles of passion and crime."[2] Doubtless, Bulwer was seeking at this time to dignify his choice of subject
matter, to which objections had been raised since the novel's first
appearance. Certainly he was aware of the market value of novels of crime
when he wrote *Eugene Aram* in 1831, yet even then his artistic idealism
was the genuine culmination of a long and intense preoccupation with
the spiritual.

This elevated approach to art, well known in his century as Bulwer's
"idealizing principle," informs the rarefied, otherworldly atmosphere of
most of his fictions, and accounts for his insubstantial heroes and
heroines, whose grandiose speeches and inflated passions jar upon the
modern sensibility. The same quality which leads a commentator in our
own century to describe *Eugene Aram* as "over-written and hectically
sentimental"[3] led the down-to-earth, Benthamite *Westminster Review* of
a hundred years before to protest: "A man, with Bulwer, is not a man,
but the personification of something beginning with a capital letter."[4]

Even the many who admired Bulwer's artistry often admitted to an
uneasy sense that its effect was not entirely healthy. Though he was very
much a part of his times, Bulwer never embraced that scrupulous concern
for rectitude so often associated with the Victorian period. On the
contrary, he viewed circumspection with contempt and typically delighted
in testing the boundaries of what was permissible without overtly crossing
them. Characteristic of Bulwer's art was a subtle unconcern for propriety,
which introduced passions a shade too violent and flirted dangerously
with the unseemly, the bizarre, and the grotesque. His work, from the
early glittering novels of fashion to the later excursions into Rosicrucian
mysticism, was often disturbing to those of his contemporaries who
valued normalcy. Typical is the opinion of Mrs. Robert Southey, who
called him "clever" and "fascinating" but "insidiously misleading,"[5] and
that of Sir Walter Scott, who found him a "powerful" author yet regretted
his "*slang* tone of morality."[6] Bulwer himself was fully conscious of a practical moral obligation to his public, but he differed radically from his
critics in defining what was moral verity and what mere decadence.
Eugene Aram, which its author perceived as high-minded psychological
inquiry and its detractors as irresponsible sophistry, is a clear case in point.

A common thread linking *Eugene Aram* with Bulwer's other novels
censured in the 1830s and 40s is their exploration of the aberrant mind.
The psychological interest was his justification for dwelling on such
subjects. To pursue it into the realms of evil required an intrepid defiance

of social taboo, a spirit of independence which Bulwer, defending his novels of crime in 1845, was happy to possess:

> Long since, in searching for new regions in the art to which I am a servant, it seemed to me that they might be found lying far, and rarely trodden, beyond that range of conventional morality in which novelist after novelist had intrenched himself,—amongst those subtle recesses in the ethics of human life in which Truth and Falsehood dwell undisturbed and unseparated. The vast and dark Poetry around us—the Poetry of Modern Civilization and Daily Existence, is shut out from us in much, by the shadowy giants of Prejudice and Fear. He who would arrive at the Fairy Land, must face the Phantoms.[7]

As Bulwer had learned by now, he must also face the Critics. His fascination with highwaymen and murderers denied him the approval of a growing critical fraternity which perceived as the artist's only conscionable purpose the wholesome improvement of mankind.

1

Although *Eugene Aram* was not unanimously welcomed on its debut in December, 1831, with the reading public it was an almost immediate triumph. The first edition (postdated 1832) was sold out within months of its appearance. No official sales record has been found, but Bulwer, writing from Nice in 1849 to his publisher Blackwood, clearly recalled the initial figure: "...sometimes I find my Novels hang fire at first & recover afterwards. This was the case with Eugene Aram for which I remember the subscription was only 1000 copies—but it sold 3000—of the 3 volume form."[8]

Allusions to the novel in both fiction and nonfiction on both sides of the Atlantic abound, attesting to its widespread contemporary influence. The American romantic painter Washington Allston (1779–1843) one evening impressed his future biographer and a few other friends with a spirited discourse upon *Eugene Aram*, which he had just read. "The easy flow of language, emphasized by his expressive countenance and manner," we are told, "made it a memorable occasion to his privileged listeners."[9] For some later Victorians, the book became synonymous with extravagant romance and symbolic of its emotional excesses. George Eliot's *Felix Holt* (1866) describes a scene at Treby Manor, home of the ultra-conservative Debarry family, where in September of 1832 the late bestseller has ill-suited its readers for other pursuits: "The focus of brilliancy at Treby Manor that evening was...not in the drawing room, where Miss Debarry and Selina, quietly elegant in their dress and manners were feeling rather dull than otherwise, having finished Mr. Bulwer's *Eugene Aram*, and being thrown back on the last great prose work of Mr. Southey, while their mamma slumbered a little on the sofa."[10]

A lower stratum, whose approval the fastidious Bulwer must surely have welcomed less, paid him an unlikely compliment shortly after the publication of *Eugene Aram*. Pierce Egan, author of *Life in London* and *Tom and Jerry*, two series of crude, irreverent underworld sketches published in monthly numbers during the 1820s, called upon Bulwer one day with the manner of a "retired prize-fighter" commending a promising newcomer to the ring. He proceeded to withdraw from a silken pouch and carefully unfold a revolting relic which he proudly displayed as the authentic caul of the murderer Thurtell. Such a treasure, he said, could only be rightfully kept by the author of *Eugene Aram*.[11]

The periodical reviews of *Eugene Aram*, unlike Egan's enthusiastic tribute, were mixed. Perhaps the friendliest reception came from the radical *Examiner*, whose article of almost unalloyed praise inspired Henry Crabb Robinson at once to secure the first volume, which he took home and read in bed until the early hours of the morning.[12] Full of encomiums to Bulwer's genius and the truthfulness of his artistic vision, the *Examiner* proclaimed Aram's character the "master-piece" in "a work abounding with excellencies."[13] The *Monthly Review* agreed, preferring the new novel to any of Bulwer's prior efforts and declaring with appalling imperception that it has "not a particle of his characteristic affectation."[14] The *Court Journal* also joined in the appreciative chorus, as did the *Literary Gazette*, whose commendation was to be expected since it had been for many years the mouthpiece of Bulwer's publisher, Henry Colburn. But most reviewers, like Leigh Hunt writing for the *Tatler* and the anonymous contributor to the *Literary Guardian*, combined respectful approval with judicious criticism. Although Hunt's essay closed with gracious acclaim for this achievement filled "with beauties of all sorts, calling for every species of sympathy, and exalting the author in our estimation as a writer and as a man," he shared with the *Edinburgh Review*, the *Guardian*, and numerous other critics the belief that no author had a right to manipulate the facts of history as Bulwer had done the circumstances of Aram's life.[15]

The proper relationship of history and fiction was, as we have seen, in debate at the time, when a host of lesser followers of Scott were taking extravagant liberties with historical truth despite the widespread opinion of serious persons that popular literature should teach useful—and dependable—facts. The problem, as manifest in *Eugene Aram*, affected different critics in remarkably dissimilar ways. The *Edinburgh Review* added to the common criticism expressed by Hunt the suggestion that Bulwer could have been more faithful to history had he made his protagonist not the hero in a novel but the villain in a tragedy. There he could present Aram "nearly as he was — the bold-faced treacherous murderer — the smooth dissembler — in whose life nothing becomes him but the leaving of it, and the mental resources he developes in struggling with his fate."[16] The author of this view could not have known that his plan had been anticipated and abandoned: the Aram of Bulwer's atrocious unfinished play not published until the following year, is much the tragic villain suggested here.

The *Spectator* review was also concerned with Bulwer's manipulation of fact, but its anonymous writer was so ignorant of the subject he addressed that he was hardly a competent judge. To begin with, he accepts without challenge an inaccurate assertion in the novel's preface that it is essentially faithful to history. Only the fictional confession, he claims, departs "materially from the exact truth," and its publication is unfair to the historical Aram, who, so far as is known, never did confess. This absurd objection is the only recorded inference that Bulwer's treatment of Aram was libelous. The review closes by citing the one "grand fault" in the work: that our foreknowledge of the outcome frustrates the author's efforts at suspense and in fact defeats the book.[17] Similar reasoning would, of course, make it difficult to appreciate *Hamlet* on the second reading.

Far more judicious and more commonly expressed is the *Edinburgh* reviewer's diagnosis of the novel's overriding flaw. The reason it fails, he says, is the "moral anomaly" of a hero whose crime is irreconcilable with his noble qualities. The "naked and coarse-grained villainy of the real Aram," who murdered for greed, shows through the fiction and defies Bulwer's effort to make him sublime: "Mammon is almost the only incarnation of the evil principles which no art can render poetical." The critic of the *Edinburgh* was not the first, and certainly not the last, to fault the novel for making a romance out of a homicide. The *Athenaeum* had always maintained a scrupulous neutrality towards Bulwer, despite the fact that its respected name had been undeservedly lampooned in *Paul Clifford* as the title of the vulgar hack journal, the "*Asinaeum*." Now the *Athenaeum* rose up in a spirit of moral outrage to reject *Eugene Aram* decisively while it was still practically damp from the press. Contrasting Bulwer's new hero unfavorably with even the infamous Byronic villains, whose sinful acts are at least left "vague and undefined," it lamented "the fine powers which the author has squandered upon this sad subject" and hoped "soon to see Mr. Bulwer laying the rich garlands of his fancy on a more hallowed shrine than a gibbet, and adorning with his wit, his humour, and his pathos, subjects which we may muse on without a shudder."[18]

The suggestion here that crime, however portrayed, is essentially inappropriate as a subject for fiction represents an extreme view of the issue. Few readers would have concurred, so long as simple poetic justice was served in the course of the narrative. The lesson most commonly taught by the popular literature of the day, in Margaret Dalziel's apt summation, was that "Duty is duty, quite easily discernible and quite within our powers of performance. If we do right, we shall in one way or other be rewarded — if we do wrong, we shall suffer for it here and hereafter."[19] And yet, from the standpoint of the prevailing mores, Newgate fiction, which tended to glorify crime, was a different matter. Bulwer, with his clumsy attempts at psychological inquiry into the "subtle recesses where Truth and Falsehood dwell...unseparated," seemed especially irresponsible.

The colorful highwayman-protagonist of Bulwer's *Paul Clifford* (1830), the first Newgate novel, escapes justice entirely and flees to America, where he is represented at the novel's close leading an exemplary life. His crimes were at least pardonable. With his gallantry and high principles, he was something of a latter-day Robin Hood. But there was no similar excuse for Aram. The romance surrounding Bulwer's mysteriously sinister, morbid, and asocial scholar-murderer was not the relatively wholesome daylight variety; and his offense, even as minimized by Bulwer, was still mostly sordid — mostly, as the *Edinburgh Review* put it, "Mammon." It is true that the Aram of the novel suffers, dies, and is no doubt damned for the murder of Clarke. Justice, on the surface, is served. The moral complication, however, is that he feels no remorse for his crime, only regret for the pain it has caused; and yet the reader is invited to sympathize and feel sorry for his downfall. Furthermore, the sophistic justification on Godwinian principles of Aram's crime was irregular enough to trouble many of Bulwer's more reflective contemporaries.

2

By far the most formidable opposition in the early days of reaction against Bulwer and the Newgate novel was a source hardly associated with sobriety: the clique of mostly youthful writers behind *Fraser's Magazine for Town and Country*, a lively new publication with Tory leanings, founded in February, 1830. Self-described with characteristic tongue-in-cheek as "the only Magazine which represents the wishes and meets the wants of the period in which we live,"[20] *Fraser's* set out in a spirit of exuberant impudence to disturb the literary peace and puncture inflated dignity wherever it might be found. Other literary notables—Thomas Moore, Macaulay, and Harriet Martineau, to name a few—were tilted at periodically, but Bulwer's excessive self-esteem and the many aspects of his writing which so cordially invited parody made him a natural object for what became known in the fraternity as "Bulwer-baiting." Indeed, *Fraser's* gave him no respite for nearly the first three years of its existence and was still gibing at him sporadically long afterwards.

Repeatedly assailed in *Fraser's* were Bulwer's "assumed virtue" and "arrogated self-knowledge," his "eternal whine about what he calls the good and the beautiful," and his "windy sentences. . . gravely delivered with all the emphasis of truth and the air of profound conviction."[21] Behind the fun and between the lines was a serious and progressive reviewing policy that anticipated the coming movement toward literary realism by pointedly preferring what was open and honest in writing to what was false or artificial.[22] The application of this philosophy to Bulwer's *Eugene Aram*, following its debut late in 1831, added to the Aram literature a small body of first-rate parody whose appearance, however ephemeral, reflects an avenue of contemporary critical response that deserves notice in regard to the Aram theme. The limitations of this study permit only a glimpse into what amounted to an ongoing feud between Bulwer and the wags of *Fraser's*. The whole fascinating story is chronicled elsewhere,[23] and preserved so well in the volumes of the offending periodical that the merest imaginative effort brings to life from their pages the vibrant personalities of this former time.

The editorial mastermind of *Fraser's* and the leader of the attack was Dr. William Maginn, a remarkably gifted and equally unprincipled Irishman whose brief career as an influential London journalist soon guttered in alcoholism, riot, and unscrupulous dealings. Around him was gathered a troupe of heedless wits, who at his instigation readily joined in the fun of making Edward Bulwer an utter mockery. Most of their names are forgotten today, but one of them was William Makepeace Thackeray, whose anti-snob artillery had its first trial against the conspicuous target presented by the author of *Eugene Aram*.

Fraser's began its offensive early. Following the January, 1832, table of contents is a notice that:

Liston Bulwer [see n. 24] has just hit upon a new line of business. His '*fancy flash*' [probably an allusion to *Paul Clifford*, which dignifies the "flash" or underworld life of thieves and highwaymen] having proved an unmarketable commodity, he has discovered that his genius lies one degree lower; and therefore, most prudently has he resolved upon doing the NEWGATE CALENDAR into a series of *fashionable novels!*' His first speculation in this way is an attempt on the life of *Eugene Aram*.

Attached to this announcement is a piece of doggerel entitled "E. A. and E. B.," whose concession to the season consists of the nearly impossible recommendation that it be sung to the tune of "'God save you, merry Gentlemen!'":

> E. Aram was a pedagogue
>   So sullen and so sad;
> E. Bulwer was a gentleman
>   Wot plied as Colburn's Cad:
> And the deeds of both, I grieve to say,
>   Were werry, werry bad.
>
> E. Aram he whipped little boys
>   With malice and with ire;
> E. Bulwer wrote Whig articles,
>   As Beelzebub did inspire:
> And both of them they did these things
>   All for the sake of hire.
>
> E. Aram killed a man one day,
>   Out of a devilish whim;
> E. Bulwer did almost the same—
>   A deed well nigh as grim:
> For Aram he murder'd Daniel Clarke,
>   And Bulwer he murder'd *him*.
>
> E. Aram's crime it was impell'd
>   That cash he might purloin;
> E. Bulwer did his wickedness
>   For love of Colburn's coin:
> Alas! that money should debauch
>   Two geniuses so fine!
>
> E. Aram he was sent to jail,
>   And hanged upon a tree;
> E. Bulwer is in parliament,
>   A shabby-genteel M.P.;
> But if he writes such murdering books,
>   What must his ending be?

> Why, that in *Fraser's Magazine*
> His gibbet we shall see.[24]

It is not always possible to determine with certainty which of the anonymous assaults in *Fraser's* are by Thackeray, which by Maginn, and which by others of their confederacy and friends. But the review of *Eugene Aram*, "A Good Tale Badly Told," that appeared in February, 1832, is more than likely Maginn's.[25] If so, it clearly indicates why his style of the hasty, irreverent "squib" was imitated in every paper with a penchant for chic *bon mots*. The review is a superficial but brilliant indictment of the novel on both artistic and moral grounds. The new book, it holds, sets an "evil and pernicious example," and would be truly dangerous were it not so "feebly executed." Bulwer is criticized for his distortion of history and for the triteness of his characterization: "How is it that novelists always make the eldest daughter pale, tall, with black eyes and hair, *penseroso* in thought and demeanour, while the younger has invariably blue eyes and a sunny smile, with a bosom too pure and innocent for sadness?" Certain other comments are, in true Fraserian style, sheer insult, like the accusation that Bulwer plagiarized from *Faust* or the absurdly unfounded inference behind the charge that "On drawing-room fascinations [Bulwer] descants historically, as from tradition—the cellar and the garret he paints to the life, as one who loves and knows his subject."

With the introduction of the moral issue, the reviewer's barrage *ad hominem* intensifies. There is doubtless truth to biographer Michael Sadleir's indignant assertion that much of this moralizing, coming as it did from the *Fraser's* camp, "was sheer cant."[26] It is not to the subject matter itself that the writer objects, for, as the first part of its title suggests, the review maintains that Aram's is "A Good Tale." The objection is that it has been "overlaid with tinselled fripperey, [and] spun out into tedious dialogue and vapid declamation," so that it becomes "to a sound taste in writing as unpleasant as a glass of curaçoa diluted in a pint of water to an unvitiated palate." Wit soon gives way to righteous indignation as *Fraser's* accuses Bulwer of "a habitual tampering with sacred subjects, and a constant hankering after profanity and blasphemy." Cited in support of the charge is a passage wherein "a Protestant clergyman is represented uttering prayers for the dead"—a doctrinal oversight which Bulwer later took pains to correct.

The moral question which closes the essay is more pertinent to art: "When is it justifiable or allowable to dress truth in the garb of fiction?" For what end, the critic asks, is a man as callous and inhuman as history reveals Aram to have been, here depicted "as a high-souled being, averse to all human laws, because indignant at the disparities of society, yearning after universal philanthropy, and destroying a worthless churl because his virtuous sensibilities are wounded by dissolute and heartless lust?" *Eugene Aram*, in his estimate, serves none of the three legitimate purposes possible to historical fiction—"innocent recreation, elevated amusement, or the attainment of a moral end." On the contrary, it is a mere vehicle for its author's "moral and legislative sophistry," and an insidious vehicle at that, since the publicity surrounding "any novel or unusual crime" generates "a sequence of similar offences" and there is in *Eugene Aram* and such books the same potential. "We dislike altogether," the reviewer concludes, "this awakening sympathy with interesting criminals, and wasting sensibilities on the scaffold and the gaol. It is a modern, a depraved, a corrupting taste."

Months later, this assault was followed by the burlesque *Elizabeth Brownrigge*, a clever parody so closely imitative of *Eugene Aram* that it can only be fully appreciated after a fresh reading of the novel. *Elizabeth Brownrigge*'s former attribution to Thackeray is no longer generally accepted, the prevailing view today being that it was the work of Maginn, possibly in collaboration with John Gibson Lockhart.[27] Like *Joseph Andrews*, this piece travesties its predecessor by reversing the male and female roles. It substitutes for Eugene Aram another figure from the *Newgate Calendar*, his contemporary Elizabeth Brownrigg, a midwife executed in 1767 for the depraved torments to which she subjected several of her female apprentices, causing the death of one girl. With the added aristocratic *e* to her name—her initials already invoked "Edward Bulwer"—Elizabeth Brownrigge was the perfect answer to Eugene Aram. Her transformation into a high-minded but hypocritical philosopher is acutely satirical of his Byronic metamorphosis. Like Aram, Elizabeth is a philanthropist as well as a scholar. Even in prison,

> She completed a large stock of baby-linen for the poor; she perused and commented upon the principal new publications of the day; and she composed an elaborate parallel between the characters of Socrates and Lady Jane Grey, after the manner of Plutarch.[28]

Each of the principals in *Eugene Aram* has his or her parallel in *Elizabeth Brownrigge*—always in one of the opposite sex. The cat Jacobina, whose eccentric canine attributes provide a comic motif in Bulwer's novel, exchanges her species as well, becoming in the *Fraser's* lampoon the dog Muggletonian, who purrs and rubs against his mistress's skirts.

The passage introducing Alphonso Belvidere, Elizabeth's fiancé and Madeline Lester's counterpart, exemplifies the many-edged satire which is characteristic of this witty production. Under fire are all the worst affectations of Bulwer's literary style and manner—the inflated sentiments, the embarrassingly purple passages, the overweening snob appeal, and the flaunted, pointless allusions—even, thinly veiled between the lines and sitting for the portrait, his dandified self:

> Alphonso, who stood six feet two without his shoes, united, in the compact and slender structure of his person, the vigour of the Hercules with the elegance of the Apollo. His features, which were cast in the perfect mould of the Antinous, were coloured with a deep, rich sunniness of tone, which no pencil inferior to that of Titian could ever have aspired to imitate; while the breadth of his forehead bespoke the intellectual powers of a Newton or a Locke; and the bright, lambent, and innocuous fires of his unfathomable eye beamed with the gentle virtues of a martyred saint. As his figure was character-ised by strength and grace, so was his countenance by intelligence and humility. He was distinguished among literary men as the editor of a new monthly magazine [Bulwer had just undertaken the editorship of Colburn's *New Monthly Magazine*.]; and his attire was of that simple style of elegance which accorded well with the cast of his person. . . .his coat, waistcoat, and nether garments, were formed *en suite* of snuff-coloured broad cloth; his stockings were of white silk, variegated with horizontal stripes of blue; and his only ornaments were the silver buckles that glistened, with a modest and a moon-like lustre, at his knees, on his shoes, and in the front of his hat. (p. 74)

The two major charges against the content of *Eugene Aram*, its mis-use of historical materials and its perversion of the moral order, also find ironic expression in *Elizabeth Brownrigge*. The supposed author, an aspiring hack, explains his method in a dedicatory letter to Edward Bulwer. Wishing to write a successful novel, he had obtained from his laundress a copy of the new best seller, *Eugene Aram*, and learned from it how to make a popular fiction out of fact:

> As you have omitted any mention of the wife of your Eugene, I have not thought it necessary to recall the reader's attention to the husband and sixteen children of my Elizabeth. As you

have given your hero more learning and virtue than he possessed,
... I have presumed to raise the situation of my heroine, and ...
I have represented her in my tale as a young gentlewoman of
independent fortune, a paragon of beauty, a severe and learned
moral philosopher, and the Lady Bountiful of the village of
Islington. (p. 68)

The ultimate secret of success, he concludes, must be to reverse nature by
looking for good in the annals of evil and then "to mix vice and virtue
up together in such an inextricable confusion as to render it impossible
that any preference should be given to either, or that one, indeed, should
be at all distinguishable from the other" (p. 67). So, as Aram reasoned
away his guilt on utilitarian principles, Brownrigge drowns her victims'
cries with impassioned speeches on the necessity of "punishment" as a
moral remedy for apprentices, and delivers at the end a defense which
practically repudiates Aram's because its straining at truth is only slightly
more counterfeit.

3

After *Elizabeth Brownrigge*, the brunt of the attack on Bulwer and
the Newgate novel with which he was so closely associated came from one
single source, his most potent and dogged Fraserian adversary, William
Makepeace Thackeray. In the late 1830s and 40s, Thackeray launched an
ultimately successful campaign to help scourge the Newgate novel out of
existence, taking Bulwer for his particular target. His weaponry included
two of his best fictions, *Barry Lyndon* (1844) and *Vanity Fair* (1847–48),
as well as the more ephemeral, more crudely executed *Catherine*
(1839–40) and a number of miscellaneous articles in *Fraser's* and the
Times. Another shorter piece, "George de Barnwell" (1847), directly
parodied *Eugene Aram*.

Thackeray's marked antipathy to Bulwer was, of course, closely
related to the diametric opposition of their artistic views. There was in it,
as well, a measure of professional envy. And yet, despite their personal
and political differences—Thackeray was a Tory and Bulwer a Whig—
Thackeray actually was not far removed in principle from some of the
liberal humanitarian attitudes implicit in Bulwer's works. Though
Thackeray repudiated the morality of *Eugene Aram*, it was because he
found it specious, not because he was puritanical. Like *Paul Clifford*, a
piece written by Thackeray for *Fraser's* in 1840 entitled "Going to See a
Man Hanged" opposes capital punishment. Furthermore, it offers objective, broad-minded reflections on the lot of a young prostitute that recall

Bulwer's unorthodox consideration of that growing problem, which in *England and the English* (1833) he had daringly blamed on the restrictive social attitudes of current morality.[29] But on occasion Bulwer could also, with an aristocratic curl of the lip, disdain "the common herd" who bought his novels by the thousands.[30] His dandiacal, class-conscious arrogance was the one quality most frequently and most justifiably held up to ridicule by his detractors. It led Tennyson to compare him to a bandbox and to a lion in curl-papers.[31] And it particularly irritated Thackeray, who was proud of his bourgeois origins.

When, in 1846, a new edition of *Eugene Aram* with minor revisions appeared in Bentley's "Standard Novels and Romances" series, Thackeray, for not entirely masochistic reasons, reread it and found his original distaste for the work renewed. His return to this detested novel was occasioned by his recent agreement to produce for *Punch* a series of short parodies of contemporary novels. The assignment made him think at once of *Eugene Aram*, and the first production in "Punch's Prize Novelists," later called "Novels by Eminent Hands," was the brief "George de Barnwell," by Sir E. L. B. L. BB. LL. BBB. LLL., Bart., which ran in three weekly issues during April, 1847. The story of George Barnwell, the London shopkeeper's apprentice whose expensive infatuation with a prostitute, Sara Millwood, led him to rob and murder his uncle, was already well known. A doggerel travesty of 1812 indicates how low treatment of the theme had sunk: "There's nunky as fat as a hog," George muses, "While I am as lean as a lizzard, / Here's at you, you stingy old dog! / And he whips a long knife in his gizzard."[32]

The incongruity of the lofty tone of Bulwer's work with the existing low comedic associations of George Barnwell's story made it an excellent vehicle for Thackeray's lampoon. In many ways, the piece is strongly reminiscent of *Elizabeth Brownrigge*, although the later parody does not, like the earlier one, admit a continuous, point-by-point comparison with its serious prototype. It is directed instead at a number of pervasive weaknesses in the original work. Compared with *Elizabeth Brownrigge*, it had the advantage of brevity without sacrifice of effect. The opening descriptive passage points up the stilted inappropriateness of Bulwer's grandiose style by applying it to a humdrum scene:

NOONDAY IN CHEPE.
'Twas noonday in Chepe. High Tide in the mighty River City! — its Banks well nigh overflowing with the myriad-waved Stream of Man!...locked and bound and hustling together in the narrow channel of Chepe. The imprecations of the charioteers

were terrible....The pavid matron within the one vehicle (speeding to the Bank for her semestrial pittance) shrieked and trembled; the angry DIVES hastening to his offices (to add another thousand to his heap), thrust his head over the blazoned panels, and displayed an eloquence of objurgation which his very Menials could not equal; the dauntless street urchins, as they gaily threaded the Labyrinth of Life, enjoyed the perplexities and quarrels of the scene, and exacerbated the already furious combatants by their poignant infantile satire.[33]

George de Barnwell himself, in keeping with the new high-sounding patronymic prefix, quotes Latin and Greek poets, and philosophizes relentlessly about the Beautiful and the True in ludicrous imitation of Bulwer's scholarly hero. His introduction into the mercantile setting, as he sits reading Homer in the original with his back to the shop counter, occasions a rhapsodic flight, for he "had just reached that happy period of life when the Boy is expanding into the Man. O Youth, Youth! Happy and Beautiful! O fresh and roseate dawn of life; when the dew yet lies on the flowers, ere they have been scorched and withered by Passion's fiery Sun!" George's innocence is doomed with the appearance of a customer, the coquettishly common "Millwood," who upbraids him for his inattention: "'I might have prigged this box of figs,' the damsel said, good-naturedly, 'and you'd never have turned round.'" His face "kindling as he spoke, and his eagle eyes flashing fire," George responds with feeling:

> "Figs pall; but O! the Beautiful never does! Figs rot; but O! the Truthful is eternal. I was born, lady, to grapple with the Lofty and the Ideal. My soul yearns for the Visionary. I stand behind the counter, it is true; but I ponder here upon the deeds of heroes, and muse over the thoughts of sages. What is grocery for one who has ambition?...The Ideal, lady, I often think, is the true Real, and the Actual but a visionary hallucination. But pardon me; with what may I serve thee?"
>
> "I came only for sixpenn'orth of tea-dust," the girl said, with a faltering voice; "but O, I should like to hear you speak on for ever!" (p. 137)

George's identification with Aram, who chafed at the necessity of teaching for a living, and Millwood's with Madeline, who was mesmerized by the scholar's fine discourse, are unmistakable. Neither the narrator nor her lover, however, seems able to keep track of Millwood's given name. She is addressed and alluded to on various occasions as "Martha," "Ellinor,"

George de Barnwell, about to murder his uncle. From *Punch*, April, 1847.

"Emily," or "Adelaide," to suggest her lover's abstracted inattention to detail and the lifeless similarity of Bulwer's romantically-named heroines. After more foolery, and after a considerable time lapse, during which George has robbed and murdered his uncle—"a surly curmudgeon with very little taste for the True and the Beautiful" (p. 146)—comes a final section entitled "The Condemned Cell." This, analogous to the confession chapter of Bulwer's novel, explores the motivation for the crime in the aftermath of discovery and conviction. Three figures are present, at first, on the eve of George's execution. Martha/Emily/Ellinor/Adelaide and the turnkey Snoggin are both reduced to tears, while George rattles his chains and carries on, in speeches replete with capital letters, about the transience of life and his composure in the face of death, comparing himself to Socrates with his hemlock and Seneca in his bath. Here Thackeray cannot resist a personal jab at his dandified rival: "'Has for a bath,' SNOGGIN interposed, 'they're not to be ad in this ward of the prison; but I dussay HEMMY will git you a little hoil for your air'" (p. 155).

The culmination of the entire sketch is in the devastating moral thrust of the concluding paragraphs. Here, George confides in the kindly prison chaplain and the crucial issue of Aram's guilt comes to the fore:

> In the matter for which he suffered, GEORGE could never be brought to acknowledge that he was at all in the wrong. "It may be an error of judgment," he said to the Venerable Chaplain of the gaol, "but it is no crime. Were it Crime, I should feel Remorse. Where there is no Remorse, Crime cannot exist. I am not sorry: therefore, I am innocent. . . .
>
> "And wherefore, Sir, should I have sorrow, . . . for ridding the world of a sordid worm; of a man whose very soul was dross, and who never had a feeling for the Truthful and the Beautiful? . . . 'Dog,' I said to the trembling slave, 'tell me where thy Gold is. *Thou* hast no use for it. I can spend it in relieving the Poverty on which thou tramplest; in aiding Science, which thou knowest not; in uplifting Art, to which thou art blind. Give Gold, and thou art free!' But he spake not, and I slew him." (p. 155)

By oversimplifying the logic and dispensing with Bulwer's ultimate point—that Aram's reliance on abstract reason led him astray—Thackeray makes the novel's thematic core travesty, and its hero a conscienceless egoist. As *raisonneur*, the thoughtful man of God intones a moral close to the heart of Thackeray's artistic quarrel with Edward Bulwer:

> "I would not have this doctrine vulgarly promulgated," said the admirable chaplain, "for its general practice might chance to do harm. . . .Think what would be the world's condition, were men without any Yearning after the Ideal to attempt to re-organize Society, to redistribute Property, to avenge Wrong."
>
> "A rabble of pigmies scaling Heaven," said the noble though misguided young Prisoner. "PROMETHEUS was a Giant, and he fell."

"Yes, indeed, my brave youth!" the benevolent DR. FUZZ-WIG exclaimed, clasping the Prisoner's marble and manacled hand; "and the Tragedy of Tomorrow will teach the World that Homicide is not to be permitted even to the most amiable Genius, and that the lover of the Ideal and Beautiful, as thou art, my son, must respect the Real likewise." (p. 155)

The words become even more resonant by grace of *Punch*'s accompanying cartoons, for George de Barnwell, with his absurdly prominent nose and deep-set eyes, clearly resembles Sir E. L. B. L. BB. LL. BBB. LLL., Bart.[34]

4

The defense of *Eugene Aram* against the anti-Newgate forces was left primarily to Bulwer himself. He received, as has been shown, a great deal of favorable criticism in the periodicals of the day and had at least a few literary allies including Dickens, Macaulay, the biographer John Forster, and the journalist Albany Fonblanque. But in general, outside opposition to Bulwer's detractors was rare and not at all outspoken. His own guarded replies, however, were frequent. In *England and the English* (1833), while the Newgate issue was still young, he contended that the popular taste for reading about murder arose not from moral depravity but rather from a healthy abhorrence of evil.[35] An unjustifiably large part of his 1838 essay "On Art in Fiction" is devoted to proving the respectability and indeed the advantages of literary study of the criminal mind. Bulwer's defensive tone suggests he must surely have had *Eugene Aram* in mind, and the criticism of his reviewers that it made good and evil indistinct:

It is true that, in...these applications of art, you will be censured by shallow critics and pernicious moralists. It will be said of you,..."He seeks to interest us in a murderer or a robber, an adulterer or a parricide;"– it will be said of you..."And this man whom he holds up to us as an example, whom he calls wise and good, is a rascal, who indulges such an error, or commits such an excess." But no man can be an artist who does not prefer experience and human nature to all criticism.[36]

Bulwer's prefaces, particularly to those novels which came under fire for their moral tendencies, also contain many expressions of his views regarding crime in fiction. The more his principles or his methods were questioned, the more stubbornly he clung to them. The 1840 preface to *Eugene Aram*, typically, makes no specific allusion to the onslaught against that novel. Nevertheless, its author's keen awareness of the contro-

versy is just beneath the surface in many a self-conscious polemic calculated to deflect criticism without directly confronting it. One such passage
was clearly elicited by Thackeray's newly published *Catherine*. Any
informed reader must have recognized Bulwer's motive for introducing
the issue. Yet it is with feigned nonchalance that he writes: "The guilt of
Eugene Aram is not that of a vulgar ruffian: it leads to views and
considerations vitally and wholly distinct from those with which profli-
gate knavery and brutal cruelty revolt and displease us in the literature
of Newgate and the Hulks." The idea is tossed, in an offhand way, into
an ongoing consideration of the historical Aram's character. In the next
breath, Bulwer seeks dignity through association as he classifies his Aram
with Shakespeare's brooding villains Iago and Macbeth.

Bulwer's reluctance to grapple directly with the issues habitually
detracts from his persuasiveness. Here he seems to have forgotten that
while Eugene Aram was not vulgar, Houseman and a good many of their
acquaintances were; and that his story *is* part of "the literature of
Newgate" in the most restricted sense of the phrase: the *Calendar* itself,
which was, after all, one of his sources. Walter Phillips, who masterfully
demonstrates Bulwer's "unavailing struggle to turn [the novel of crime]
into worthy channels," refutes Bulwer's insistence that his Aram should
not be confused with the ordinary Newgate felon. Phillips argues that
because we never see the detailed workings of Aram's mind until the final
confession, which is tacked on too late and is too inept for valid psychological inquiry, the distinction "is finally a potential rather than actual
difference."[37] The logic of Bulwer's second point of defense is at least as
awkward: "Did I want any other answer to the animadversions of
commonplace criticism, it might be sufficient to say that what the
historian relates, the novelist has little right to disdain."[38]

In January of 1847, in the face of a renewed onslaught occasioned
by his latest and most lurid Newgate novel, *Lucretia*, Bulwer published
an elaborate pamphlet defense, "A Word to the Public." Beleaguered as
he was by the new wave of criticism, to the point of mental imbalance,
his first reaction had been to consider challenging Thackeray to a duel,
a purpose from which his friends John Forster and Albany Fonblanque
had luckily dissuaded him. As an alternative to pistols, the new pamphlet
was actually rather dull, being little more than a statement of Bulwer's
grievance and a tame reiteration of points that his prefaces had been
making all along about the psychological appropriateness of crime as a
subject for literature. Whereas the source of "woe" affecting the fortunes
of kings in ancient tragedy was external Fate, the tragic potential of

contemporary man, Bulwer claimed, is in the dark recesses of the soul, which modern literature must therefore explore.

The interesting outcome of this venture was the pamphlet's metamorphosis months later in the prefatory section of "George de Barnwell," where Bulwer's argument from classical tragedy is soundly burlesqued:

> In Kingly and Heroic ages, 'twas of Kings and Heroes that the Poet spake. . . .The People To-Day is King, and we chronicle his woes. . . .
>
> Fate, Passion, Mystery, the Victim, the Avenger, the Hate that arms, the Furies that tear, the Love that bleeds, are not these with us Still? are not these still the weapons of the Artist? the colours of his pallette, the chords of his lyre? Listen! I tell thee a tale — not of Kings — but of Men — not of Thrones, but of Love, and Grief, and Crime. Listen, and but once more. 'Tis for the last time (probably) these fingers shall sweep the strings. (p. 136)[39]

Forster's letters reveal that Thackeray had been made aware of Bulwer's precarious mental state well before this parody appeared, and Thackeray's indicate that "George de Barnwell" was ready for the printers before "A Word to the Public" could have reached him. His consciousness of the circumstances behind Bulwer's pamphlet makes his motive for incorporating it in the already finished manuscript nothing short of vicious.

5

In 1849, after seventeen years of obstinate resistance, Bulwer at last submitted to the dictates of critical opinion with a revised edition of *Eugene Aram*, published by Chapman and Hall. Although his capitulation is evident in the text, he was still too proud to admit it. "If none of my prose works have been so attacked as EUGENE ARAM," begins the preface to the new issue,

> none have so completely triumphed over attack. It is true that, whether from real or affected ignorance of the true morality of fiction, a few critics may still reiterate the old commonplace charges of "selecting heroes from Newgate," or "investing murderers with interest;" but the firm hold which the work has established in the opinion of the general public, and the favour it has received in every country where English literature is known, suffice to prove that, whatever its faults, it belongs to that legitimate class of fiction which illustrates life and truth,

and only deals with crime as the recognised agency of pity and terror, in the conduct of tragic narrative.

Bulwer's guard never drops as he prepares in this new preface to outline the changes at hand. First, in further defense of his subject, he quotes a long passage from "A Word to the Public" of two years before, and then praises his novel for exciting the tragic emotions. There are, he admits, a few stylistic flaws—"verbal oversights, and defects in youthful taste (some of which I have endeavoured to remove...)"—but the work surpasses all his others, especially "in the minuteness and fidelity of its descriptions of external nature." At length comes a single paragraph detailing the "one alteration, somewhat more important than mere verbal correction," which is, in reality, crucial to the entire controversy surrounding this book at the time. Bulwer's transparent attempt to make it seem unrelated to any issue besides his own casual interest in the Aram case is almost pathetically disingenuous:

> On going, with maturer judgment, over all the evidences on which Aram was condemned, I have convinced myself, that though an accomplice in the robbery of Clarke, he was free both from the premeditated design and the actual deed of murder. The crime, indeed, would still rest on his conscience, and insure his punishment, as necessarily incidental to the robbery in which he was an accomplice, with Houseman; but finding my convictions, that in the murder itself he had no share, borne out by the opinion of many eminent lawyers, by whom I have heard the subject discussed, I have accordingly so shaped his confession to Walter.

It is natural to wonder whether Bulwer truly believed that anyone literate enough to read his book could be so easily deluded. Clearly his actual intent is to call off the critics who have worried the novel for so long. They have objected to his making a hero of a murderer, so, in his revision, he simply removes the reason for the second epithet. His hero, no longer a willing accomplice to homicide, will be, as a result, more admirable in voicing the scruples of his conscience because there is less occasion for them.

Collation of the 1832 and 1849 editions reveals that, as Bulwer says, the most substantial revision occurred in the climactic chapter which records Aram's autobiographical account and, especially, his confession. The changes, of course, arise from the diminished villainy of the central character, and therefore, as his guilt is not directly confronted until this late phase in the narrative, Bulwer found little need for material alteration before that point.

It is in Book 5, chapter 7, of the 1849 edition, entitled "The Confession; and the Fate," which opens with an epigraph from *Richard II* (". . .the lamentable fall of me"), that the transformation occurs. Gordon Ray and Keith Hollingsworth have suggested that Bulwer actually revised the chapter in direct consideration of the "Condemned Cell" section of "George de Barnwell." Anthea Trodd supports that conclusion by citing lines from "George de Barnwell" and ranking them in point-by-point comparison with the sections in the original *Eugene Aram* which were removed from the edition of 1849.[40] The changes in this crucial chapter of the novel are more pervasive, however, than a mere excision of objectionable passages would suggest. The features that are altered or added, rather than removed, were Bulwer's own, especially Aram's demotion from arch-villain to unwitting accomplice intent not on murder but only robbery. Given this revised approach, Bulwer could no longer, of course, represent his non-homicidal hero as a fanatic bent on human sacrifice. It was the transformed premises, and not the omitted details, which made a different novel of *Eugene Aram* in 1849.

These new principles are relatively few, but their implications are far-reaching, and their implementation creates, in the long run, quite a different effect. The 1832 edition contained an authorial note clarifying that even in the earliest planning stages of the crime Aram was aware that murder as well as robbery would be involved. This note is removed from the 1849 version. Other passages are modified in accordance with Aram's—and Bulwer's—revised intent, and Aram's dire reference to the "deed" is transformed to the "robbery." The point at which Aram relates the murder itself is completely altered in tone and significance. In the original, it read:

> "We [Aram, Houseman, and Clarke] walked forth; the rest—why need I repeat? Houseman lied in the court; my hand struck—but not the *death*-blow: yet, from that hour, I have never given that right hand in pledge of love or friendship—the curse of memory has clung to it.
>
> "We shared our booty; mine I buried, for the present."

The revised account suggests a far more contrite speaker, agonized in the telling and so grieved by the outcome of this night's work that he cannot bear to profit materially from it:

> "We walked forth; the rest—why need I tell?—I cannot—O

God, I cannot! Houseman lied in the court. I did not strike the
blow—I never designed a murder. Crime enough in a robber's
deed! He fell—he grasped my hand, raised not to strike but to
shield him! Never more has the right hand cursed by that dying
clasp been given in pledge of human faith and friendship. But
the deed was done, and the robber's comrade, in the eyes of
man and law, was the murderer's accomplice.

"Houseman divided the booty: my share he buried in the
earth, leaving me to withdraw it when I chose. There, perhaps,
it lies still. I never touched what I had murdered my *own* life
to gain."

Afterwards, Aram does not, as in the earlier editions, forswear remorse.
On the contrary, his life is blighted by the crime, his scholarly dreams
ended because "The ambition died in remorse."

The new Aram differs from the old in the preliminaries to crime as
well. The increased sense that his researches once had a definite practical
object has been mentioned in the previous chapter. At the same time, the
original emphasis on Aram's utilitarian reasoning is virtually dropped.
The weight of his potential contribution to society as opposed to the
reprobate Clarke's vicious influence is now largely a matter of inference,
as entire paragraphs of reflection on the principle of the greatest good disappear
from the text. In the revised version, Aram's introduction to evil
follows, not from his own ratiocination, but rather from the active
influence of Houseman. Several references to that "inner voice" which
urged Aram to crime are now removed. It is, rather, Houseman who
suggests to Aram that, confronted with the inequity of the fate which has
made him undeservedly poor, he should take matters boldly into his own
hands. Aram resists the temptation but at last succumbs. In the larger
body of the novel, most of Bulwer's modifications were stylistic and, for
the most part, desirable.

Throughout the revision process, it is also clear that Bulwer took
pains to rid his novel of whatever might be considered irreligious or overpassionate.
He expunged, for instance, Aram's description of romantic
love as "an unquiet yet delicious emotion [that] agitated all within" (5.7).
Aram's expressed confidence in the power of human love was likewise
omitted when it seemed, on consideration, to impose limits on divine
retribution: "If I die even the death of the felon, it is beyond the power
of fate to separate us for long. It is but a pang, and we are united again
for ever..." (5.3). Also deleted were a passage in which Aram questions
the doctrine of free will and another in which he anticipates death with

hubristic eagerness for the sake of its revelation of the mysteries of afterlife (5.7). An interesting emendation was given the episode that so offended the *Fraser's* reviewer because a Protestant clergyman at the deathbed of Houseman's child acted the part of a Catholic priest. In the novel of 1832:

> The Curate wiped his eyes, and prepared to utter, with a quivering but earnest voice, his prayer for the dead; and Walter, whose heart was opened to the weaker and kinder feelings, knelt by the bedside, and felt his own eyes moist, as he echoed the Christian hope and the holy supplication.

From the edition of 1849, all suggestion of papistry was scrupulously removed:

> The Curate wiped his eyes, and kneeling down prayed, if not for the dead (who as our Church teaches, are beyond human intercession)—perhaps for the father she had left on earth, more to be pitied of the two! (4.11)[41]

Walter, represented originally as kneeling in an attitude of devotion by the child's bed, is now described as standing. He does not join, as before, in the prayer.

Bulwer's concession to the anti-Newgate forces in 1849 was followed by a relative abatement of hostilities. The Newgate novel as a vital genre had by now nearly run its course. Its appeal to the masses, however, founded in their perennial fascination for criminal themes, was far from extinct. The driving force behind the popularity of the Newgate novel instead found new life on the nineteenth-century stage, and Aram made the transition with it. For a populace who little knew or cared about the critical reviews, he remained as attractive as ever.

5 THE "AESTHETICAL HOMICIDE"
Nineteenth-Century Variations

S OME PEOPLE are of more value dead than alive," reflected the Reverend
John Walker of Malton, Yorkshire, in a private letter of December 26,
1852. That a country parson should be so cynical was at least partly owing
to the circumstances under which the remark was made. It had been
Walker's recent good fortune to inherit the authentic skull of Eugene
Aram, wrenched from the gibbet in the preceding century by his maternal
grandfather, Dr. Hutchinson, and he was now required to defend his right
of ownership.[1] Hutchinson's nephew, who disputed it now and repeatedly
in later years, was equally aware that thanks to Hood's ballad and Bulwer's
romance Aram had become, so to speak, a live property.

St. Robert's Cave, scene of the murder at Knaresborough, was another
instance of the same phenomenon. It was an ancient landmark, remembered earlier for its religious and, more recently, for its criminal associations. An account by Joseph Farington, the English landscape painter, in
a diary entry of September 1, 1801, suggests that the conducting of visitors
to the site was even then commonplace: "From hence [Knaresborough]
I went to St. Robert's Cave, about a mile distant near the River. At this
place Eugene Aram murdered Danl. Clarke in the year 1745 . . . .We were
attended to this Spot by a Boy, called the *Wooley Headed Boy*, His Hair
having that appearance and texture."[2] With the publicity afforded by
Bulwer and Hood, the cave became an important tourist attraction,
drawing from the nearby spa of Harrogate a constant stream of sightseers.
Few inhabitants of Knaresborough today are aware of the cave's existence,
but the carved and dated initials of nineteenth-century visitors still line
the walls of its cramped interior, testifying to the windfall advantage its
happy owners once enjoyed. Whether the new literary sensations were
genuine art remained to be seen. That they had, on the other hand,

awakened a widespread popular interest in the Aram story which was a perennial invitation to entrepreneurs, amateur authors, and hacks of every sort, would soon be unmistakably apparent.

1

Many readers, their curiosity whetted by the fiction, turned eagerly to the history, and the booksellers were quick to provide. Thus, a number of supposedly factual publications relating to the real Aram directly followed Bulwer's novel. Between 1832 and 1880 there were at least fifteen separate British, and two American, issues of his "Life and Trial"—or some variant of that title. Most of these were hastily produced pamphlet reprints of earlier versions, frequently with Hood's poem appended. Nor did their compilers hesitate to mention another debt, factitious or real: "The very interesting and deservedly popular novel recently published entitled Eugene Aram, gave rise to the present publication," states the Advertisement to Michael Fryer's *The Trial and Life of Eugene Aram* (1832).[3] This pamphlet, in many ways representative of the rest, is for all its pretense at original research little more than a modernization of Bristow (the accepted standard edition of 1759). To anyone familiar with the Aram literature it is a tissue of inaccuracies, most of them plagiarized. One whole paragraph is unabashedly lifted intact from Bulwer. Other borrowings are from the new pamphlet by Norrisson Scatcherd, *Memoirs of the Celebrated Eugene Aram* (1832), and from an unsigned article in the August, 1759, issue of the pompously titled *Grand Magazine of Magazines*.

One feature which distinguishes Fryer's and similar subsequent biographies from their predecessors is a definite bias in favor of Aram. Obviously they were catering to the prejudices of their audience. In previous years, especially in the environs of Knaresborough, there appears to have been a general consensus that Aram was guilty. Some went so far as to extend their private conviction beyond that pronounced at his trial. The Thistle Hill skeleton (whose discovery frightened Houseman into revealing the location of Clark's remains) was widely rumored to have belonged to a Jewish peddler who, with his wares, had disappeared about the same time as Clark. There was a firm local belief that the peddler had met a fate similar to Clark's and at the same hands. Some thought that Clark, with Houseman and Aram, had participated in this murder and been himself dispatched in a quarrel over the spoils. The acceptance of Aram's guilt persisted into the early nineteenth century, as manifested by the fire-and-brimstone title of a tract published in London in 1809: "The Blood of the Innocent Calleth Loudly for Vengeance, Exemplified in the

Discovery of the Murder of Daniel Clark, Fourteen Years After it was Perpetrated by Eugene Aram."[4]

With the emergence of the new, romanticized Aram, however, attitudes changed. Enthusiasts fresh from Bulwer's idealized pages were glad to be told that their hero was not really a murderer, a view that had been heard before but now became remarkably more prevalent. Fryer, writing in the editorial third person, confides "that strong doubts have always rested, and still rest, on his mind, as to the actual guilt of Eugene Aram," and indeed, he says, he "conscientiously believes that this illustrious scholar was *not guilty* of the crime for which he suffered."[5] The words oddly anticipate Bulwer's 1849 announcement that he himself had reconsidered and found Aram innocent. Interestingly enough, the very climate of partiality created by the novel's first edition must have made this admission of seventeen years later more credible than it would otherwise have been.

Of all who championed Aram in the nineteenth century, surely the most zealous was Norrisson Cavendish Scatcherd, a Yorkshire antiquary and titular lawyer, author of *Memoirs of the Celebrated Eugene Aram* (1832) and *"Gleanings" After Eugene Aram* (1836). The first pamphlet was revised in a second edition of 1838, and the two were reissued together in 1871. Scatcherd's original biographical work is not to be classed with the perfunctory, derivative compilations of other hands. Although he may be, as Watson found him, "anecdotal and desultory,"[6] his weaknesses spring not from a mercenary unconcern but from the lifelong fervency of a true believer in a consuming cause.

By his own account, Scatcherd had as a child become intrigued with Aram's history during a visit to Harrogate with his parents in 1792. He began at once to pursue the subject with a tenacity remarkable for his ten years of age. Through his mother he secured an introduction to the local authority, Knaresborough historian and publisher Ely Hargrove, but found him, although eager to converse on any other subject, peculiarly reticent in regard to Aram. The suppression of information apparently instigated by Francis Iles was, it seems, still in force. Disappointed but undaunted, Scatcherd began to question other elderly inhabitants of the area, recording their reminiscences of already distant events. For such a resolute child, this quest was no passing fancy. During the next forty years it became a vocation. Scatcherd collected documents relevant to the case and traveled the vicinity of Knaresborough and Lynn, searching villages and workhouses for aged persons who might contribute firsthand knowledge.

With the sudden unprecedented popular interest occasioned by

Bulwer's novel came Scatcherd's long-awaited opportunity. At last he could publish his conviction that Aram was really a "sublime visionary"[7] whose ruin lay in the disreputable connections and the infidelity of a low-bred wife. In a spirit of near fanaticism, Scatcherd systematically underrated such reports as ran contrary to his romantic partialities, yet he is to be credited with preserving in his two pamphlets a wealth of contemporary opinion and eyewitness experience that would otherwise be irretrievable.

Like Fryer, Scatcherd was grateful to the novelist. "Of late," he wrote, "the public mind has been remarkably excited; partly by Notices of Aram in Literary Gazettes and Newspapers; partly by a fine Poem, called 'The Dream of Eugene Aram,' by a Mr. Hood; but, most of all, by Mr. Bulwer's Romance." Naïvely he found Bulwer, despite an unfortunate inattention to historical accuracy, to have "displayed the characters and sentiments of Aram, with a faithful and masterly hand" and added, in delight at Aram's vindication, "that never, perhaps, did I derive more pleasure from a book, than from his first volume, which I read twice."[8]

Varied sources besides the pamphlets also clearly reflect a burgeoning sympathy with Aram after 1831. In 1832, the *Gentleman's Magazine* carried an article defending him and, in 1837, the recollections of an old woman who as a child had seen and admired him.[9] It was an enduring trend as well. In 1890, the author of a volume on rural excursions referred to the Aram story as a "tale of woe, of which I was so heartily tired before I ever came to Yorkshire that I vowed I would not mention it,—nor should I have done so were it not that I find the folk of Knaresborough a trifle apt to expect all strangers to drop a tear in memory of that atrocious scoundrel."[10] The *Leeds Mercury* of November 11, 1899, printed a lengthy defense that styled Aram "the Dreyfus of the eighteenth century,"[11] and as late as 1912 the *Lancet* exaggeratedly characterized him as a gentle scholar and "valetudinarian" (the latter epithet completely unfounded!): "the last person in the world whom one would have suspected of a deliberately planned murder, fiercely carried out at night with a great display of physical energy and boldness."[12]

The fact-obsessed contributors of *Notes and Queries* discovered in the Aram tradition a fertile ground for the peculiar type of "research" and debate characteristically sustained in its pages. With one notable exception, however, they were unlikely to be fascinated or deceived by Bulwer. In the 1850s, "D.," of Rotherfield, "J. S. W.," of Stockwell, and R. C. Warde, of Kidderminster were convinced of Aram's villainy and skeptical of his scholarship. J. S. W. accused the novelist of "one of the most presumptuous falsifications of biography...ever...attempted."[13] But it was "Francesca," writing in 1885, who proved that among these dry pages chivalry, if not romance, could blossom. "Eugene Aram.—" her appeal began:

> Will any reader of "N. & Q." oblige me with a list of books containing any account of the above? Traditions and letters would also be very acceptable. I judge from Lord Lytton's novel that much traditionary matter concerning Aram existed, and probably still exists.
>
> Francesca.

Her naiveté was politely overlooked. In subsequent issues no fewer than eight responses appeared, amounting to a fairly extensive cottage-industry bibliography on the subject. Unfortunately, the efforts of the gentlemen correspondents were of little help; in fact, Francesca's answer makes her original question seem pointless:

> To the correspondents of "N. & Q." who have kindly responded to my appeal on this subject, I return my most grateful thanks. I had no idea of the existence of such a mass of Aram literature. My especial thanks are due to ESTE for his trouble in copying the long list of books, &c., in his possession. I am sure this list would be invaluable had I access to libraries; but unfortunately, living in an Irish midland county, I am far from books. . . . [14]

Francesca, who probably dreamed of the Byronic Aram in Lytton, may simply have escaped a hard awakening.

So great an impression had Hood and Bulwer made on the popular notion of Aram that afterwards the real and the fictional characters would be, to the distress of antiquarian gentlemen in Rotherfield, Stockwell, and Kidderminster, habitually confused. On more than one occasion it was supposedly sober literary men who repeated imaginary detail as fact. Fryer's carelessly researched history, for instance, describes the Thistle Hill body as being exhumed from a "wooden chest."[15] The remains were not encased, according to all previous accounts except the parallel episode in the novel, which uses the identical phrase (4.10, or 4.11 in later editions). Bulwer's version was also responsible for the mistaken assumption, repeated time and again thereafter, that Houseman was the only witness to speak against Aram at his trial. In an 1869 essay on sensation literature, Leslie Stephen's understanding of the case is a strange hybrid of Bulwer and Hood. Aram, he says, is the type of criminal whose tragic potential justifies his treatment in fiction, because his motives,

if we would take Lord Lytton's ingenious representation as at all
an accurate picture,...depended upon a perversion of a laud-
able ambition, and he attempted to justify his crimes by a
sophistry...paying, by implication, a certain homage to
honourable sentiment.

The "if" that begins the passage is sizable, since none of this was true
except in the novelist's imagination. "Of course it is not right," Stephen
concedes, drawing now from Hood, "to knock an elderly miser on the
head with a pickaxe in order to appropriate his gold."[16]

On the sixth of July, 1910, the way was cleared for a work that would
at last distill the fact from the fiction. On that date Messrs. Sotheby,
Wilkinson & Hodge sold for £31 a package of eleven legal documents
relevant to the Aram case—the coroner's inquisitions and witnesses'
depositions leading to Aram's arrest and trial, which had been passed
down in the family of John Theakston, the coroner of Knaresborough at
the time of these events. "A fresh account of this remarkable case, based
upon the documents recently sold at Sotheby's," wrote one Horace Bleackley in a letter to N&Q, "would be welcomed by students of the period,
but if such a one is written, it is to be hoped that it will not be treated
in the lazy, slipshod fashion in which such subjects are too often dealt
with nowadays."[17] Bleackley's wish was soon to be granted, for Eric
Watson's precise, thoroughly researched legal-historical study was forthcoming, to deflate the fictional image and refute the notion that Aram
was a superman.

2

Fryer, Scatcherd, Bulwer, and most others who argued for Aram's
innocence turned to received tradition for their evidence, attempting to
interpret the reported details of the case in a favorable light. There was,
however, another method of inquiry which purported to determine
Aram's guilt or innocence solely by the qualities of his skull. Though the
first and only separately published account of this nature was Dr. James
Inglis's *Phrenological Observations on the Skull of Eugene Aram* (1838),
the pseudoscientific principles of phrenology, which had been in
existence since the turn of the century, were actually applied to the
mystery as early as 1817.

In May of that year, two gentlemen who lived in the vicinity of
Knaresborough, the Reverend James Dalton and his friend Mr. Fry,
resolved to test the controversial new discipline empirically. Their plan
was to submit for the analysis of Dr. Johann Spurzheim, the chief

proponent of the theory at that time, two skulls to which Dalton had access, neither of whose identities Spurzheim would know: that of Eugene Aram, and that of Adam de Thirsk, former abbot of Fountains Abbey, executed for his opposition to Henry VIII. Accordingly, the doctor's consent was obtained and the skulls were forwarded to him. His estimate, in a letter of May 22, is typical of the kind of ambiguities and half-truths which allow such quackery to prevail as long as there are those who will interpret them loosely. Aram's skull he found to resemble "that of a woman." This "female," he writes,

> had a good share of common sense, without being able to reason deeply; she was pleased with witty, amusing, and super-stitious stories, and fond of theatrical performance. She had strong feelings, without great hope—a great deal of vanity, attachment, and personal courage; she might have been able to commit an error to please those whom she liked. Example was to her particularly important; she was not indifferent as to sexual intercourse—was more easily guided by soft means and flattering treatment than by command, which revolted her feelings, and would induce her to have recourse to desperate means.[18]

Abbot de Thirsk, Spurzheim judged by the "ivory density" of his skull, was probably insane at the time of his death—a point which would doubtless have gratified King Henry.

Twenty years later, after Bulwer had made the establishment of Aram's innocence a matter of interest to many, the skull was again brought forth, this time not to challenge but rather to defend the apocryphal science. At a meeting of the Medical Section of the British Association for the Advancement of Science at Newcastle in August, 1838, Dr. Inglis produced the skull and detailed its phrenological character-istics, hoping to prove the medico-legal applications of such analysis. His argument that Aram's was not the skull of a premeditating murderer achieved minimal success, for many of his hearers doubted not only its plausibility but also the authenticity of the skull itself, a point which now seems indisputable.[19] Inglis's pamphlet, published later the same year, is an indignant attempt to reconcile phrenology with the doctrines of Christianity and free will, as well as to verify the provenance of Aram's skull and to reaffirm the author's conclusion that Aram, having been assaulted by Clark, merely overreacted in self-defense. In predictable accord with this belief and several of Aram's well-known traits, Inglis finds the skull suggestive, above all, of combativeness, secretiveness, cautious-

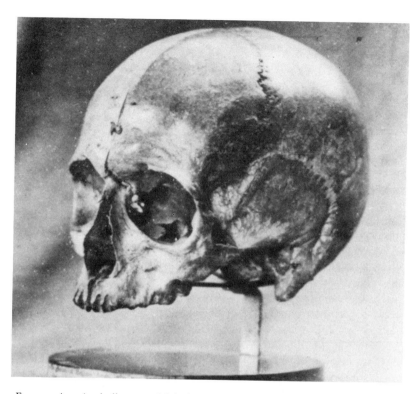

Eugene Aram's skull, on exhibit in the Royal College of Surgeons Museum, London. Photograph by A. P. Monger in Watson's *Eugene Aram: His Life and Trial.*

ness, self-esteem, and a highly developed love of children and languages.

Not all of the phrenologists, however, found Aram so benign. A Mr. Simpson at the British Association meeting took his skull for that of a "dangerous man," while the eminent practitioners George and Andrew Combe, ignorant of the skull's identity at the time of their examination, gave a report that coincides remarkably with transmitted accounts of the real Aram's character:

> He was irascible and vindictive. He was proud and essentially selfish; yet to serve a purpose he might exhibit great plausibility of manner. His intellectual faculties were intense in action rather than comprehensive and vigorous. ...He was not a stranger to benevolent feeling, but his benevolence was greatly

inferior to his selfishness. He was not scrupulous.

The head on the whole indicates a man of low natural dispositions; with as much of the higher powers as to render him dangerous by his talents and plausibility; but not enough of them to render him in ordinary circumstances amiable and virtuous.[20]

3

Each in turn, the poet, the novelist, even the phrenologists, adapted Aram to their ends. The last to do so were the dramatists, if that term can be applied to the journeymen writers who scrounged a living concocting melodramas for the nineteenth-century stage.

Bulwer, as we have seen, had considered adapting the Aram story to tragedy during the planning stages of his novel but gave up the possibility in favor of fiction. And yet the result was in many ways a prose tragedy, in keeping with its author's belief that fiction as a genre must model itself on classical drama. The novel *Eugene Aram*, which relates a known event, has relatively few characters, begins in a state of calm, and moves with increasing rapidity towards a foreknown cataclysmic end designed to excite pity and terror, is surely as good a play as any of the several drawn from it.

Since adaptation and even outright plagiarism were rarely restrained by law, purveyors of nineteenth-century melodrama frequently borrowed their subject matter from best-selling novelists. Scott, Dickens, and Collins were particular favorites, whose works were recycled time and again in predictable melodramatic form by "house authors" underpaid for writing one or two fresh plays a week, in addition, perhaps, to acting. *Oliver Twist*, for example, endured at least fourteen such different dramatizations between 1838 and 1891. The extreme popularity of *Eugene Aram* is nowhere more evident than in the fact that it underwent in seventy years at least ten. The aura of mystery surrounding the hero, along with the inherent sensational and pathetic elements of his story, particularly as exaggerated by Bulwer, made it a natural choice for melodramatic treatment. Violence heightened by suspense could always be depended upon to draw an audience, and most melodramas seem, consequently, to have included at least one murder. Because it was romanticized crime that audiences loved, however, those playwrights who treated the subject of Eugene Aram did not return to the factual histories. Instead they adopted the romantic, adventurous, and humorous trappings of Bulwer's novel or invented similar circumstances of their own. The figure of Madeline provided a convenient unfortunate heroine and that of Houseman an irredeemable villain. Walter Lester, as in the novel, usually shared with Aram the position of hero, for all their antagonism, and Corporal Bunting fitted neatly the melodramatic type of the "comic man"—the friend or manservant who, by humorous means, advances his master's cause against the forces of villainy.

The first rendering of *Eugene Aram* as melodrama occurred only weeks after the appearance of the novel. W. T. Moncrieff's *Eugene Aram; or, St. Robert's Cave* made its debut on February 8, 1832, at the Surrey Theatre, where it ran successfully for over a month. The play, "founded on Bulwer's celebrated novel," was in fact the only authorized version. Bulwer, to show his approval, was present at the opening night. It must have been a lavish occasion, for the Surrey, though situated in a working-class neighborhood on the south bank of the Thames and catering, like most of London's theaters at the time, to a largely unsophisticated clientele, was hardly shabby. Commodious, with "excellent acoustics and sight lines," it was known for its "elegant lounges,...spacious coffee-rooms and foyers...chandeliers, crimson and gold draperies, an elaborate proscenium, and an ornamental ceiling painted with the story of Bacchus and Ariadne."[21]

The reviewer for the *Times*, evaluating the first performance of Moncrieff's play, had little but praise for the actors. Indeed, most of the cast were established favorites. Edward Elton (born Elt), in the title role, a newcomer to the Surrey, was already known as "the East End Kean." Surely his style was the bombastic rant then in fashion—described by a foremost modern historian as "the quintessence of burlesque,...absurdly grandiose,...utterly unlike anything human"[22]—but within its limits he is said to have done justice to the part. "It was painful," the *Times* reports,

> to see the truth with which he went through the scene preparatory to the execution. His manly avowal to *Walter Lester*, that he was the murderer, and the forgetfulness of his own wretched fate when seeing his wife stretched out at his feet, drew forth a good deal of merited applause.

Mrs. W. West, his leading lady and a popular actress of the era, "made a very lachrymose affair of her part, as she is occasionally apt to do." (Mrs. West, in a crude line drawing reproduced in Michael R. Booth's *English Melodrama*, is pictured in another role characteristically clutching a handkerchief to her bosom.)[23] Mr. Cobham—"'the Kemble of the minor theatres,'" and Mr. Vale—"the famous popular low comedian,"[24] capably sustained the roles of Walter Lester and Corporal Bunting.

The *Times's* primary objection was to the Newgate theme, which the reviewer found more blatant in the play than in the novel:

> We never had imagined that the last Newgate scenes of condemned criminals would have been thought a fit subject for the stage; nor do we believe that an experiment of them would be tolerated for a single night at any of our two principal theatres [i.e., Covent Garden and Drury Lane, the only London theatres permitted at the time to stage legitimate drama]. ...Here, however, they seemed to excite an extraordinary share of interest among the auditors of the gallery, whose vehement applause will, no doubt, speak better than any criticism of our own of the good taste displayed by such a choice....Mr. Bulwer's excellent novel...has deviated from the real history, but has redeemed that error with great talent, much knowledge of character, and very eloquent description. His dramatic imitator cannot lay claim to similar praise.[25]

Bulwer, who almost certainly read this review, must have wished the man were writing for *Fraser's*. In fact, as the emphasis of the piece reflects, the insidious effects of Newgate drama were more commonly condemned than those of the fiction which inspired it. Crime-oriented theater had met, at this point, with only verbal disapproval. In the 1840s, however, a proliferation of plays about Jack Sheppard sparked a decided reaction against the Newgate drama, which as a result was greatly repressed by court actions through the end of the sixties.[26] That Newgate fiction was not subjected to such legal restraints is doubtless owing to its more literate audience. It was the ignorant masses whom the governing class most feared—and not the parlormaids or their mistresses who thrilled to Bulwer's art. Melodrama was typically a lower-class pursuit whose usual theme was the oppression of the poor and helpless by the rich and powerful. It had therefore a potentially dangerous, rabble-rousing air. The fictional Aram, who inhabited the relatively genteel world of country squires and parsons, was atypical—a kind of silver-fork melodramatic hero with whom the masses could not so readily identify as with, for instance, the low-life Jack Sheppard. As a hero who was also a criminal, however, Aram was nonetheless suspiciously subversive.

W. T. Moncrieff (pseudonym for William George Thomas), Bulwer's "dramatic imitator," whom the *Times* found so unequal to the task, was responsible during his lifetime for a good many lackluster adaptations of popular novels and over one hundred and seventy plays altogether. His version of Bulwer was the only one of the several Aram stage scripts to be

"Houseman. Release my throat or you will commit murder!" Engraving taken in the theater during a performance of Moncrieff's *Eugene Aram.* Frontispiece to Cumberland Acting Edition (1832).

published. In 1853 it was condensed into a few pages of simpleminded narrative in Purkess's Penny Library of Romance as one of a series of such travesties. But the four "acting editions" which appeared were largely for professional and amateur theatrical use as working scripts, not really intended to be read.[27] The three-act drama follows the plot of the novel closely, selectively compressing it for stage effect at the expense of characterization and thematic depth. The novel's prominent scenes remain intact, and much of the dialogue is retained verbatim. For the sake of exciting stage action much is made of an element that is proportionately underplayed in the fiction: Houseman's thievery in the neighborhood of Grassdale, where he has come to blackmail Aram. Several minor characters are added in connection with this intrigue, including various ruffians to consort with Houseman, and the outraged citizens of Grassdale by way of a chorus. An awkward collection of villagers mustered by the innkeeper to thwart the robbers provides business and humor somewhat in the manner of Shakespeare's ragtag armies.

In constructing this play, it was Moncrieff's purpose, of course, to entertain his audience with the violent sounding of nearly every chord in their emotional range. The excessive commitment of melodrama to the precepts of "pity and terror" is apparent at every turn as events move headlong to the breathless conclusion, wherein Madeline visits Aram in prison and falls dead in anguish at his feet. Nineteenth-century audiences were as fond in their day of startling and lavish stage gimmickry as modern filmgoers are of elaborate special effects. This production appears to have been quite a thriller, particularly the horrific Gothic scene (act II, scene ii) in which Aram (and presumably the audience as well) is frightened nearly out of his wits as he returns alone on a stormy night from a conspiratorial meeting with Houseman. It is not difficult to imagine the pre-electronic devices of the Victorian theater producing the thunder and red-forked lightning for which the stage directions call—as, suddenly illuminated in their midst, the leering parricide's skeleton dangles from the gibbet and points its accusatory finger at the guilty hero. This Aram is, of course, the Aram of Bulwer's first edition, the homicidal Aram who struck—but not the death blow.

The popular success of Moncrieff's drama inspired, within no more than a few months, a small rash of cheap imitations by anonymous compilers, one of which opened on March 13, 1832, at the Edinburgh Theatre Royal, and two in London: at the Royal Pavilion in Whitechapel Road (February 13, 1832) and at Sadler's Wells (May 14, 1832). Neither of the latter two was noticed by reviewers, although they were advertised in the *Times* for the duration of their run, which in each case amounted to slightly more than a week. Shamelessly derivative as these productions were, they must have transformed Aram beyond the recognition of his fictional creator, if Bulwer had deigned to mingle with such a common crowd as these two theaters ordinarily housed. The Pavilion, in a working-class East End neighborhood, was a particularly seedy place where, in later years, the murderer Henry Wainwright (who recited Hood's "Dream of

Eugene Aram" for the actors) found the chorus girl who became his mistress and finally his victim. Its version of the current sensation was innovatively entitled *Eugene Aram; or, The Cave of St. Robert*, as opposed to Moncrieff's *Eugene Aram; or, St. Robert's Cave*. It was billed as "an entirely new and interesting melodrama,"[28] although its characters and situations were straight from Bulwer.

Sadler's Wells would have staged an entertainment at least as rude. The Wells in 1832 was a sink of vice unfrequented by respectable persons. In these days before its rehabilitation by the great actor-manager Samuel Phelps, who reintroduced Shakespeare to its stage in the 1840s, catcalls, insults, and obscenities were shouted from the pit and gallery, and an occasional brawl enhanced the evening's entertainment. At the Wells, a Mr. Johnson, enacting the part of Aram, braved what must have been for him the very trying perversities of an audience whose taste could induce a sane management to feature with *Eugene Aram* an afterpiece entitled *Winki the Witch*.[29]

The West End was the scene of another inglorious Aram incarnation after a space of some twenty years, at the struggling Marylebone Theatre, on the area's outermost skirts. An anonymous *Eugene Aram* appeared on the night of March 30, 1855, at the top of the bill. On March 31, it was second piece to *Rob Roy*. The following day the theater was out of business.

4

The best, or at least the best remembered, of the Aram plays was one produced a generation later: William Gorman Wills's *The Fate of Eugene Aram* (or simply *Eugene Aram*), which first ran at the Lyceum from Saturday, April 19, to Friday, June 20, 1873. A memorable moment in the rising career of Sir Henry Irving, who played the lead, it would be revived many times afterwards at the insistence of his adoring public. This was a time of advancement not only for Irving but, to some degree, for the dramatic art in Britain. It was evident that the theater, after decades of catering to vulgar tastes, was at last becoming generally recognized as a respectable entertainment for audiences whose level of sophistication was somewhat more elevated. The "morning performances," or matinees, of Wills's *Aram* advertised in the *Times* were a novelty at this period, and a sure sign that the management expected the leisured classes to attend. Wills in particular had a reputation as a "rehabilitater" of classic plots and especially of classic melodramas reworked, one modern commentator puts it, for their impact on the "heart" rather than the "simple nervous system."[30] *Charles the First* (1872), which secured his fame, was a "white handkerchief piece," as his plays were often called. As it neared the end of a phenomenal 180-night run at the Lyceum early in 1873, H. L. Bateman, the theater's American manager, recognized in Wills and in Irving, now in his second season on that stage, a pair of talents worth fostering.

Irving had won acclaim not only for his sensitive portrait of the doomed Charles I but also for his role as Mathias the Polish Jew, an agonized, blood-guilty Shylock type who figured in *The Bells*, produced in the same year. In this latter creation and similar dark ones, including that of Aram, he was largely responsible for humanizing and amplifying the characterization of the theatrical villain, as well as for saving Bateman from financial disaster. Like Wills, he preferred refurbishing an old part to forging a new one. His powerful recitation of Hood's "Dream of Eugene Aram" was already a favorite with his many admirers. Thus, when Bateman, shrewdly considering the particular talents of both men, suggested that Irving and Wills collaborate on a new version of the Aram story, it was a mutually congenial arrangement. Irving found his salary doubled to £30 a week and Wills retired to Brighton to write the new play, receiving Irving's advice by mail.

Wills, an Irishman who composed more than forty plays during roughly twenty-five years before his death in 1891, was first of all a painter—and a bohemian one at that. In what he called his "daisy-picking" way of life, he wrote for magazines and the stage only when desperate. The intervals were devoted to his more consuming art, pursued in the midst of a riotous indulgence that his income was ill able to support. He lived in filth, surrounded by monkeys, stray cats, and dirty linen. He had a reputation for inviting people ceremoniously to dinner and not being home to receive them. He was so absent-minded that he is said on one occasion to have boiled his watch for an egg. Though his critics were often beguiled by his arty peculiarities and the emotional intensity of his work into calling him a genius, the keen discernment of Henry James, not easily swayed, found him worthy only of sarcasm. "Charged" as he was "with the delicate task of pouring the old wine into new bottles," James wrote, who else could have adapted Goethe's *Faust* so that "from the beginning to the end of the play,...it might never occur to the auditor that he was listening to one of the greatest productions of the human mind"?[31]

In *Eugene Aram*, as in most of his adaptations, Wills eliminated those elements on which older melodrama thrived—low comedy, fast-paced action, violence, suspense, and spectacle. Such crude attractions as the scaffold scene (in *Charles the First* as well as *Eugene Aram*) and the parricide's gibbet gave way to conversational prolixity and a penchant for soliloquy that would have bored the "pittites" of earlier decades straight out of their three-penny seats. In Wills's play, according to Clement Scott, who wrote reviews for the *Observer* and seems to have been easily impressed, there was "little for the posters, but much, very much, for the imagination."[32] Moncrieff's version, by now almost entirely forgotten, was no model for Wills; and from Bulwer's novel, which remained very much alive, he boldly departed as well. The result was an entirely new play connected with the tradition that preceded it only by the brooding central figure of the tragic scholar-murderer. In this incarnation Aram was restored to at least a measure of the gentility with which Bulwer had endowed him and which had suffered in recent decades by association with the Jack Sheppards and Dick Turpins of the vulgar stage.

Oddly enough, Wills's plays, which he tended to write in bed, were superficially disciplined in their execution. This one was no exception. In structure it followed the classical unities no less rigidly, as one critic observed, than *Oedipus Tyrannus*.[33] A space of some twelve hours compasses all the events, and the setting throughout is confined to the vicarage and churchyard at Knaresborough. Wills's script called for only three changes of scene, or one per act, whereas Moncrieff's had involved no fewer than fifteen. This was largely owing to a contemporary preference for elaborate authenticity in the construction of stage sets which necessitated large pieces of scenery and furnishings too costly and unwieldly to be shifted frequently in the course of a production. The set designers for *Eugene Aram*, Hawes Craven and H. Cuthbert, were consequently so important to its success that they received equal billing with the principal actors and the dramatist. Their lavish creations were, in fact, the only aspect of the play with which none of its several reviewers found serious fault.

On opening night the audience was excited, eager to see and judge the successor to the much acclaimed *Charles the First*. The response was breathless when the curtain rose on the first act to reveal a painstakingly complete and realistic garden crisscrossed by actual gravel paths. The garden, it is soon discovered as the play begins, belongs to Parson Meadows of Knaresborough, whose daughter, Ruth, will be wed to Aram the following day. The gardener and his young son are gathering flowers for the wedding when a stranger, posing as a collector of geological specimens, asks to borrow their pickax and spade. Proving, as one reviewer notes, an unfortunate sort of father-in-law for a man whose safety depends on cautious retirement, Parson Meadows ingenuously offers the visitor shelter for the night, though as an amateur geologist he is politely skeptical about the likelihood of finding fossils in St. Robert's Cave. Houseman, of course, is the stranger, and his real object is to recover the gold buried with Clarke. After he departs like a snake from the garden of Aram's future hopes, the engaged couple take the stage. The act closes with an idyllic love scene that impresses the audience with Ruth's innocent joy and Aram's inability to share it, distracted as he is by the specter of secret guilt. Arm-in-arm as evening falls, tomorrow's bride and groom stroll slowly towards the church, where a children's choir wafts a sweet chorale composed expressly for the occasion, according to the bill, "by Mr. R. Stoepel, musical director."[34]

The great fault of Wills's dramatic art, in the view of those who longed for the old action-packed melodramas, was too little plot. What movement there is in *Eugene Aram* is sandwiched in Act II between the love idyll of Act I and the protracted death scene of Act III. The central episode takes place in the parlor of the Meadows home, which, dominated by a grand piano, was elegantly outfitted, as one critic complained, well beyond the usage of the era it was to represent. As Aram and his future father-in-law play chess in this anachronistic setting, Ruth mischievously insists on reading aloud to them a testimonial to Aram's many virtues, prepared for him on this happy occasion by the villagers he has taught. Unable to endure the private irony of the situation, he stalks out of the room. Parson Meadows, having won the game by default, also withdraws, leaving Ruth alone when Houseman reappears. The latter reveals in the course of the understandably strained conversation that Aram, an old acquaintance of his, was once in love with another woman. Ruth's jealousy is aroused, so that, again alone with her lover, she demands an explanation. The news that her rival is long dead consoles her, but Aram's troubles are only beginning. Suddenly the stranger enters, and in a moment of tense mutual recognition Aram braces himself for the confrontation he knows is ahead.

"No one can better make two persons more satisfactorily fill an entire stage than Mr. W. G. Wills," wrote a hyperbolic critic (*Times*, April 21) in regard to the furtive dialogue which ensues between the two former accomplices, one of whom is intent on blackmail. In a cut-and-parry exchange, Houseman "threatens, bullies, and coaxes in vain," while "his adversary, firm as a rock, will give nothing, concede nothing."[35] At the height of this conflict, there is a startling new development. The gardener, suspicious of the stranger's intent, has himself excavated the cave and discovered Clarke's skeleton, identifiable by an engraved knife buried beside it. Remembering Houseman now as Clarke's acquaintance, the gardener accuses him of murder, and Houseman in turn accuses Aram. When a hasty inquest is summoned, Aram lingers behind momentarily. His resolution, firm against Houseman, is plainly undone at the thought of viewing his victim's remains: "He is no sooner alone than he is a despairing man, wistfully scanning in the mirror the effect which the secret workings of conscience have produced upon his face" (*Times*, April 21).

The final curtain rises on nearly total darkness. A gradual, faint glow of dawn reveals the white stones and crosses of the churchyard and, dominating the stage, a huge, spreading yew whose overhanging branch Irving once likened in conversation to "'the cruel hand of Fate stretched out.'"[36] Beneath the tree is an obscure, motionless form which, touched by the thin beams of light, becomes the figure of a man face down on the ground and covered in a black cloak. It is Aram, whose despair has driven him here. Houseman, freed after the inquest, happens along and flees in terror at the ghostly vision Aram presents. Next it is Ruth who appears, seeking her lover. He interprets her presence as divine consolation and, thus encouraged, makes full confession. The entire last act, a bravura piece tailored expressly for Irving, is a virtual monologue punctuated by Ruth's occasional word of comfort. Its speaker, too broken to raise himself, writhes at the foot of the tree. In an agony of remorse he relates the story of fourteen years before, how the base seduction and subsequent death of his first love drove him, in a spirit of righteous vengeance, to murder her tormentor. As day breaks and the curtain slowly falls, Aram expires (a victim of mysterious natural causes) in the arms of Ruth, whose forgiveness he loosely interprets as a sign that Heaven too will grant him absolution.

The opening-night reception, according to all accounts, was wildly enthusiastic: a demonstrative crowd summoned numerous curtain calls and the appearance onstage of Bateman himself, who had directed the play. The reviewers were not so uniformly appreciative. Most expressed at least some reservation, usually directed at Wills for his handling of the story, to which they objected on either artistic or moral grounds. The *Illustrated London News* practically accused the author of plagiarism, finding *Eugene Aram* "very similar to...Mr. Lovell's 'Love's Sacrifice.'" Though the writer was enthusiastic about the "many poetical lines and speeches," he lamented that so interesting a case as Aram's was reduced to a commonplace tale of lover's revenge with a mere "regular stage criminal" as changeling for "the aesthetical homicide whose career has given rise to so much psychological speculation."[37]

One major departure from tradition was Wills's decision to set the play in Knaresborough, no doubt thinking he improved on Bulwer and Moncrieff, both of whom were forced into awkward contrivances of plot in order to link the scene of the murder with the scene of the hero's arrest years later in a remote county. Yet that he should remain during the intervening fourteen years at the site of the undetected crime brought on even greater problems. It is strange, for example, that no one recognizes Houseman until the end of the second act, and even stranger that Ruth, living in Knaresborough, is so ignorant of her lover's past. Aram's attempt to escape his guilt and begin life anew, the point on which the moral issue hinges, becomes implausible in Knaresborough, where it is virtually inevitable that some unforeseen circumstance will raise suspicion and precipitate discovery. Many of the play's illogicalities, in fact, spring from this central weakness.

Temple Bar was one publication which found Wills's effort hopelessly mediocre. Its especially penetrating article demonstrated that his play would hardly bear rational analysis. First, the retrospective time scheme, while appropriate to the novel's descriptive and reflective powers, was entirely wrong for the drama, which depended, according to the standard of the day, on the consecutive unfolding of incident. "Imagine," the writer suggested, "Shakespeare bringing the guilty Queen on in the first act in Macbeth, bemoaning herself and washing her hands in her sleep, and then the unraveling of motive and the description of the murder of Duncan, all done backward in a frenzied soliloquy." Next, Aram's character was inconsistent and unreal. It was "inconceivable," given his habitual melancholy and his anguished, still vital memory of a woman who was faithless, that Wills's hero should fall in love again, especially with such a girlishly naive type as the parson's daughter. Other lapses made the play seem utterly ridiculous upon consideration: that Aram, for instance, should display "terror at the extremely natural occurrence that a stranger has introduced himself to the notice of the Vicar of Knaresborough; and yet [be] wholly unprepared to find that the stranger is Houseman." And finally, the dramatist's concentration on Aram reduced the secondary figures to cardboard by comparison, so that even Ruth Meadows, who ought to be a fairly important character, became "an interruption whenever she [was] not merely a chorus."[38]

It was the sober *Athenaeum* and the *Saturday Review*, however, that objected morally to the subject matter of Wills's new play, at a time when most reviewers no longer disapproved of criminal themes. The *Athenaeum*, unaware that the play had been commissioned, questioned his choice of a story so "commonplace and repellent" that only a complete departure from truth could invest it with "force, dignity, or interest." Even so, the argument ran, Wills's adaptation could never be psychologically convincing because of the basic contradiction in Aram's character, the impossibility that so noble a spirit would have allowed an innocent young woman to jeopardize her happiness by casting her lot with his:

> If fourteen years spent in the practice of good works and the acquisition of respect and honour had left the hero as he is represented, a man who, even in the sweetest hours of court-ship, could not summon to his face a smile, the sense of guilt and danger would have over-mastered the promptings of love.[39]

The critic for the *Saturday Review* seized indignantly on a phrase from the playbill announcing that Wills had imparted to the historical murderer "'a halo of romantic incident.'" "There is no limit," he wrote, "to the process of palliating crime and obliterating the memory of punishment." Like the reviewer for the *Illustrated London News*, he would rather have seen the Newgate Aram, in whom there was a certain "grandeur," translated literally to the stage than this artificially "'idyllic' view of murder." It was more specifically the religious trappings at which he took offense: the choirboys' anthem in the first act and the churchyard with its white crosses in the last. Wills's Aram "dies in the odour of sanctity," he concluded,

> but we cannot help thinking that Christianity is able to do tolerably well without such Christians as Aram. . . . The English public has not yet arrived at the point of regarding Christianity as a mere machinery for producing stage effects. It has been said that religion was not designed to make our pleasures less, but it certainly was not designed to make them greater at the theatre.[40]

As far as the acting was concerned, the reviewers were, with one important exception, appreciative. What minor failings they did discern were attributed to limitations of the text rather than the actors' interpre-tation of it. Ruth was originally played by Miss Isabel Bateman, the manager's daughter. In the role of Aram's fiancée, she was described by one reviewer as "pretty" (*Sunday Times*, April 27) and by another (the *Athenaeum*) as "pleasant and tender, if weak," because of the frustra-tingly empty characterization Wills had given her. (Afterward, Ellen Terry was Ruth to Irving's Aram.) Houseman was acted, in the general consensus, melodramatically but well by E. F. Edgar, whom Irving had imported from the Surrey Theatre. As Jowell, the gardener, Mr. Irish was merely "effective" (*Sunday Times*); and Mr. W. H. Stephens as the parson contributed a convincing display of "bland respectability" (*Times*).

The one major exception to the general approval had to do with

Irving's performance, and even this fault was partly attributed to Wills. It was the almost universal critical opinion that, while Irving was excellent in the first two acts, in the third he extravagantly overplayed. Irving's style, although accurately characterized as melodramatic, represented a departure from the norm that not all of his contemporaries admired but few could ignore. Henry James described it as "staginess gone mad."[41] More specifically, it involved an oddly stylized diction and an even more eccentric physical pattern of constant, exaggerated motion that led his stage dresser to judge as his best performances those during which he had perspired most. The best account of Irving's mannerisms is in the reminiscences of Gordon Craig, Ellen Terry's actor-son and Irving's some-time protégé. Irving, he relates, offended purists nightly with his bizarre stage pronunciations of the Queen's English: "He would say '*Gud*' for '*God*'; '*Cut thrut dug*' for '*Cut throat dog*' (*Shylock*); '*Tack the rup frum mey nek*' for '*Take the rope from my neck*' (*Mathias* in *The Bells*)." His detractors, characterizing his movements, would say that Irving, "like the marionette, loses command of his legs, and that he depresses the head, protrudes the shoulders, that his locomotion is the result of an involuntary spasm, accompanied by extraordinary sidelong and backward skirmishings, reminding one of the movements of a napkin-ring when suddenly shot from under the forefinger." Whether in motion or repose, he seems to have literally choreographed his performances in keeping with this style. As Craig describes it:

> His movements were all measured. He was forever counting—one, two, three—pause—one, two, a step, another, a halt, a faintest turn, another step, a word....Or seated on a chair, at a table—raising a glass, drinking—and then lowering his hand and glass—one, two, three, four—suspense—a slight step with his eyes—five—then a patter of steps—two slow syllables—another step—two more syllables—and a second passage in his dance was done. And so right through the piece—whatever it might be—there was no chance movement; he left no loose ends.[42]

It is comforting to learn from Craig that Irving could and sometimes did walk perfectly normally. Otherwise it would be strange to imagine his evening stroll with Ruth at the close of Act I. But it is also apparent from the contemporary reviews that a good deal of his impersonation of Aram was much as Craig describes him. One picture of him in the role, from a striking drawing by Sir Bernard Partridge, bears out the image too. In it Irving wears breeches and hose, a waistcoat and frock coat—all dark—

relieved only by a white, ruffled shirtfront. His long black hair and clothes disordered, the figure staggers backward, both hands clutching the chest in an attitude of stylized dismay.

Sir Henry Irving as Eugene Aram. Engraved from a drawing by Bernard Partridge, 1883.

Partridge's drawing very likely represents Aram's initial confrontation with Houseman in Act II. At that point most of the reviewers were still with him. "The manner in which the threats of Houseman and the sense of his own danger stir the blood of Aram till the fierce light of murder comes into his face, and one recognizes in the teacher the assassin" even the hostile critic of the *Athenaeum* found "highly creditable." "Mr Irving's delineation of the fall from a haughty defiance of daring to a state of hopeless humiliation," said the *Times*, "is not to be surpassed in force and elaboration." The discerning writer for *Temple Bar* gives us a few clear glimpses of what was admirable in Irving's art, before turning to condemn what was not:

> ...the fine touches in the interpretation, the despairing glance over the girl's head as it lies on his breast, the vague absent smile, and the lapse into thought far away from her, even while the love words are on his lips and the caressing hands are touching her; the writhing under the torture of praise and love in the address from his pupils as it is inflicted by the lips of his bride, the shrinking from the pretty details of the wedding—all these are his own. In the agony and terror of detection, in the morbid dread of the poor remains of the man he has slain, in his dreadful question to Houseman, "Did—it—stir?"—throughout the whole of the concluding scenes, Mr. Irving displays increasing power and intensity of expression; but the situations are unduly prolonged, and in the concluding scene in the churchyard he has too much ground to cover.

The reviewer may have been unaware of the pun in his last few words, but it is certain that most of his brotherhood were disgusted by the spectacle of a human being groveling on the earth throughout an entire act of a dramatic production. "To us," said the *Sunday Times*, "the sight of a man upon the ground should never be prolonged. It is humiliating to our nature." To Joseph Knight of the *Athenaeum* it seemed "as though the curse intended for the serpent had fallen upon him, and he was compelled to go upon his belly and eat dirt." "It is difficult to maintain dignity," the *Saturday Review* complained, "while sitting or lying upon the ground," adding that "Mr. Irving probably contends as well as possible against the absurdity of his position in the last act." The problem was not, however, that Irving remained too still. On the contrary, in keeping with Craig's account, Knight wrote that throughout the long death scene the actor was "insensible to the virtue of repose." Though he never stood and walked, he was constantly moving—flailing his arms about and contorting his body—now lying, now sitting at the base of the tree. It is not surprising that several commentators found the confession difficult to follow, spoken as it was through "the spasmodic utterances of a dying man" (*Illustrated London News*).

Two reviews, those in the *Sunday Times* and the *Athenaeum*, directly exhorted Irving to tone down the last act if he valued his professional reputation. "The applause of ignorant crowds," Knight warned, "is terribly misleading." Irving, for all his individualism, was sensitive to the criticism of those excesses which apparently came naturally to him. (Once he asked Gordon Craig, "Do I say 'Gud' when I say 'Gud'?")[43] In this case, he took the advice that was proffered. An article in the *Sunday Times* midway through the play's two-month run reports:

> The marvellous impersonation by Mr. Irving of the hero in Mr. Wills's highly wrought and poetical drama of *Eugene Aram* is a lasting attraction at the Lyceum, to which it nightly draws the fashion and intellect of London. Some alterations have been made in the acting in the third act which, without being less powerful, is now more even and less spasmodic.[44]

Aram's restoration to dignity at the hands of Wills and Irving did not go unchallenged by their rivals, however. As Moncrieff's play had done, this too inspired a few short-run productions of the story at cheaper theaters eager to capitalize on someone else's success. Two of them appear, in fact, to have been revivals of Moncrieff's play dusted off for the occasion. The first opened within a week after Irving's debut at the Lyceum, when a Mr. Charlton was "excellent," according to the *Sunday Times*, as the lead in *Eugene Aram; or, St. Robert's Cave* at the transpontine Elephant and Castle.[45] Not long afterward, Hoxton's Britannia the Great Theatre ("the old Brit"), in the East End, offered the same title as the concluding piece to a luridly incongruous package-for-everyone, the other two productions being "The KU-KLUX-KLAN; or, The Secret Death Union of South America" and "A new musical TERPSICHOREAN SKETCH." The *Sunday Times*, while it had nothing but disdain for the South American Death Union, tossed a favorable word in passing to the third portion of the bill: "In this old drama," it said, "Mr. Newbound was an excellent Walter Lester, and Mr. Reynolds gave a clever portraiture of the scholar and murderer."[46] Lastly, George Conquest's Grecian Theatre, north of central London, whose audience was said to consume "mountains of pork pies" in the course of a night's entertainment,[47] advertised, for Thursdays only, what must have been curtailed versions of "Eugene Aram" and "Oliver Twist" together with a concluding drama, *Watch and*

Wait, and the usual "Dancing and illuminations every evening."[48]

Although no dramatic retelling of Aram's fate would again be as well received as the Wills-Irving collaboration of 1873 had been, despite its weaknesses, there were yet three later stage versions of the story, one for Victorian audiences and two in Edwardian times.

The Standard Theatre, in London's Shoreditch, was something of an anomaly in 1879. Though located in the East End, usually known for vulgar audiences and tawdry stage productions, it was the only theater in the neighborhood that could consistently attract moneyed patrons from the northern suburbs and visiting players from the more prestigious West End companies. Doubtless its success was owing to the penchant its joint proprietors and managers, John and Richard Douglass, had for large-scale enterprise. Billed somewhat speciously as "the largest and most magnificent theatre in the world," the Standard typically launched such outsize spectacles as a ballet in the course of which one hundred and fifty fairies were flown in on wires, or an equestrian drama with real horses prancing across the stage and out into the street as a policeman stopped traffic.

The rendition of *Eugene Aram* which played at the Standard for a week in July of 1879 probably did not involve any such grand effects. It passed unnoticed by any major publication and seems to have been quickly forgotten. No member of the cast won enduring dramatic fame. The author, Adolf Faucquez, was a French *émigré* and Royalist who "turned out dramas wholesale"[49] and supplemented his writing income by teaching his native language. He and his play were recalled by a boy he hired to copy his playscripts, H. Chance Newton, whose casual and not too complimentary mention of them in a specialized theatrical history many years later is practically their only memorial:

> His Eugene Aram drama...was very dramatic, as indeed all his plays were. I very soon "spotted" that Adolf's writing of this Aram play had been inspired by what was perhaps the most astounding stage distortion ever known of the Eugene Aram murder facts, namely, W. G. Wills's drama named after that murder [*sic*], and produced at the Lyceum in the mid seventies.[50]

The next emergence of Aram on an English stage was no more considerable. T. C. M'Quire, creator of a romantic opera with a prologue and three acts entitled *Eugene Aram* that opened at the Margate Theatre Royal on July 4, 1901, was and is utterly obscure. Margate at the turn of the century was a booming seaside resort whose principal theater was open only during the summer months. Its current owner, Edmund McKnight, since the death of his mother two years previously had been losing a depressing uphill battle to defend the tradition of success that had prevailed throughout her many years of management. His new rival, the Grand, specialized in musical comedy. Against its sparkling allurements the operatic *Eugene Aram*, it need only be said, was insufficient proof.[51]

5

For the last of the Aram plays and the only one not named for its protagonist, *After All* is a peculiarly appropriate title. The other singularity of this drama, which opened at London's Avenue Theatre on January 15, 1902, is its happy ending. During the past three quarters of a century, admirers of Eugene Aram in his various incarnations had been hoping, at least subconsciously, to see him exonerated. Finally they had their way, those who were still alive to appreciate it — for the hero of this version is acquitted, to the presumable relief of the audience, though he confesses his guilt in the concluding scene. What a long way public morals had come since poor Bulwer was criticized for sympathy with a duly condemned murderer!

Just as the Aram of *After All* was linearly descended from the other Arams who preceded him, so each of the principals in this play seemed to have his connection with the past dramatic history of the Aram story. Martin Harvey (later Sir John Martin-Harvey), who played the lead, had been apprentice for fourteen years under Sir Henry Irving at the Lyceum, and Mabel Terry-Lewis, the leading lady, was the latest product of the great nineteenth-century acting family. Even one of the playwrights, Freeman C. Wills, was younger brother to William Gorman Wills. He and his collaborator, Frederick Langbridge, were both Irish, and the play premiered at Dublin's Theatre Royal on October 7, 1901, before coming to the West End. Both authors were also, strangely enough, clergymen. Wills has been described as "a very 'advanced' cleric of the muscular Christian type," and Langbridge later became canon of Limerick.[52]

After All, unfortunately for everyone concerned, was not as successful as had been Wills and Langbridge's previous play for Martin Harvey, *The Only Way*, based on Dickens's *A Tale of Two Cities*. An unpropitious last-minute postponement of the opening date for *After All* gave way to a fully realized calamity when the first night's performance resulted in unanimously poor reviews. Shortly thereafter a defensive campaign was launched in the advertisement page of the *Times* that could hardly have appeared subtle to anyone who was paying attention. Looking like a review were it not for its location in the newspaper was a lengthy quotation from Mr. Clement Scott (his name in large block letters), who had been so ecstatic about W. G. Wills many years before and was now in retirement except, apparently, when called upon to help salvage floundering plays. "I entered the Avenue Theatre somewhat of a sceptic," Scott had written:

> I came out an enthusiast.
> I found a prologue which is a play in itself, a miniature tragedy, interesting to pulsation, and acted to perfection.
> That murder of Daniel Clarke: the three sudden stabs, and then the lifeless, pulseless rag of a man on the floor, the awful silence, the wild look of horror on the face of the just murderer of the seducer of his sister I am not likely to forget. . . .
> It may be that the whole play has been hauled over the coals since the first night. If so, I rejoice I am no longer a first nighter, for I can tell the public what a play is, and not what it was. . . . [53]

The following day, January 26, an odd announcement appeared in the theatrical section of the *Sunday Times*:

> Since the performance of this charming play [*A Cigarette Maker's Romance* — a popular farce in which Harvey also starred] at Sandringham by Royal command Mr. Martin Harvey has had many requests that he should revive the piece, but in consequence of the success of 'After All' it has been found impossible to give more than one matinée a week. [54]

The oddity resides in the fact that a play so successful as *After All* is here reputed to have been should have struggled on for a total engagement of only three and a half weeks at a period when successful plays generally ran at least as long as they had in the 1870s.

Wills and Langbridge's new production was billed as an adaptation of "Lord Lytton's novel" and so it was, but it also owed something to W. G. Wills's play, specifically the Knaresborough setting (where the Meadows family has germinated, becoming the Orchard family) and the revenge motive for murder — in this case, revenge of a ruined foster-sister as opposed to a fiancée. In the prologue so vividly described by Clement Scott, Aram, in Houseman's presence, murders the seducer of the drowned Miriam. Afterward, he succeeds to a fortune and takes up residence in the country. Beyond this point there seems little reason to paraphrase the delightfully flippant synopsis which appeared in the *Sunday Times*, whose dramatic reviews, as they had done nearly thirty years before, still revealed almost the entire plot and in the process could effect their most cutting criticism:

> The play itself opens fifteen years later. Eugene Aram is admired and respected by the world in general, and there is something picturesquely mysterious and remorseful about him, which is not without its elements of attractiveness for Madeleine Orchard, who seems to be in love with him as he with her. But Madeleine is also in love with her cousin, Walter Orchard, . . . it being just as well to have two strings to one's bow. Her sister, Nancy Orchard, is also in love with Eugene Aram, but with an instinctive feeling that to be in love with Eugene Aram is not a wholly remunerative investment of the capital of the affections, she also retains another admirer, one Squire Upjohn [later described by this reviewer as "Tony Lumpkinish"], upon whom she may decline should Aram prove unkind or impossible. Walter Orchard, without any notion that Aram had anything particular to do with it, is investigating the circumstances of his father's death and disappearance. . . . Meanwhile Houseman, who has already levied handsome blackmail upon Aram, has taken to the practice of burglary in the peaceful vicinity of the Manor House. . . of Squire Orchard, father of the two young ladies with the duplicate affections. . . .
>
> Houseman burgles the Manor House and Eugene Aram shoots him in the leg, Houseman denounces Aram as the murderer of Walter's father, and Eugene Aram explains to Walter the provocation which led up to the murder, and Walter holds Aram to have been perfectly justified by circumstances. In the final act we have the close of the trial, Aram's speech in defense, the judge's summing-up, and the jury's verdict of "Not guilty." Later on Aram confesses to Madeleine that he really is guilty after all, and Madeleine faints into the arms of Walter, whilst Aram goes up some steps and off at the back, apparently meaning to efface himself for ever.[55]

For the sake of an ending both happy and sentimental, it may be added, Madeleine remains with Walter, whom she really loved all along, while her sister, Nancy, still pines for the departed Aram. Given the degeneration of Aram plots from Bulwer through Wills to Langbridge and Wills, it seems appropriate to give thanks that the story was not again revived.

The three major reviews of the play differ only in emphasis. The

Sunday Times found no fault with the acting, considered of course within the limits of the text, whereas the *Illustrated London News* was displeased with everyone except Harvey and Terry-Lewis, who the reviewer seems to have felt were undeserving of the straits they were in. The *Athenaeum*, which appears not to have noticed the advance of liberalism in the intervening thirty years, still prudishly objected to any renewed interest in Aram, "whose sordid crime," it insisted once again, had already "received more attention than it merits."[56] The consensus of all, apparently because it was the only reasonable conclusion, was that even Martin Harvey, for whom everyone felt sorry, could not redeem a play as bad as this one. It was more the pity, besides, for Harvey, "could he but find a fitting frame, would present a very picturesque and a very impressive portrait of Eugene Aram."[57] "An air of mystery or romance is easily worn by him," wrote the *Athenaeum* reviewer,

> and self-abnegation has become of late the 'breath of his nostrils' [an allusion to his popular role as Sydney Carton]. Here he is...moodily sentimental and nothing more. The maidens by whom he is protected or caressed are as incomprehensible as he, and as unreal as the son who, on an *ex parte* statement, hugs his father's murderer to his breast.

Harvey, in a drawing by S. Begg of a "Scene from the Prologue: Miriam Seeks Refuge From the Mob," does look the part, as he stands with a globe and books in evidence in his study, Miriam clinging to him on her knees, and Houseman enforcing the door against the angry mob outside. That the drawing appeared on the cover of the January 18 *Illustrated London News*, the week before that periodical reviewed the play so unfavorably, indicates the anticipation with which this new effort was awaited following Harvey's success in the Dickens adaptation. The actor is remembered ultimately, in a prominent encyclopedia of the theater, as less than he might have been:

> A handsome man, with clear-cut sensitive features and a distinguished presence,...his death [in 1944] broke the last link with the Victorian stage. He might have risen to greater heights had he not become so identified with the somewhat melodramatic role of Sydney Carton, which he was constantly forced to revive in order to satisfy an adoring public.[58]

With one successful play, perhaps Langbridge and Wills had done him more harm than they could have done with several fiascos like *After All*.

"Scene from the Prologue [of *After All*]: Miriam Seeks Refuge From the Mob." Martin Harvey as Aram. From a drawing by S. Begg, *Illustrated London News*, 120 (Jan. 18, 1902).

6

In the aftermath of his dramatic celebrity Eugene Aram has been nearly but not utterly forgotten. Allusions to Aram occur in at least two popular mystery novels from our own century. *Bertie Wooster Sees It*

Through (1946), by P. G. Wodehouse, quotes Hood's poem in passing; *So Much Blood* (1976), by Simon Brett, not only features epigraphs from Hood but also involves the poem as a clue in the eventual solution of the mystery.[59] These references are doubtless obscure to most modern readers, however, as they would surely not have been a hundred years ago.

It would in fact have been rather unusual at any point in the nineteenth century after 1832 to run across an Englishman, literate or illiterate, who had never heard of Eugene Aram. He occupied during that time a small but established niche in the awareness of most of his countrymen and of a good many people in America and Europe as well. Even in fairly recent times he has been represented not only by the printed word but also in other media. Between 1832 and 1883 he was the subject of numerous paintings and drawings by professional artists who looked to Hood, Bulwer, Irving, and Wills for their inspiration. Continuing the melodramatic tradition, as stage melodrama succumbed to the newer fascination of moving pictures, there were three silent film versions, in 1914, 1915, and 1924.[60] On August 6, 1959, the BBC commemorated the two-hundredth anniversary of Aram's execution with a broadcast of *The Man on the Gibbet*, a radio play by Arnold Kellett that may be the last fictive expression of the story.

Throughout the period of his fame, Aram interested a wide variety of individuals for as many different reasons. Among the vast holdings of the Library of Congress is an obscure volume entitled *Eugene Aram. A Play in Five Acts Founded on Bulwer*, privately published in New Orleans in 1874. Its author, Espy William Hendricks Williams, whose very name connotes mint juleps and mimosa blossoms, may have thought, judging by the date of his play, that he could improve on W. G. Wills. Another artifact, this from 1915, which reposes on the local history shelf of the Knaresborough public library, is surely one of the most eccentric literary curiosities ever published. Ostensibly it is a poetic work entitled "Knaresborough Castle" by Sampson Waters, B.A., Harrovian, Christ Church, Oxford, Barrister-at-Law. There is indeed a poem of absurdly pedestrian quality so named in the book. The sixteen of its two hundred and seventy-two lines that directly concern Aram are representatively abysmal,[61] and the poem proves on closer inspection to have been a mere excuse for the impassioned soapbox oratory of its single-minded author. Three prefaces on politics and government inveigh in the strongest terms against the specter of socialism. Together they total one hundred and seventy-four pages of "introduction" to the poem itself, which occupies pages 179–188.

The Aram story, first romanticized and subsequently popularized in the nineteenth century, appears to have followed a course of steady deterioration. Hood wrote a serious ballad that is not a masterpiece of English literature but nonetheless has many artistic excellences. Bulwer transformed Aram into an impossible creature of fantasy and gave rise to the tenacious myth that his crime was an act of heroism carried out in the service of a principle. And the melodramas reduced him at last to a mere empty mannikin absurdly packaged for mass consumption. By contrast, these make Bulwer's novel look like a work of surpassing subtlety. But in the artistic world there was ultimately good to come of it all. If he had ever been the subject of a truly great accomplishment of art, Eugene Aram would be well remembered today. He was not, of course, but his treatment by lesser hands provided, as we shall see, a kind of generic precedent for certain other writers in whose more enduring creations he is clearly reflected.

6 "UNCOMMON ABILITIES"
The Scholar-Criminal
in History and Literature

THAT EUGENE ARAM'S STORY persisted beyond his own century is largely owing to the singularity of his dual nature as murderer and scholar. Traditionally, his appeal hangs on the fascination of paradox. The two sides of his character are incompatible and yet inseparable. Had his memory depended on either alone he would have been soon forgotten. The murder would in itself have lacked enduring or widespread interest had it not been the unlikely work of a schoolmaster and scholar. Remarkable as it may have been at the time for the fourteen-year lapse between commission and discovery, and the macabre circumstances under which the body was concealed, it was a brutal affair clumsily effected for paltry gain, obscure and uncomplicated by any grand theme of passion. Its chroniclers stress, time and again, the incongruity between Aram's intellectual calling and his violent deed as its single most intriguing feature.

Aram's scholarly reputation, alone, was no more likely to have established his celebrity. Self-taught in the remote Yorkshire countryside and without university affiliation, he lacked the money, the influence, and the patronage he needed to publish his work. Nor did he have the genius or the strength of character that enabled his great contemporary, Samuel Johnson, to prevail in similar circumstances without them. Ironically, Aram's slight fame as a linguist during the eighteenth and nineteenth centuries directly resulted from his greater notoriety as a felon. In this respect, as in others, the two contradictory elements were inextricably bound. Those men of letters who were aware of his Celtic theories could hear of and read them only as appended to the trial accounts, since they were never published separately. Most of this audience regarded his research as a mere curiosity, the product of "the murderer, Eugene Aram." Thus, in a letter of February 18, 1760, the once prominent Yorkshire antiquary Samuel Pegge condescendingly wrote:

> One Eugene Aram, a very bad man, was executed at York last year for a murder. He has done something, being a scholar and a schoolmaster, towards a Lexicon on a new plan. Hearing of this, I sent for the pamphlet, which contained some account of his life, and the specimen of a Lexicon. He goes to the Celtic, the Irish, and the British languages, as well as others; and there are things in the specimen that will amuse a lover of etymologies.[1]

Another reader of the pamphlet, Tobias Smollett, viewed its author with more sympathy. His *History of England* (published 1758–1765) laments the untimely execution of a man whose work, "had he lived to finish it, might have thrown some essential light upon the origin and obscurities of the European history." Smollett adds, regarding the still recent denial of king's pardon in Aram's case, that "if ever murderer was entitled to indulgence, perhaps it might have been extended not improperly to this man, whose genius, in itself prodigious, might have exerted itself in works of general utility."[2] The sentiment came, of course, too late to be of practical value. More meaningful perhaps was the hope advanced in a periodical edited by Smollett that Aram's contribution would "not be lost in the learned world."[3]

A letter of July 27, 1784, from the Reverend Michael Lort, a Cambridge linguist well known in scholarly circles, suggests, however, that the learned world was unimpressed. Addressing Bishop Thomas Percy, compiler of the influential *Reliques of Ancient English Poetry* (1765), Lort mentions a mysterious encounter with a woman who, he writes,

> called on me to offer me some MSS. of Eugene Aram's Celtic Dictionary, which she says had been once in your hands, and I suppose would have continued so, if you had thought them of any value. Had I seen her before Vallancey [see note] went back to Ireland I would have sent her and her papers to him, who seems to be deep in Celtic etymologies; can you recollect any particulars of these papers?[4]

There is no record of Percy's reply, but the woman who visited Lort may well have been, as Watson speculates, Aram's daughter Sally.

Among such men as Lort and Percy, Aram seems to have aroused only a mild and fleeting curiosity. The "Plan" which they read had been hastily written under great pressure in a prison cell and suffered, as its author admitted, from his lack of access to notes or sources. Its appearance in the appendix to an ephemeral version of his "Life and Trial" hardly lent it scholarly respectability.

Whether Aram was more deserving of fame or infamy became a public issue in 1777, with the appearance of a revised and expanded second edition of the prestigious *Biographia Britannica*. The first edition, published in 1747, had been, of course, too early to include him. But the noted nonconformist minister and biographer Andrew Kippis, commissioned by the booksellers to enlarge and improve the work for reissue, saw fit to incorporate Aram's life in the new edition and at the same time to exclude several other figures treated in the original version, among them a seventeeth-century bishop, John Atherton, who had been executed for "unnatural [i.e., sexual] crime." Kippis's selective judgments were received with some disapproval in the form, first, of an anonymous pamphlet which considered them objectionable and improper. Thirteen years later, the dispute was still heated, or at least revived. It was inexcusable, wrote a correspondent to the *Gentleman's Magazine* of March, 1790, that Eugene Aram, "a wretch of infamous principles, who. . . ended his life on a gallows, and probably still remains suspended on a gibbet," should appear among the worthies of England simply because he was a scholar. It was even less excusable, the writer continued, that "such a character was substituted to [*sic*] Bishop ATHERTON."[5] The following month, another reader refuted the first in a letter to the magazine's pseudonymous editor:

Mr. URBAN,

. . . you have inserted several observations relative to the new edition of the Biographia Britannica; and, among others, objections are made to the admission of Eugene Aram into that work, and the exclusion of Bishop Atherton. But it appears to me, that the remarks of your correspondent upon this subject are far from being just. The insertion of Eugene Aram is objected to, because he was a man of bad principles, and ended his life at the gallows. But it should be remembered, that it was never understood, that in the Biographia Britannica the lives only of virtuous men were to be recorded. In the old edition are the lives of several persons who ended their days by the hands of the executioner. . . . As to Eugene Aram, it is truly said of him in the Bioagraphia [*sic*], in the article objected to, that "the progress that he made in literature, considering the little instruction that he received, and the disadvantages under which he laboured, may justly be considered as astonishing; and that his powers of mind were uncommonly great, cannot reasonably be questioned. . . ." It was certainly the extraordinary talents and attainments of Aram that occasioned his introduction into the Biographia; and I know, that, by persons of undoubted taste and judgement, the account of him in that work has been thought a curious and very proper article. . . .

With respect to Bp. Atherton, he never had the least claim to insertion in such a work as a Biographia Britannica, and was, therefore, very properly omitted in the new edition. He was not in the least distinguished for genius or learning; his merely being a bishop could give him no just pretensions; and still less the unnatural crime for which he suffered. Your correspondent says, that "Bp. Atherton's reputation is suspected to have been destroyed, and his catastrophe effected, more by the contrivance and malice of a party [his enemies among the Irish Catholics], than by the aggravated guilt with which he is charged." If this were perfectly just, which I think may reasonably be questioned, it would not give Atherton the least claim to insertion in the Biographia Britannica. Aram was inserted on account of his uncommon talents and learning; but Atherton, who was not distinguished for either, never had the least pretentions to being recorded in such a work. Yours, &c.

H.S.[6]

If the cultivated sometimes found Aram unworthy of note, those less capable of understanding his scholarly pursuits had been, especially before his disgrace, all the more impressed by them. In the environs of an isolated Yorkshire village such as Knaresborough, classical attainment easily inspired reverence. The awed esteem which Aram once enjoyed there was due, the York Pamphlet says, to "the general estimation and opinion, gentlemen had of his uncommon abilities and extensive learning." While a fair number of villagers could then read and write, they did so primarily in the context of daily business transactions or religious pursuits. They kept records, made up accounts, penned an occasional letter, or read the Bible, but, as the price of books was still prohibitive, most had a limited acquaintance with the printed word.[7] In their eyes, a man conversant in Latin and Greek and genteel in bearing might well seem removed from common life and above gratuitous violence. When the same man had for years educated their children, winning a reputation for responsibility and restraint at a time when schoolmasters were often tyrants, his peaceable conduct would seem even more assured. No doubt, among the angry mobs which taunted and threatened the ruffian House-man in the aftermath of Aram's trial, there were some who still rejected the possibility of the schoolmaster's guilt.

Since the Middle Ages, when education was virtually restricted to the clergy, the life of learning had carried with it a positive association with that of religion, an association jarringly contradicted by Aram's case. During the thirteenth through the eighteenth centuries, anyone, layman or ecclesiastic, who could read might well be termed a "clerk." The word, whose original, more limited meaning was "cleric," is itself indicative that the mysteries of religion and print were traditionally conjoined. Historically, even the merest literacy afforded a supralegal, protective connection with the church, as reflected in the test of the "neck-verse" to establish benefit of clergy. As late as 1706, when the practice was amended by statute, the man who could read the twenty-third psalm might, in some capital cases, save himself from the gallows.

Although there had always been instances of "criminous clerks," the scholarly profession implied, more than others, at least the expectation of moral uprightness. Such attitudes, especially considering the relatively low incidence of murder in eighteenth-century England,[8] gave Aram's crime a special impact, not only at the time of its commission but also in the century which followed. The closing comment of the *Biographia Britannica* entry on Aram expresses a typical view of his life: "It is exceedingly to be lamented, that a man possessed of such abilities, and such application, should have made so disgraceful an exit; and we are hurt to find so excellent a head, joined to such depravity of heart."[9]

During the nineteenth century, the period of Aram's subsequent prominence in literature, there was widespread belief in the close relationship of ignorance and crime. That a properly guided education, on the contrary, repressed vice and violence in human nature was a major tenet of the popular education movements of this era. It was, in fact, essential to the educational views of both Godwin and Bulwer, his ideological heir. "The characters of men," Godwin wrote, "are determined in all their most essential circumstances by education....Speak the language of truth and reason to your child, and be under no apprehension for the result. Show him that what you recommend is valuable and desirable, and fear not but he will desire it."[10] Given such belief, Aram's life story becomes a disturbing but captivating riddle. Many of Bulwer's readers, drawn by his novel to study its hero's actual history, convinced themselves of his innocence, a conclusion at which the novelist himself claimed eventually to have arrived. Failing that conviction, it was difficult for them to account for Aram's criminal side, in reality or in fiction. It became a common tendency on the part of his biographers to either deny his guilt or downplay his scholarship, since they were unable to reconcile the two.

Aram's close connection with children in his role as schoolmaster has been a related problem throughout the history of the Aram theme. It was this bizarre discrepancy—between the vicious felon and the respected, even beloved guardian of fledgling minds—which inspired Hood's poem and was at least partly responsible for the fact that Bulwer's Aram is no longer an usher. Closer to our own time but indicative of the same contrast is a quip by the young Robert Frost, responding to an editor's request for biographical information. "It is necessary," he wrote, "to admit that I teach 'orthography' in a district school: and that in the fitness of things, the association of Eugene Aram with children in this capacity seems no more incongruous than my own."[11]

Certainly Aram was not the first in history, or yet the last, who joined an intellectual with a criminal bent and by such aberrance gained interest. Notable instances come to mind quite readily of literary figures in England and France whose tempestuous lives led to violent outbreaks. Marlowe and Ben Jonson are representative of the type, along with the minor poet Richard Savage, who won notoriety in 1727 by killing a man in a tavern brawl. Nor has any association with the church ever exempted a man from such propensities. François Villon, in 1455, was attacked by a priest with whom he had a long-standing feud and in the ensuing scuffle fatally stabbed him. Afterward the poet was twice sentenced to death for burglary and released. Four centuries later, Verlaine went to prison for shooting his young protégé, Rimbaud. These men, however, differ markedly from Aram. They led riotous lives and never affected propriety. Their crimes were for the most part passionate, precipitate outbursts, not calculated schemes coolly engineered for personal gain. Their actions do not seem inconsonant with what they showed the world of their lives.

At the time of Daniel Clark's murder, however, as at any other time in human history, the man whose gentle and scholarly exterior concealed an iniquitous secret was an unsettling figure. Of this type, more recent history provides several other striking examples. A few are familiar to students of literature, and two were, like Aram, linguists. The increasing frequency of their appearance during the nineteenth century may be a logical corollary to the spread and democratization of learning. Ironically, in light of the idealism of the education movements, the very fact that learning was more accessible might simply ensure that a larger proportion of learned men would be of devious or criminal bent. As a commentator on Bulwer's work observed (in the era of the First World War),

> to show that great learning and attainments, together with con-
> duct that conforms to the requirements of society, are not neces-
> sarily inconsistent with criminality or viciousness was a needed
> lesson then, and is increasingly important now since accom-
> plishments can be more easily acquired, and Arams are more
> numerous.[12]

The forger, Dr. William Dodd, executed in 1777, is an early instance
of one who fell almost by accident into crime. Compiler of *The Beauties
of Shakespeare* (1752), an enduringly popular anthology of select passages,
he was also chaplain to the king and private tutor to Philip Stanhope, the
future fifth earl of Chesterfield, by whose family he was well loved and
respected. When Dodd published in 1772 a sermon on "The Frequency
of Capital Punishment Inconsistent with Justice, Sound Policy and
Religion," he could have had little notion how close to his own interests
the issue would soon become. Overwhelmed and distracted by debt, he
forged the earl of Chesterfield's signature to a bond, without intending
permanent misappropriation of the money. When he was apprehended,
the sympathy of many prominent persons, and even the king himself,
could not save him from the impersonal movement of the law. In a letter
to Dodd, Samuel Johnson wrote consolingly, "Your crime morally or reli-
giously considered has no very deep dye of turpitude; it corrupted no
man's principles. It evolved only a temporary and reparable injury." By his
death, Dodd became a martyr to the cause he had espoused five years
earlier. Leon Radzinowicz, the eminent historian of English criminal law,
attributes to his execution the origins of the penal reform movement
which rose to prominence early in the next century.[13] It is also likely that
the notoriety of the Dodd case, coming so soon after Aram's execution,
recalled the Yorkshire tragedy and by association helped the memory of
Aram to survive.

A later and far more reprehensible literary malefactor than Dodd was
Thomas Griffiths Wainewright. A friend of Lamb, Hazlitt, and De-
Quincey, he was a precocious wit-about-town whose art criticism frequently appeared in the *London Magazine*. To satisfy his flamboyant and
expensive tastes, Wainewright swindled the Bank of England out of some
£5,000 by forgery. Afterward, while he still enjoyed the general regard of
the London intellectual world, he poisoned in succession his uncle, his
mother-in-law, and his sister-in-law for inheritance and insurance
money.[14] His career directly inspired the character of Honoré Gabriel
Varney, the unscrupulous artist and villain of Bulwer's 1849 novel *Lucretia*;

or, The Children of Night. It was of Wainewright that Oscar Wilde observed, "The fact of a man being a poisoner is nothing against his prose."

It has been suggested, and dramatized in Bulwer's *Eugene Aram*, that the frustration of the poor scholar's life provided motivation for Aram's crime. To whatever extent this may be true, the nineteenth century saw at least one such pathetic case. Stockwell, a London suburb, was the scene of tragedy for the Reverend John Selby Watson, a classical scholar and translator who had published a good many dry treatises and who, on a Sunday afternoon in 1871, murdered his wife in his library. The grammar school of which he had been headmaster for twenty-six years having suffered a decline in enrollment, he was dismissed from his post. His future, without hope of pension at the age of sixty-six, was unbearably bleak. He broke under the pressure, unable to support the nagging of a shrewish wife. He killed her in a fit of rage, then failed miserably in his attempts at concealment of the crime and, later, at suicide by poison. He was tried and convicted, and died thirteen years afterward in a prison for the criminally insane.[15]

Two additional figures in the scholars' chamber of horrors shared Aram's interest in language studies. The first, Eugène Marie Chantrelle, a French emigrant, taught his native tongue at an academy in Edinburgh. He was the author of several textbooks in that field and had, as well, a proficiency in German, Greek, and Latin. Like Aram, he had married a meek wife, whom he dominated and abused. His early training in France had been as a physician, and, in 1878, he put his medical knowledge into practice by poisoning his bride of ten years. The overdose of opium which he administered was calculated to give the appearance of accidental death by natural-gas poisoning from a heater in her room. Chantrelle's aim, comparable to Wainewright's, was the collection of an insurance policy he had recently drawn in the victim's name. But Mme. Chantrelle had, prior to her murder, expressed fear of just such an act on her husband's part. Consequently, the suspicions of her relatives brought a speedy investigation of her death. Less than five months thereafter, Chantrelle went to the gallows — like Aram, subdued but unrepentant. The sentiment with which his biographer summarizes Chantrelle's life could as well apply to his eighteenth-century predecessor: "So ended the melancholy career of a man whose knowledge, skill, and accomplishments, had they been properly directed, would have assured for him success in many positions in life, but whose misdeeds, laid bare by the inflexible hand of justice, eventually brought for him their terrible retribution."[16]

Of all such cases throughout history, however, that of America's Edward Howard Rulloff in the 1870s most strikingly, and ironically, recalls

Aram's own. Indeed, the *New York Times* report of Rulloff's execution dubbed him "the modern Eugene Aram."[17] Then in his early sixties, Rulloff lodged in New York City, under the alias "Leurio," with a respectable family who took him for a sedate bachelor-philologist conscientiously supporting himself and funding his language studies by a career in real-estate law. Legal matters, it was understood, were the cause of his frequent extended absences from home. In actuality, Rulloff was a sham. Not only had he had no formal higher education, but he was the mastermind of two younger companions, Dexter and Jarvis, who accompanied him on periodic burglaries of homes and businesses in neighboring communities. On the night of August 17, 1870, their target was a general store in Binghamton, New York.

In this instance, the burglary would lead to murder. Two clerks, sleeping on the second floor of the building, were awakened by the break-in. They surprised Rulloff and his companions in the act of robbing the store, and in the scuffle that followed, one of the shop boys, Frederick Merrick, was shot and killed. As the robbers fled, the second clerk gave the alarm. Hours later, Rulloff was discovered, disheveled and covered with grime, hiding in a shed, and the bodies of Dexter and Jarvis surfaced in the nearby Chenango river, whose width they had attempted to swim. The surviving witness could positively identify the two drowned men but not the fugitive. Although Rulloff denied his guilt and any association with Dexter and Jarvis, he was detained as a result of public feeling against him.

Police investigation eventually established that Rulloff had in fact known Jarvis since the latter's childhood, Jarvis's father having been Rulloff's jailer during a prison stay twenty-seven years earlier. At that time, Rulloff had ingratiated himself with the senior Jarvis and, some months after his release, returned the friendship by running off with Jarvis's wife and small son. The boy had stayed with Rulloff, who raised him and tutored him in crime. On occasion, it was discovered, Rulloff had artfully and successfully posed as a lawyer to defend his youthful companions. When the apartment he shared with Jarvis was searched after the Merrick murder, it was found to contain "many burglar's tools, including jimmies, dark lanterns and masks." As the *New York Times* reported, "The quiet retreat of the sedate and gentle linguist was shown to be a den of outlaws."[18]

At Rulloff's trial, the evidence was so compellingly against him that his only hope of escape was through a technicality. Rulloff, like Aram, took part in his own defense, although he did not conduct it alone. He had in the past demonstrated his powers as a canny if uncertified lawyer, but in this instance neither his own efforts nor those of his counsel could save him. The courtroom audience detested Rulloff, applauded when events went against him, and had to be quieted by the judge on numerous occasions. The jury shared their opinion, if not their deportment. On January 11, 1871, Rulloff was convicted and, shortly thereafter, sentenced to hang.

Like Aram, Rulloff had conceived an original theory concerning the origins of language, although it was by no means as cogent as Aram's. Compared to the work of the eighteenth-century schoolmaster, Rulloff's was, in fact, almost a parody. It is aptly described by the newspaper as the "vagaries with which he has amazed the ignorant and amused the learned world."[19] Rulloff was, like Aram, fascinated by the close similarities he perceived among root words and syllables in diverse languages, both ancient and modern. But rather than attributing those similarities to a natural, accidental dispersion of peoples through conquest or trade, he believed the languages in which they occurred to have been simultaneously created by an obscure, primordial brotherhood of priests, whose influence transcended regional boundaries. "In ancient times," he wrote, "the seclusion of sacred temples and the leisure of an intellectual priesthood were devoted to supplying the various nations of the earth with languages."[20] Thus Greek, Latin, Sanskrit, Hebrew, Arabic, Celtic, German, French, and English, as well as many lesser tongues, had been consciously formulated according to a pervasive system involving root combinations of "three elements" each: "a liquid, a vowel, and a mutable." As the great work of Rulloff's life, his manuscript *Method in the Formation of Language*, was never published, we can only speculate on such interesting matters as how the synthetic languages were taught and established among the diverse barbaric tribes of antiquity, or what form communication took in the years before their creation.

Despite the absurdity of Rulloff's views on comparative philology, his knowledge of the classics and of language theory appears to have impressed at least some bona fide scholars. In 1843, although he had never been formally educated beyond high school, Rulloff had applied for a professorship at Jefferson College, then in Canonsburg, Pennsylvania.[21] Since there was no opening at the time, the professors "gave him some clerical work to do, and in a little while satisfied themselves of his remarkable scientific and literary attainments." Afterward, they are said to have recommended him for a position at "Chapel Hill College in North Carolina," as professor of languages.[22] His arrest for a robbery which, strangely enough, he did not in this case commit, prevented his accepting the post. Years later, when Rulloff was imprisoned for the Merrick murder,

Professor Mather, a Greek scholar of Amherst College, Massachusetts, having heard of his reputed learning, visited Rulloff in Binghamton Jail. Mather questioned him extensively and found "a subtlety of analysis and reasoning...the marked characteristic of his mind." "Here," continued Mather, "is a profound and appreciative student of all that is beautiful and glorious in classical learning working for years as a philologist, and with a zeal rarely equalled; and yet all the time living a life of crime as dark and terrible as any criminal in our land."[23]

Rulloff's ingenuity is demonstrated by a curious scrap of evidence brought forth at his trial. Among the contents of Dexter's pockets when he was pulled from the river was a bit of stenographic writing in Rulloff's hand, legible though waterlogged. The cipher, a device allegedly invented by Rulloff for secret communication among the conspirators, was sworn by an expert on the witness stand to be unlike any of over two hundred such systems known to him.

Whatever may have been the extent of Rulloff's linguistic expertise, his zeal for philology, recognized by Professor Mather, was certainly genuine, so much so that it led some to question his sanity. A letter from another scholar, G. F. Comfort, published in the *New York Times*, differs so markedly from Mather's estimate of Rulloff's learning that it is difficult to imagine how two experts could be as divergently affected. Comfort recounts that during the months of May, June, and July of 1869, prior to an important meeting of the American Philological Association in Pough-keepsie, New York, Rulloff, under the pseudonym of "E. Leurio," had been

> very active in bringing his discovery [via a manuscript entitled "A Key to the Origin and Formation of Language"] to the personal notice of most, if not all persons of linguistic attainments in this City and vicinity. . . . But one opinion was formed by all. Mr. Leurio seemed utterly ignorant of the history of languages and of words, and had no knowledge of the results of the labors of philologists during the last thirty years. His earnestness and persistence seemed to remove him from the class of ordinary charlatans. The only explanation...seemed to be that he was a monomaniac. . . . About the 1st of July, Mr. Leurio issued a circular, in which he described his manuscript as containing the most remarkable discovery of the age, and offering it for sale at the modest price of $500,000.[24]

At the convention in late July, Rulloff persuaded a panel to read the work. When they denied its worth, he stormed out, cursing them as he went.

He was not heard of again until his arrest for murder became public.

In early May of 1871, in a last effort to reverse the death sentence, Rulloff's lawyers called for a sanity hearing. His questioners dwelt at length upon his linguistic theories to test the charge of monomania in his adherence to them. He told the examiners that although he did not care what happened to himself, "his earnest wish was that the Governor might fully appreciate this new philological system, and that his book might be placed in proper hands to be developed and published."[25] The remainder of the hearing, as transcribed, dealt with religious issues, as Rulloff affirmed his atheism and subtly countered the doctrinal questions put to him. On May 12, the commissioners declared him "entirely sane." He was executed on May 18, 1871. The *New York Times* of that date termed him "a prodigy lured into crime from pure love of learning."[26] The phrase might more appropriately describe the eighteenth-century counterpart to whose career his own rang like a dissonant echo.

In literary history as in recorded history, Aram was a novelty: the earliest true example of the literary type of the scholar-criminal. The dichotomy so evident in the historical Aram translates directly to his role in fiction. He figures in the vast literature of crime — among its rogues, vagabonds, pickpockets, footpads, and more desperate cutthroat villains — all of those whose actions and attitudes defy human law. But he ranks as well with the comparatively few fictional beings whose driving force is the love of books and the acquisition of knowledge — the pedants, the alchemists, the poor, starving scholars.[27] Even fewer characters in fiction share with Aram the distinction of bridging these disparate worlds. Those that do, are varied in the extreme. Some are among the world's most memorable literary creations. In them, the whole is greater than the sum of the two parts.

Two great classic figures must be mentioned as forerunners of the Aram type. Though neither is a lawbreaker in the ordinary sense, they draw much of their depth and power from the juxtaposition of evil (or violence) and intellect. Analogous to Bulwer's hero is the grand archetype of Faust, who also forfeited his soul for the sake of knowledge and so destroyed himself. Bulwer's Aram, especially in the fragmentary drama, as we have seen, is clearly Faustian in his yearning to "unsphere / The destinies of man, or track the ways / Of God from world to world; pursue the winds, / The clouds that womb the thunder to their home."[28] Boteler, the Houseman counterpart who leads him into crime ("Thou may'st have thy wish!"), is, in that respect at least, his Mephistopheles. The less selfish Aram of the novel, though he hopes to do good with his ill-gotten riches, considers himself, like Faust, exempt from common morality by virtue of his superior gifts. The influence of Goethe on Bulwer was and is well known,[29] and *Fraser's Magazine*, upon the publication of this novel, was quick to cry plagiarism, although on the basis of very general similarity.[30] The vast gulf between the two authors is nowhere more evident, however, than in the conclusions of the two works. Bulwer's protagonist makes a weak concession to Providence, hoping for, and almost assuming, God's eventual forgiveness, whereas Goethe's plummets impressively through brimstone and fire to his ultimate and only reward.

Also on the periphery of this typological cluster is Hamlet, the student called from his books and his meditations to enact bloody vengeance. Since Bulwer considered Shakespeare his supreme artistic model and conceived of the novel form as a kind of prose tragedy which should aspire to the greatest heights of the drama, it is plausible that something of the moody Dane is in the brooding scholar. Their similarities multiply the more one considers them. Both characters are prone to philosophical soliloquy. Both find in the course of destiny that their bloody acts necessarily afflict the lives of others whom they love. Both justify murder in the context of a universal moral code whose instrument they are, and on the assumption that the victim is marked by the corruption of his soul to die. Both are themselves destroyed as a direct result. In each case, the supreme tragedy is that the blight has fallen on a life that would have been sublime had not inevitable circumstances impelled them to the vengeful deed.

As with the several historical parallels to Aram, so it is with his fictional counterparts: the nearer ones come after him. The study of literary influence is necessarily imprecise, since an author himself can hardly know what intricate patterns of experience converge in his latest creation. Bearing in mind, however, the wide familiarity of the Aram theme in the nineteenth century—when its pairing of disparate elements was especially unusual—a number of scholar-criminals after 1832 may be perceived as echoes of this significant prototype. Two clearly transcend it. The Aram beneath the surface of these later productions is usually Bulwer's Aram, although in a few instances Hood's morbid, less idealized figure is discernible as well.

A well-respected novel of 1855[31] is so similar to Bulwer's *Eugene Aram* in many ways that neither its author nor most of its audience could have been unmindful of the connection. The scholarly criminal of Mrs. Caroline Clive's *Paul Ferroll* is the undetected murderer of his wife. Like Aram, he is aloof, mysterious, fatalistic, egotistical, and cynical. Remorse does not trouble him, but only the threat his private guilt poses to his security. "Everything about me," he tells an acquaintance in a rare moment of confidence, "assures me there is a crisis coming in the grand malady of life. I have a struggle going on at this moment which no one can know or share."[32] Also like Aram, Paul Ferroll inhabits a private mansion whose central tower is transparently symbolic of his intellectual faculties. All London is eager to lionize him if only he would permit it:

A great deal of Mr. Ferroll's time was given up to literary employment; his name and fame as an author were some of the best parts of his existence, and made him necessary, as well as acceptable, in certain circles. He had written a few things which gave him fame, and from time to time there issued from the Tower a brilliant article, a few exquisite verses, or a fine fiction, which kept the attention of the reading public upon him. (p. 23)

Like Bulwer's novel, Clive's is a study in the unseen potential for violence that lurks in the heart of every human being, however rational: "How little we know of what passes in each other's minds" is her epigraph from Sidney Smith, recalling similar passages from Bulwer (cf. p. 70 above). That she drew from Bulwer seems plausible from a comparison of the two novels' opening paragraphs, each of which contemplates a luxuriant and tranquil rural scene whose sinister undertones are as yet only hinted. "In the county of _____," Bulwer begins,

there is a sequestered hamlet, which I have often sought occasion to pass, and which I have never left without a certain reluctance and regret. . . . I know not in any part of the world, which it has been my lot to visit, a landscape so entirely lovely and picturesque, as that which on every side of the village I speak of, you may survey. The hamlet to which I shall here give the name of Grassdale, is situated in a valley, which, for about the length of a mile winds among gardens and orchards laden with fruit, between two chains of gentle and fertile hills. (1, 3–4)

Bulwer's novel opens in the early summer; Clive, whose style might be easily mistaken for Bulwer's, achieves a similar effect of newness and (alas, false) innocence by starting at dawn:

Nothing looks more peaceful and secure than a country house seen at early morning. The broad daylight gives the look of safety and protection, and there is the tranquillity of night mixed with the brightness of day, for all is yet silent and at rest about the sleeping house. One glorious July morning saw this

calm loveliness brood over the Tower of Mainwarey. . . . It stood
in the midst of a garden bright with summer flowers, which at
this hour lifted their silver heads all splendid with dew and
sunshine; and it looked down the valley to the village, which
stood at a little distance, intersected and embowered with
orchards, and crowned with the spire of the church. (p. 1)

When Paul Ferroll's notoriously shrewish wife is found murdered
that peaceful morning in her bed, a gardener is accused of the crime but
later acquitted. Immediately afterwards the bereaved husband departs
"no one knew whither," and after "a considerable time" returns remarried
to his former sweetheart. Reestablished in the community, he demonstrates extraordinary courage aiding the victims of a cholera epidemic, but
his general charity, like Aram's, is offset by an avoidance of individual
intimacies. When, eighteen years after the fact, jewelry belonging to
Ferroll's late wife is found in the possession of the accused gardener's
widow, she in turn is charged with murder. Upon her conviction Ferroll
reveals his guilt to save her life, whereupon his second wife dies of grief.
He manages to escape execution, however, and emigrates to America like
a host of other unfortunates from nineteenth-century British novels. He
succumbs not long afterwards to a fever. "'Some men,'" he muses as death
approaches, "'will say I can be forgiven — some will say I cannot. I have
thought much. . . .There is a God, and *He* knows'" (p. 316).

Thus the central question, whether Heaven can forgive murder under
extraordinary circumstances, remains essentially open in Clive as in
Bulwer. Most of the clamor over the Newgate novel had subsided by the
1850s, and *Paul Ferroll*, despite its moral ambiguities, did not evoke widespread concern. Souring its generally too appreciative reception, however,
were two particularly hostile reviews. The *Athenaeum* was sarcastic,
expressing "some perplexity as to the author's intentions." Was her
purpose, it wondered, to prove that murder is "one of the rights of man"
or simply to "beg the question of capital punishment"?[33] The *Saturday
Review* was brutal, flatly indicting the book as a "nightmare"—
improbable, unnatural, and "very horrible, indeed."[34]

Somewhat as Bulwer was moved in the face of adverse criticism to
alter the ending of *Eugene Aram*, Mrs. Clive prepared a sequel to her
novel which attempts to reconcile some of the more obvious incongruities
of the original without assuming a definite moral stand. *Why Paul Ferroll
Killed His Wife* (1860) is a flashback whose primary purpose is to supply
a motive for the crime, although several of the central characters' names
are different and even the Paul Ferroll of the title, oddly, is Paul Leslie

in the text. This volume relates the consuming love affair of Paul and his first sweetheart/second wife, Elinor. The happiness of this pair is soon destroyed by the influence of Laura Chanson, a perfect vixen who, herself enamored of Paul, uses every deceitful stratagem to confound its progress. At length she succeeds, rather like Iago with Desdemona, in making Elinor appear unfaithful, whereupon Paul deliberately marries the wrong woman in a spirit of self-annihilation. After more than a year of utter misery with Laura, he discovers her deceit. Elinor, who has retired to a convent, of course refuses to forsake it for a married man. As the convent gates close behind her, leaving her lover distracted to the point of insanity, the stage is set for the beginning of the earlier companion volume:

> Violent were the passions of the strong but fettered man; fierce the hatred of the powerful but baffled intellect; wild was the fury of the man, who believed in but one world of good, and saw the mortal moments passing away, enenjoyed [*sic*], and irretrievable.
>
> Out of those hours arose a purpose. The reader sees the man, and knows the deed. From the premises laid before him, he need not have indeed concluded that even that man would do that deed; but since it was told, in 1855, that the husband killed the wife, so now, in 1860, it is explained *why* he killed her.[35]

The Paul Ferroll (or Leslie) of the 1860 sequel is a noticeably less sympathetic figure than the Paul Ferroll of 1855. There had been a good deal of justice in the critics' initial objection that a cold-blooded, remorseless murderer ought not to be depicted enjoying eighteen years of domestic bliss with his angelic new bride and finally escaping a felon's death without so much as a point to be made by it all. Therefore, intending to right the situation, Mrs. Clive now hopelessly entangled it by representing her hero as an infinitely unhappy man (in this period before the murder at least) whose agony of spirit was ample punishment for the evil he contemplated. The new Paul Ferroll was coldly intellectual and an apparent atheist who, shockingly for that time, "believed in but one world of good." And yet "even that man" would not necessarily do murder — if we didn't, that is, know otherwise. . . .

Despite the confusion that resulted from a retrospective sequel which altered the hero's entire nature and even his name without accounting for the change, the *Saturday Review* was placated. If murder, in its view, could not be forgiven, at least the lesser crimes of authorship could.

"We are glad," the reviewer of 1860 wrote, "that the author has made all the reparation she could for her former ambiguity of tone. And it is a pleasure to be able to discuss her new work without feeling that it is objectionable from a moral point of view." In fact, the reviewer was intoxicated with moral satisfaction. Mrs. Clive was not as bad a writer as she might seem, given her less than satisfactory handling of technical matters, but here she was praised out of all reason. In the current incarnation of Paul Ferroll the *Saturday Review* discovered "a picture of life and human nature as they might be if there were no God and no moral law!" Comparing the hero's passion for Elinor with Faust's fascination for Margaret, he found in the book itself "a power of psychological analysis which is almost unsurpassed." But the comment of most interest for our purposes is his disparaging allusion to another familiar prototype:

> The character of Paul Ferroll, as drawn in *Why Paul Ferroll Killed His Wife*, is infinitely superior as a work of art to that of Bulwer's Eugene Aram [*sic*], with which it may possibly be contrasted. Eugene Aram is a very lackadaisical and sentimental philosopher, who commits murder from feelings of maudlin philanthropy. No such being ever existed, or ever will exist, except in a lunatic asylum; and, in such a creation, Bulwer either misconceived, or else purposely departed from, the real historical original. But a Paul Ferroll may, we grieve to think, very well exist, and be highly respected in society, until he is found out, after which discovery society would not hesitate to hang him.[36]

However believable may have been the scholar-criminal drawn by Mrs. Clive, and however facile this reviewer's estimate of her success, both of them at least were looking in the right direction. Realism, which the *Saturday Review* had found lacking in her first work and somehow discovered in its sequel, was indeed the criterion for the modern novel, and it was the absolute lack of realism in Bulwer's impossibly ideal criminal hero that was already making him dated — a creature for the fantasy world of melodrama but not for serious art.

Murder, Mrs. Clive seems to have understood on second thought, could not be realistically reconciled with the positive attributes of a "hero" in the traditional benign sense of the term. Instead, the answer was not to submerge but to spotlight the character's evil propensities, making of him a kind of aberrant psychological case study — a chilling example of moral sickness that would be all the more devastating because the mind it infested was learned.

Several characters from better-known mid-nineteenth-century fiction, while they are not true Aram types like Paul Ferroll, deserve passing notice here for their distinct subsidiary relationships with the Aram tradition. At least two other novels, Dickens's *Barnaby Rudge* (1841) and Trollope's *Orley Farm* (1862), adopted the unusual narrative pattern of the undiscovered crime in order to explore the long-term effects of private guilt upon the human soul. Lady Mason, the tragic protagonist of *Orley Farm*, who forges her late husband's will in order to benefit her son, is generally unsuspected for twenty-five years. Like Bulwer's Aram, "she had striven to be true and honest,—true and honest with the exception of that one deed. But that one deed had communicated its poison to her whole life."[37] Although Trollope detested Bulwer, there are additional similarities in theme and execution between *Eugene Aram* and *Orley Farm*. Even the moral uncertainty that pervades the earlier work is present, more subtly, in the attitude of Furnival the barrister, Lady Mason's longtime friend. Half in love with her as he is, he struggles throughout the novel with, on the one hand, an irrepressible sense that she is blameless and, on the other, his unspoken awareness as a discerning professional that she is unquestionably guilty. An intriguing sidelight to this novel in relation to the present study appears in a minor character, an Old Bailey lawyer of unquestionable efficacy and unscrupulous means who is employed on Lady Mason's behalf. His name, which is just possibly a hidden jest, is Solomon Aram.

Rudge and two other Dickensian villains—Bill Sikes (in *Oliver Twist*, 1843–44)—are not of course scholarly criminals, but they have all been observed to recall the mad fears and deluded self-torment of Hood's compulsive soliloquist. Plagued, like the Aram in the poem, with terrifying visions of the victim's undying corpse, these are the sort of murderers who "walk the earth / Beneath the curse of Cain,— / With crimson clouds before their eyes, / And flames about their brain" (Hood, ll. 67–70). They suffer such tortures before their apprehension that, as Dickens says of Rudge, "nothing man has ever done to man in the horrible caprice of power and cruelty, exceeds [their] self-inflicted punishment."[38] Jonas Chuzzlewit, whose motivating interest is to hasten the fruition of his father's insurance policy, is obviously drawn from the real-life poisoner Thomas Griffiths Wainewright. But though Jonas attempts to poison his father and believes he has done so, the old man in fact dies of natural causes. Montague Tigg, whom he really does murder, is bludgeoned to death, like the Daniel Clarke in Hood, in a gloomy wooded setting symbolic of the dark, uncivilized recesses of the human soul. An obsessive preoccupation with the unburied dead body also links Chuzzlewit to the Hood prototype and of course to his earlier counterparts in Dickens:

> He tried — he had never left off trying — not to forget it was there, for that was impossible, but to forget to weary himself by drawing vivid pictures of it in his fancy: by going softly about it and about it among the leaves, approaching it nearer and nearer through a gap in the boughs, and startling the very flies that were thickly sprinkled all over it, like heaps of dried currants. His mind was fixed and fastened on the discovery, for intelligence of which he listened intently to every cry and shout; listened when any one came in or went out; watched from the window the people who passed up and down the street; mistrusted his own looks and words. And the more his thoughts were set upon the discovery, the stronger was the fascination which attracted them to the thing itself: lying alone in the wood. He was for ever showing and presenting it, as it were, to every creature whom he saw. "Look here! Do you know of this? Is it found? Do you suspect *me?*" If he had been condemned to bear the body in his arms, and lay it down for recognition at the feet of everyone he met, it could not have been more constantly with him, or a cause of more monotonous and dismal occupation than it was in this state of his mind.[39]

The next noteworthy appearance of the true Aram type, after *Paul Ferroll*, also occurs in the work of Charles Dickens, upon whom Bulwer has long been recognized as a significant influence. The two were close friends who shared active interests in many diverse areas, from the staging of amateur theatrical productions to the recruitment of government aid for impoverished authors. There are numerous clear instances in which Dickens's work was directly affected, for better or worse, by Bulwer's advice or example. One or two literary scholars have in fact attributed minor details in Dickens's novels to *Eugene Aram* in particular.[40] But they have missed the largest connection of all.

The triumph of the Aram theme in Dickens, and its one obvious appearance there, is the character of Bradley Headstone in *Our Mutual Friend* (1864–65). He shares with Aram and Paul Ferroll the dubious distinction of being a scholar as well as a murderer, but he is the first such creation outside of Hood to be represented as a schoolmaster besides. In several additional respects Headstone is much closer to the actual Eugene

Aram than any of Aram's other fictional counterparts. Like the historical murderer, Headstone comes from humble origins, and is consumed with a sense of social inferiority not only on that account but because of the awkwardly ambivalent position in which his profession places him. The relatively low social status of the teacher in nineteenth- as well as eighteenth-century England, which was precisely why Bulwer did not make his hero a schoolmaster, is a central issue in the development of Headstone's villainy.[41] His learning and acquired respectability have lifted him out of his original social class, yet his meager salary and common roots deny him the equal society of true gentlemen. Of such frustrations Headstone's crime is born—as was, no doubt, that of the original Aram. It is this prosaic quality in his make-up, in contrast to the abstract philosophy motivating Bulwer's hero, that makes Bradley Headstone so much more credible.

Headstone is introduced in the first chapter of Book II as a dangerously repressed Jekyll-and-Hyde personality, "a man of rapid passions and sluggish intelligence."[42] To outward appearance, he is rigidly "decent," but his inner nature, burning for release, is "fiery" and "animal" (pp. 217–218). He is, as his rival Eugene Wrayburn observes, "rather too passionate for a good schoolmaster'" (pp. 291–292). From day to day, Headstone carries out the duties of his profession "mechanically" (p. 217). In fact, the very restraint and regimentation inherent in his role as teacher contribute to the murderous intentions with which he dogs Wrayburn's footsteps night after night: "Tied up all day with his disciplined show upon him, subdued to the performance of his routine of educational tricks, encircled by a gabbling crowd, he broke loose at night like an ill-tamed wild animal" (p. 546).

Rejected by Lizzie Hexam and angered that Wrayburn, who is socially superior to them both, should lay claim to her affections, Headstone attempts to drown his antagonist and mistakenly believes for a time that he has succeeded. Like Bulwer's Aram and his Dickensian predecessors, this would-be homicide is remorseless, yet prey to feelings "more wearing and more wearisome than remorse." His greatest torment is the contemplation of detail:

> The state of that wretch who continually finds the weak spots in his own crime, and strives to strengthen them when it is unchangeable, is a state that aggravates the offense by doing the deed a thousand times instead of once; but it is a state, too, that tauntingly visits the offence upon a sullen unrepentant nature with its heaviest punishment every time. (pp. 708–709)

This preoccupation with minutiae attends him afterward in the classroom in a scene capitalizing on the incongruity of his presence there:

> . . . as he heard his classes, he was always doing the deed and doing it better. As he paused with his piece of chalk at the blackboard before writing on it, he was thinking of the spot, and whether the water was not deeper and the fall straighter, a little higher up, or a little lower down. He had half a mind to draw a line or two upon the board, and show himself what he meant. (p. 709)

The passage is reminiscent of Hood's schoolmaster, similarly distracted: "'. . . all that day I read in school, / But my thought was other where.'" (ll. 181–182).

Headstone's ultimate agony, as with Bulwer's hero before him, comes not from remorse at all but from the unavoidable human consequences of his crime. First, his prize pupil and only friend, guessing the truth, deserts him in a pathetic scene that leaves Headstone desolate and groveling upon the floor. Later the overwhelming realization that his deed has only hastened the marriage he hoped to prevent subjects him to recurring fits that are clearly symbolic of his spiritual infirmity. That Headstone finally drowns locked in a death-grip with the blackmailing Rogue Riderhood suggests not only their nefarious identification as alter egos, which many critics have noted, but also the idea, common to every rendering of the Aram theme, that the murderer inevitably destroys himself along with his victim.

Compared with Bulwer's Eugene Aram, Bradley Headstone is a far more sophisticated invention. While Bulwer's Aram is largely sympathetic, Headstone is, realistically, only pitiful. His character is developed with an objective mixture of restrained compassion and distaste. His temperament is inherently vicious, and the fact that he is psychologically aberrant is no excuse for his guilt. Dickens knew instinctively what Mrs. Clive had realized too late: that the only way to make a fictional murderer credible was to make him unpleasant. Bulwer, unable to reconcile the basic anomaly of the scholar-murderer's nature, had attempted to transcend it with speculative ethics. Dickens, on the contrary, painted Headstone as a real human being whose respectable exterior was at direct and dangerous variance with his vile hidden self, and so resolved the problem by making anomaly the very soul of his creation.

Noticeably absent from the episode of Bradley Headstone is the question so prominent in most other narratives associated with the Aram story, that is, whether crime may, under certain extraordinary circumstances, have justification. Several of the world's best writers have stood for or against the proposition that the welfare of society in general, or of a deprived and deserving member of it, can sometimes turn wrong to right. Others, in the tradition of the decadent romantic attitude of Napoleon-worship, have suggested that a man of unusual ability and intellect has a natural right to transcend the laws and conventional ethics of ordinary men, acting independently to his own advantage or in the service of his own ideals. Such varied figures at Balzac's Rastignac and Vautrin, Stendhal's Julien Sorel, Hugo's Jean Valjean and Claude Gueux, Schiller's Karl Moor, and even Doyle's sinister but gentlemanly criminal Moriarty have been governed by similar considerations. The continued vitality of related themes is evidenced in so recent a novel as Mario Puzo's *The Godfather*, whose contemporary success has been comparable to that of *Eugene Aram* in its century. His son defends the Mafia don on the ground that he could never accept the conventional life, a way "'not suitable to a man like himself, a man of extraordinary force and character. . . . he considers himself the equal of all those great men like Presidents and Prime Ministers and Supreme Court Justices and Governors of the States. He refuses to live by rules set up by others, rules which condemn him to a defeated life.'" The book's portrait of this cold but majestic figure bears out the defense, and yet the logical objection not surprisingly recalls Thackeray's rejoinder to Bulwer: "'But that's ridiculous,'" the son's fiancée says. "'What if everybody felt the same way?'"[43]

The notion that extraordinary individuals are answerable only to themselves received its most profound examination in 1866 with the publication of Dostoyevsky's *Crime and Punishment*. Here Dostoyevsky pointedly rejected the stance which Bulwer's *Eugene Aram* seemed to have adopted, however much Bulwer may have denied it, "'that there are persons who are able, or rather not who are able but who have every right, to commit any wrong or crime, and that laws, so to say, are not made for them.'"[44]

A number of published sources have drawn connections between Bulwer's hero and Dostoyevsky's anti-hero, one of which has maintained that it was almost certainly a case of conscious influence.[45] Unfortunately, nothing in Dostoyevsky's private writings confirms such a link, although it has long been established that he read widely in the English popular novels of the period, particularly Dickens,[46] and so it seems unlikely that he would have ignored a work as widely acclaimed at the time both at home and abroad as Bulwer's *Eugene Aram*. Still, the only support for those who would discern Aram in Raskolnikov rests in the striking similarity between the two novels. It is a likeness so great, in fact, that upon reading both together one can only conclude that Dostoyevsky, by coincidence or design, accomplished what Bulwer attempted.

Raskolnikov, like the Aram of the 1832 novel, is a former tutor who, chafing at the monotony of his duties, has given them up. Also like Aram, he talks to himself, avoids other people, and finally seizes upon crime as a desperate escape from intolerable circumstances. He premeditates murder out of a sense of his own superiority and justifies it by his undeserved poverty and the baseness of his victim. Like Aram, he is led into evil by his own entanglement in sophistries and his too-great dependence on logic—aspects which have led George Gibian to see Dostoyevsky's novel as an "attack against rationalism."[47] So enamored of the abstract was Bulwer's hero that he resented, above all, the degrading trivialities involved with committing and concealing homicide, and yet he gave voice to his resentment in only the most general terms. With Dostoyevsky, however, the sordid necessities are realized in abundant detail. The mundane act of "casing" the old pawnbroker's apartment during the planning stage of her murder, for example, disgusts Raskolnikov:

> He could hear her opening the chest of drawers. "That will be the top drawer," he fancied. "I know she keeps the keys in her right-hand pocket...There is one with toothed wards, three times as big as the others; that can't belong to the drawer, of course. There must be something else, a chest or a trunk...I wonder if there is. Those big wooden trunks always have that kind of key...All the same, how sickening all this is!..." (p. 6. Cf. Aram's speech, in italics, p. 76 above)

After the act, Raskolnikov's state of mind is also very similar to Aram's. He persists in denying remorse. "'Crime? What crime?'" he cries:

> "Killing a foul, noxious louse, that old moneylender, no good to anybody, who sucked the life-blood of the poor, so vile that killing her ought to bring absolution for forty sins—was that a crime? That is not what I am thinking of, and I do not think of atoning for it." (p. 438)

He further rationalizes murder with another of Aram's arguments, about the acceptability of wartime killing: "'I definitely don't understand why smashing people with bombs in a regular siege is formally more respectable!'" (p. 439). (Cf. p. 75 above.) The only guilt he feels is for bringing sorrow upon his family, and yet he learns, as the thinking criminal in fiction always seems to do, that the ultimate victim of the crime is his own lost soul: "'Did I murder the old woman? I killed myself, not that old creature! There and then I murdered myself at one blow, for ever!'" (p. 354).

Also like Aram before him, Raskolnikov is preoccupied with the workings of fate, which seems to have dictated his role in the murder. He experiences the uneasy feeling, first, that the present train of events is foreordained to make a killer of him and, later, that the same two-faced destiny has projected his apprehension and punishment. Several bizarre coincidences which further his plans suggest to Raskolnikov that fate has "laid an ambush for him" (p. 52). Any number of times after the crime he struggles with an almost undeniable urge to give himself up, and on several occasions he almost does so, like a moth fascinated with the flame. This amounts to a psychologically more subtle variation on Aram's ranting certainty that he is impelled toward an irrevocable end.

In other thematic respects as well, Dostoyevsky echoes and improves upon Bulwer. His interest in the eternal warfare of good and evil in the human heart, and Raskolnikov's in particular, recreates the central paradox of Aram's nature as Bulwer drew it: "'How could you give away your last penny, and yet commit murder for gain?'" Sonya asks (p. 348). The answer is the same in Raskolnikov's case as in Aram's: it is a matter of the greatest good for the greatest number. Throughout *Crime and Punishment* runs the issue of man's intellectual responsibility to sacrifice individual interests and employ any means to promote the general good. "'Kill [the old pawnbroker], take her money,'" the argument runs, "'on condition that you dedicate yourself with its help to the service of humanity and the common good....What is the life of that stupid, spiteful, consumptive old woman weighed against the common good?'" (p. 56). The doctrine of utilitarianism informed several different schools of belief and was as prominent in Russia at the time as it had been in England thirty years before.[48] Dostoyevsky's treatment of it is quite similar to Bulwer's. Both intended to demonstrate, by the self-destruction of a character who acts according to its precepts, that the utilitarian ethic is inherently unworkable, since man's limited perspective does not permit him to master fate or even foresee the consequences of his own actions. As Keith Hollingsworth has noted, the mental process of Aram's confession, which explains his utilitarian motive, "strikingly resembles, in outline, that of the later Raskolnikov."[49]

On a level more submerged than reason, however, Raskolnikov's dreams and meditations reveal that it is also and more accurately the predatory evil at the heart which compels him, in anger, to murder. That Aram's stated motive, his desire to benefit society, is developed almost exclusively of other considerations makes Bulwer's handling of the theme much less realistic and less sophisticated. As Régis Messac perceives it, much of the disturbing ambivalence of Bulwer's novel derives from the author's unconscious inability to accept his own idea that a good man may be led into crime for a worthy purpose.[50] The essential problem with Aram's characterization—the incompatibility of the two sides of his nature—Dostoyevsky finally resolves by making his murderer deranged. The physical sickness to which Raskolnikov is also subject is, like Bradley Headstone's fits, an outward manifestation of his inner madness. There is of course no hint in Bulwer's work of this entirely plausible explanation for the violent actions of such a protagonist.

Raskolnikov's crime, furthermore, is an individual—rather than, like Aram's, a conspiratorial—act. This facilitates the psychological study of Dostoyevsky's central character by focusing on the private workings of his mind divorced from outside influence. There is no tempting Houseman in *Crime and Punishment* to obscure the issue of the hero's guilt. Bulwer believed, as his prefaces indicate, that in *Eugene Aram* he was exploring the internal crisis of a guilty soul, but compared to this later work he had barely scratched its surface. These important considerations, along with Dostoyevsky's scrupulous attention to realistic detail—the introduction, for example, of Sonya and her pathetically destitute family in contrast to Bulwer's insipid love story—are the principal reasons why Dostoyevsky's novel so far outclasses Bulwer's, although they are in many respects so similar.

Of the four truest-to-type scholar-criminals in Western literature since 1832—Eugene Aram, Paul Ferroll, Bradley Headstone, and Rodion Raskolnikov—one is now utterly forgotten, and only two seem likely to further endure, for reasons that are by now obvious. And yet this category of fictional hero is hardly to be considered insignificant or defunct because of its relative rarity. There is a good deal of power still resident in the figure of the ingenious wrongdoer, grandly isolated and eternally at odds with conventional society. The *literatus* who ventures down such a road is the quintessence of the kind. He is twice removed from the ordinary—by mind as well as deed. When great intellect and great crime converge, the effect is profoundly disturbing. The scholar who stoops to crime exemplifies a crux of human nature. In his being the id and the super-ego, the beast and the angel, are perpetually at variance.

APPENDIX
Bibliographical Note
to Chapter 1

The biographical account in chapter 1 is woven from the truest strands in a tangle of sources. Those sources are here outlined.

The one primary record of Aram's life in full is the brief, hastily written autobiography in letter form which he composed at a friend's request while imprisoned in York Castle awaiting execution. The letter is reprinted from an eighteenth-century source in Eric Watson's *Eugene Aram*, pp. 181–185. Although the letter is almost certainly authentic, the published version is fragmentary, having undergone significant censorship by eighteenth-century editors. The original manuscript is lost. Despite its incompleteness and Aram's untrustworthiness, this is a valuable document, since it provides virtually the only information available regarding Aram's early years.

Journalism, the most obvious printed medium for the reporting of crime today, was yet in its infancy at the time of Aram's execution. The contemporary newspapers therefore are not a viable source. In researching the above-mentioned study for Hodge's Notable English Trials series just prior to the First World War, Watson investigated what contemporary newspapers were yet extant, the files of many for the appropriate dates having been lost or destroyed. Those accounts he was able to locate he found unsatisfactorily vague and frequently erroneous.

There were, however, from 1759 through the first decades of the twentieth century, numerous magazine articles with reference to Aram, as well as entries in biographical encyclopedias, various histories, legal works, and calendars of crime. These too are exhaustively catalogued in Watson, and many are still accessible. A few stand out in importance. The first issue of the *Annual Register*, dated 1759, carried an accurate, sober, and trustworthy report of the trial, as did the *Gentleman's Magazine*, the

London Magazine, and Smollett's *Critical Review*. Smollett's *History of England*, completed in 1765, cited the case as a remarkable recent instance of increasing disregard for law and order, and, like the *Critical Review*, presented a somewhat extravagant appraisal of Aram's scholarly potential. The *Newgate Calendar*, from its inception in 1773 through most of its later versions, chronicled the Aram story in sordid and often exaggerated detail, repeating almost the same account in each new edition.

Indeed, it is not unusual to find several different sources repeating each other almost verbatim. Although they occasionally shed new light on the events of Aram's life, they also — more frequently — compound the error and uncertainty that surround his history. So venerable a work as the *Dictionary of National Biography*, for example, reports that Houseman, Aram's accomplice, was the sole witness for the prosecution. This detail, significant in Bulwer's fictional version, is directly at variance with the trial reports, yet so common to such summaries of the case since Bulwer's time that it appears to have spread like contagion among them. Still less to be excused is the historian who wrote that Houseman, as well as Aram, was hanged (in *Yorkshire: West Riding*, ed. Arthur Mee, p. 222).

An important source from which periodical and encyclopedic articles were sometimes filched is the series of Aram "Life and Trial" pamphlets which poured off the presses, usually of York bookseller-publishers, in a steady stream from 1759 until well into the next century, even before the influence of Hood and Bulwer had been felt. These are the first and most valuable of the secondary materials which have come down to us from Aram's day, especially for the record they give us of the proceedings at Aram's trial. The most prominent of the eighteenth-century booksellers who profited from the convicted man's notoriety were Ann Ward, Charles Etherington, and Ely Hargrove. The Bristow version, named for its editor and sold in London for Ann Ward, became established as standard, but in actuality few editions differ markedly from the others. Some of these "Genuine Accounts," as they were also commonly titled, append letters and poems allegedly by Aram, or include anecdotes that others omit. Also, the language becomes modernized in later publications. But otherwise each is a nearly exact copy of its predecessors, in the form of a short biography which quotes Aram's autobiography to dispense with his formative years and then proceeds to revel moralistically in the infamy of his criminal career. The one anomaly is generally referred to as the "York Pamphlet," its publisher being unknown. This pamphlet, which appeared within a fortnight after Aram's execution, relates some interesting apocryphal episodes and tells its story with unusually intense hostility. In the Victorian era, after the 1832 publication of Bulwer's novel had mantled

Aram's villainy in a rosy romantic glow, his pamphlet biographies became decidedly more sympathetic. It seems a telling indictment that, in general, the further Aram receded in time, the better he looked.

Of all the biographical sources pertaining to Aram, Eric Watson's definitive 1913 legal study most nearly approaches objectivity, untainted by personal interest or sentimentality, although even there, behind the barrister's meticulous professionalism, is faintly discernible the bias of the prosecuting attorney as Watson in effect tries Aram's case anew. Yet this achievement, representing careful scrutiny of a wide range of printed materials, and dogged detective work among the very bones of Aram's victim, is surely by far the most important reference for any assessment of Aram's life.

NOTES

Introduction

1. In older usage the spelling is Knaresbrough or Knaresboro'. Clark's name in some accounts is spelled with a final *e*.

2. As quoted in Eric R. Watson, *Eugene Aram: His Life and Trial*, Notable English Trials Series (Edinburgh, 1913), p. 169.

3. *The Girlhood of Queen Victoria: A Selection from Her Majesty's Diaries Between the Years 1832 and 1840*, ed. Reginald Baliol Brett, 2nd viscount Esher (London, 1912), II, 83.

4. (London), II, 344.

5. J. S. Fletcher, *Picturesque History of Yorkshire* (London), III, 185.

6. Watson, p. 1.

Chapter 1

1. From Aram's autobiography, reproduced in Watson. See Appendix. Subsequent references from the autobiography are to Watson's version. My research has largely verified the genealogy Aram cites, obscure facts of which another writer would hardly have been in possession and whose accuracy is therefore a strong indication that the autobiography is authentic.

2. (Edinburgh, 1914–65), V, Part II, 51–52. Other charters in Farrer record grants by early members of the Aram family to other abbeys. This reference is the only one which specifically mentions St. Mary's.

3. Michael Fryer, *The Trial and Life of Eugene Aram* (Richmond, Eng.: M. Bell, 1832), p. 51n. I have found no record that an Aram was ever sheriff of Nottinghamshire as Aram seems to claim, nor have I been able to identify the Oxford professor of divinity to whom he also alludes.

4. "John de Averham, 21 E. 3. [the twenty-first year of Edward III's reign, i.e., 1348]...the collectors charged with the payment of 6 £ for three knight's fees of John de Moubray." This entry from Robert Thoroton's *History of Nottinghamshire* (Nottingham, 1790–97), III, 109, which perfectly accords with Aram's claim, may well represent the advent of the Aram family in that county. I have located no record of the surname there prior to the mid-fourteenth century.

5. Thomas Aram appears in Foster's *Gray's Inn* register for Nov. 25, 1682. Collins's *Peerage* (London, 1735), II, Part 2, p. 814, further records in the same year the marriage of "*Thomas Aram of Gray's-Inn*, Esq.; and, in Right of his Wife, of the *Weld* [*sic*] in the county of *Hertford*."

6. John Nichols, ed., *Literary Anecdotes of the Eighteenth Century* (London, 1812–15), III, 722.

7. *Eugene Aram*, p. 7.

8. From a deposition in Norrisson Scatcherd, *Memoirs of the Celebrated Eugene Aram: With the "Gleanings" After Eugene Aram*, 2nd ed. (Harrogate, 1871), p. 52.

9. Fryer, p. 54n.

10. Fletcher, III, 185.

11. Scatcherd, pp. 42, 44, and 48.

12. Scatcherd, p. 44.

13. Scatcherd, p. 72.

14. Scatcherd, p. 44.

15. *The Genuine and Authentic Account of the Murder of Daniel Clarke* (York: "Printed for, and sold by the Booksellers," [1759]), p. 9. Hereafter identified as the York Pamphlet. See Appendix.

16. Scatcherd, p. 45.

17. York Pamphlet, p. 19.

18. York Pamphlet, p. 33.

19. Both statements are from the official legal records pertaining to the Aram trial, which are reproduced in Watson, pp. 149–169. Subsequent references from pretrial examinations are to this source. Of the trial itself there is no formal transcript, only the reports of unofficial observers.

20. York Pamphlet, p. 37.

21. Although few inhabitants of Knaresborough are now aware of its significance, St. Robert's Cave, where Clark was presumably murdered and buried, still exists on the northern bank of the Nidd, approximately 100 yards west of Grimbald Bridge. Its narrow entrance is accessible by means of stone steps descending from the road above. Robert Flower (1160?–1218), for whom the cave was named and who is said to have carved the steps himself, was a hermit who withdrew here for a time as part of his ascetic regimen. The cave's single compartment is approximately round, and so small that a person of average height can easily touch the ceiling.

22. This is according to Aram's statement to the authorities upon his arrest in 1758. There he also claimed to have spent in London the entire twelve-year period between his removal from Knaresborough and his appointment at Lynn. His autobiography contradicts both points: it does not refer to the visit to Nottinghamshire, and does mention several other places where he resided before moving to Lynn.

23. York Pamphlet, pp. 38–45.

24. York Pamphlet, pp. 12–13.

25. Aram's "Essay Towards a Lexicon upon an Entirely New Plan" is reprinted in full in Watson, pp. 188–203, from which the quoted passages are taken.

26. Rayner Heppenstall, "The Children of Gomer," *Times Literary Supplement*, Oct. 17, 1958, p. 600.

27. Scatcherd, p. 61.

28. Watson, p. 35.

29. *Eugene Aram*, pp. 36–39.

30. York Pamphlet, pp. 11–12.

31. Fryer, p. 14n.

32. The Bell, now the Crown Hotel, still stands in Knaresborough's High Street.

33. *Memoirs*, p. 40.

34. *Eugene Aram*, p. 60.

35. The young Paley was so fascinated by Aram's case that, despite his characteristic clumsy horsemanship, he borrowed his father's mare and rode sixty miles across country, "taking many a tumble along the way," to be present at the proceedings. On his return, he is said to have "entertained and astonished all around him, by his spirited harangues and judicious remarks on this important trial." George Wilson Meadley, *Memoirs of William Paley, D.D.* 2nd ed. (Edinburgh, 1810), pp. 8–9.

36. This and subsequent passages from Aram's defense speech are quoted from Watson, pp. 91–98.

37. Aram does not mention the possibility that these bones belonged to the ascetic tenant for whom the cave was named, doubtless because he knew the local tradition that Robert Flower (see n. 21 above) had been buried in the narrow tomb carved by his own hand from the indigenous rock in front of the cave and still visible there.

38. Fryer, pp. 45–46.

39. *The Complete Works*, ed. P. P. Howe (London, 1933), XVII, 130–131; and VIII, 314.

40. "*Eugene Aram* — Mr. Bulwer's New Novel," *Tatler*, 4 (1832); rpt. in *Leigh Hunt's Literary Criticism*, ed. Lawrence and Carolyn Houtchens (New York, 1956), p. 397. Some have, in fact, doubted the authorship of Aram's speech, albeit with little foundation. (See Watson, pp. 98–99.)

41. Archibald Bolling Shepperson, *The Novel in Motley* (Cambridge, Mass., 1936), p. 210.

42. Fryer, p. 46. Here the judge himself seems to imply that Aram's speech was ghostwritten.

43. Fryer, p. 47.

44. "The remarkable trial of Eugene Aram," *The Annual Register...of the Year 1759*, 2nd ed. (London, 1760), p. 362.

45. York Pamphlet, p. 55.

46. Quoted from W. Bristow, ed., "The Genuine Account of the Life and Trial of Eugene Aram, School-Master," (London, [1759]), p. 32.

47. Watson, p. 119, mentions in this connection the two French writers but does not identify them.

48. One source differs interestingly in a single detail from this, the usual version. Capt. A. W. Twyford's *York and York Castle: An Appendix to the 'Records of York Castle'* (London, [1883]) states, p. 24, that Aram used a "steel pen" to cut himself. Since Aram was allowed writing materials in his cell and was in fact writing on the eve of his execution, this explanation is at least as plausible as the common one and certainly more appropriate to the story.

49. Bristow, p. 48.

50. *Memoirs*, p. 45.

51. "Eugene Aram: Phrenology," *Literary Gazette*, Jan. 21, 1832, p. 25.

52. Harry Speight, *Nidderdale and the Garden of the Nidd: a Yorkshire Rhineland* (London, 1894), p. 476.

53. *Memoirs*, p. 31.

Chapter 2

1. *The Great Doctor Burney* (London, 1948), I, 84.

2. *Interpretations of Literature* (1915; rpt. Port Washington, N.Y., 1965), I, 204.

3. Ian Ousby, *Bloodhounds of Heaven: The Detective in English Fiction from Godwin to Doyle* (Cambridge, Mass., 1976), p. 20.

4. Keith Hollingsworth, *The Newgate Novel 1830–1847* (Detroit, 1963), p. 12.

5. Julian Symons, *Mortal Consequences: A History—From the Detective Story to the Crime Novel* (New York, 1972), p. 19.

6. Eric Rothstein, "Allusion and Analogy in the Romance of *Caleb Williams*," *University of Toronto Quarterly*, 37 (Oct., 1967), 18–30.

7. See James Walton, "'Mad Feary Father': *Caleb Williams* and the Novel Form," *Romantic Reassessment*, Salzburg Studies in English Literature, No. 47 (Salzburg, 1975), pp. 1–61.

8. From *Political Justice*, as quoted by Robert Naylor Whiteford, *Motives in English Fiction* (New York, 1918), p. 197.

9. *Caleb Williams*, ed. David McCracken (London, 1970), p. 3. Subsequent references are to this edition.

10. *William Godwin: His Friends and Contemporaries* (London, 1876), II, 304–305.

11. Godwin cites (p. 180) the biography of Brightwel (Godwin's spelling) in the 1779 edition of the *Newgate Calendar* as the real counterpart to that of his fictional soldier. The same edition of the *Calendar* (then titled *The Malefactor's Register*) includes an account of Aram (IV, 131–147) as well as of Brightwell (I, 382–387) and Jack Sheppard (I, 392–410).

12. In casting Caleb as a philologist Godwin may also have had in mind his friend Horne Tooke, a noted linguistic scholar and fellow radical "to whose etymological conversation and various talents" Godwin declared himself "greatly indebted"—as quoted by George Woodcock, *William Godwin: A Biographical Study* (London, 1946), p. 41.

13. *Memoirs of Bryan Perdue: A Novel* (London, 1805), II, 188. Subsequent page references will be to this, the first and only edition.

14. Bowring and Barton quoted in Walter Jerrold, *Thomas Hood: His Life and Times* (London, 1907), pp. 238–239.

15. Sir Thomas Noon Talfourd, *Memoirs of Charles Lamb*, ed. Percy Fitzgerald (London, 1892), p. 215.

16. Austin Dobson, *Fanny Burney* (London, 1903), p. 9.

17. *Memoirs*, p. 215.

18. *The Letters of Thomas Hood*, ed. Peter F. Morgan (Toronto, 1973), p. 539.

19. "The Dream of Eugene Aram, The Murderer," *Selected Poems of Thomas Hood*, ed. John Clubbe (Cambridge, Mass., 1970), pp. 160–169. Clubbe's text is the 1831 edition, accompanied by Harvey's carefully interpretive illustrations. This anthology is the source for subsequent references.

20. Lloyd N. Jeffrey, *Thomas Hood*, Twayne's English Authors Series (New York, 1972), p. 81.

21. This detail, it would seem, is anachronistic. *Der Tod Abels* (1758) enjoyed much success in England from its first appearance and was still popular in Hood's time. It is hardly possible that the boy was reading it in German, however, and the English translation (1761) did not appear until two years after Aram's death.

22. Lafcadio Hearn ("interpreter of the Western world to Japan"!) grossly misunderstood the poem's conclusion to mean that the boy had gone home and given information leading to Aram's arrest. I, 206.

23. Quoted in Anne Renier, *Friendship's Offering: An Essay on the Annuals and Gift Books of the 19th Century* (London, 1964), p. 13.

24. *Letters*, pp. 249 and 351.

25. *Letters*, pp. 456–457.

26. Stanley Weintraub, *Beardsley: A Biography* (New York, 1967), p. 13.

27. Richard D. Altick, *Victorian Studies in Scarlet* (New York, 1970), pp. 212–213.

28. M[aurice] Wilson Disher, *Melodrama: Plots That Thrilled* (London, 1954), p. 152.

29. Austin Brereton, *The Life of Henry Irving* (London, 1908; rpt. New York, 1969), II, 274.

30. "The Judgement of Paris," *Temple Bar*, 40 (1875), 400.

31. *Personal Reminiscences of Henry Irving* (New York, 1906), I, 30–31.

32. *Oscar Wilde: A Summing-Up* (London, 1940), p. 132.

33. "'Sikes and Nancy,' Dickens's Last Reading," *Times Literary Supplement*, June 11, 1971, p. 682.

34. *Thomas Hood* (London, 1963), p. 186. For further discussion of the Aram influence on Dickens (through Bulwer as well as Hood) see pp. 159–162 below.

35. The most current is the Clubbe anthology (1970) previously cited. Although the poem, as might be expected, has appeared less frequently with the passing years, it was included in at least six British and American anthologies published during the 1940s, as well as a few more recent collections: Burton Stevenson's *The Home Book of Verse*, 9th ed. (New York, 1953); Russell Noyes's *English Romantic Poetry and Prose* (New York, 1956); and William Cole's *Story Poems, New and Old* (Cleveland, Ohio, 1957).

Chapter 3

1. At the end of his career, his full name was Edward George Earle Lytton Bulwer-Lytton. Upon inheriting Knebworth, the ancestral estate, from his mother in 1843, he had hyphenated with the patronymic, Bulwer, her family surname, Lytton. He was also, after 1838, addressed as a baronet—and, after 1866, as a baron. In the interest of simplicity, I refer to him throughout as Edward Bulwer, by which name he was generally known during the years most pertinent to this

study.

2. Matthew Whiting Rosa, *The Silver-Fork School* (New York, 1936) p. 74; and Keith Hollingsworth, *The Newgate Novel*, p. 65.

3. From Christensen's thesis as expressed in the centennial essay, "Edward Bulwer-Lytton of Knebworth 25 May 1803–18 January 1873," *Nineteenth-Century Fiction*, 28 (1973), 85–86.

4. The first phrase appeared in *Pelham* (1828). The second is from a letter written in 1842 to John Forster in 1842, quoted by Victor Lytton, *The Life of Edward Bulwer* (London, 1913), II, 35.

5. *Pencillings by the Way*, Letter CXIX (1835); rpt. in *Library of Literary Criticism*, ed. Charles Moulton (New York, 1966), III, 485.

6. "Lord Lytton," *Belgravia*, 20 (1873), 74.

7. "Confessions and Observations of a Water-Patient," *New Monthly Magazine*, n.s. 75 (1845), 3.

8. *Bulwer: A Panorama* (Boston, 1931), p. 247.

9. In a letter quoted by Paul, II, 302. Paul does not record the date of the letter. Lady Caroline died in 1828.

10. For discussion of the utilitarian aspects of Godwin's thought, see D. H. Monro, in *Godwin's Moral Philosophy* (London, 1953), p. 15 and *passim*; and K. Codell Carter, introducing his edition of *Political Justice* (Oxford, 1971), p. xiii.

11. In a letter of May 13, 1830, quoted by Paul, II, 306.

12. *The Newgate Novel*, pp. 71–73. Louis Cazamian's venerable study, *The Social Novel in England, 1830–1850*, tr. Martin Fido (London, 1973), which first appeared in 1903, isolates *Paul Clifford* as marking "the point when utilitarianism became genuinely influential in literature" (p. 41).

13. Paul, II, 305.

14. From the 1833 appendix to *Eugene Aram* (London: Chapman and Hall, 1849), p. 277. Subsequent references to the dramatic fragment are to this edition. In the text, some scenes are unnumbered. I have supplied these numbers as well as all line numbers.

15. Unless otherwise specified, my text for *Eugene Aram* the novel is the first edition, 3 vols. (London: Colburn and Bentley, 1832). Since this and even the standard editions of Bulwer's works are difficult to locate, I ordinarily cite not the page numbers but the book and the chapter in which the passage occurs. (*Eugene Aram* is divided into five books.)

16. The 1840 preface to *Eugene Aram* (London, 1849), p. xiii.

17. From the chapter's epigraph, a quotation from *Richard II*. This and all the passages from Aram's "confession" which follow are from Book 5, chapter 7.

18. *Victorian Conventions* (Athens, Ohio, 1975), p. 95.

19. "*Eugene Aram* — Mr. Bulwer's New Novel," p. 396.

20. Textual evidence suggests that Bulwer's earliest plan was not, as he ultimately decided, to make Madeline and Ellinor the daughters of Squire Lester, and Walter their orphaned cousin. On several occasions in the first edition Squire Lester and Walter are erroneously referred to as father and son (vol. I, 100, 113; II, 4), and Madeline and Ellinor call Lester their uncle (II, 89, 123, 140. The latter instance remained uncorrected in the 1849 edition, p. 139). Reference is similarly made to Geoffrey Lester's (alias Daniel Clarke's) "children" (I, 14), meaning, presumably, Madeline and Ellinor. Later this was corrected to "child." Originally, it seems, Bulwer intended Aram to have murdered his fiancée's father rather than

her uncle. But this would place Walter in the position of avenging his *uncle's* death and therefore would somewhat weaken the role he plays at the end of the novel.

21. "The Late Lord Lytton as a Novelist," *The Cornhill Magazine*, 27 (1873), 345–354; rpt. in *Men, Books, and Mountains*, ed. Samson O. A. Ullman (Minneapolis, 1956), p. 119.

22. See p. 2 above. For the deposition, see Watson, pp. 158–159.

23. "The Late Lord Lytton," p. 119.

24. Whiteford, p. 271.

25. 1840 preface to *Pelham*, ed. Jerome J. McGann (Lincoln, Neb., 1972), pp. 451–452.

26. In later editions this is Book 3, chapter 2, misnumbered in the first edition. (In the first edition, the chapter numbers in Book 3 begin with chapter 9, continuing in sequence from Book 2, whose last chapter is 8. Each of the other four books begins with chapter 1.)

27. *Dickens, Reade and Collins, Sensation Novelists* (New York, 1919), p. 164 and *passim*.

28. Book 3, chapter 2, in later editions. (See n. 26.)

29. Book 3, chapter 7, in later editions. (See n. 26.) Cf. also the historical parallel, p. 27 above.

30. As quoted from an unspecified writing in Victor Lytton, *Life*, I, 349.

Chapter 4

1. *Monthly Chronicle*, 1 (1838), 42–51 and 138–149.

2. The 1840 preface to *Eugene Aram* (London, 1849), p. xi.

3. J. C. Reid, *Thomas Hood* (London, 1963), p. 104.

4. "Modern Novelists: Sir Edward Bulwer-Lytton," *Westminster Review*, 83 (1865), 476.

5. In a letter of 1842, quoted in S. M. Ellis, *William Harrison Ainsworth and His Friends* (London, 1911), II, 63.

6. *The Life and Letters of John Gibson Lockhart*, ed. Andrew Lang (London, 1897), II, 35–36.

7. Preface to *Night and Morning*, Saint Botolph ed. (Boston, 1897), pp. xiv–xv.

8. Unpublished letter. National Library of Scotland. MS. Blackwoods Correspondence 4086/165. For this source I am indebted to Sybilla Jane Flower.

9. Jared B. Flagg. *The Life and Times of Washington Allston* (New York, 1892), p. 414.

10. *Felix Holt, The Radical*, ed. Peter Coveney, Penguin English Library ed. (Harmondsworth, Middlesex, 1972), p. 183.

11. Victor Lytton, *Life*, I, 389.

12. *Henry Crabb Robinson: On Books and Their Writers*, ed. Edith J. Morley (London, 1938; rpt. New York, 1967), I, 401.

13. January 22, 1832, pp. 51–52.

14. February, 1832, p. 302.

15. "*Eugene Aram* — Mr. Bulwer's New Novel," p. 400.

16. April, 1832, pp. 214–215.

17. Volume 5 (1832), 16–19.

18. January 7, 1832, pp. 4–5.

19. *Popular Fiction 100 Years Ago* (London, 1957), p. 170.

20. January, 1831, p. 714.

21. [William Makepeace Thackeray], "*Ernest Maltravers*," *Fraser's Magazine*, 17 (1838), 85–86.

22. See Cheryl Lively, "Truth in Writing: The Standard of Realism for the Novel in *Fraser's Magazine*, 1830–1850," *Victorian Periodicals Newsletter*, 6 (1973), 3–10.

23. See Sadleir, ch. VI and *passim*; and Miriam M. H. Thrall, *Rebellious Fraser's*, Columbia Univ. Studies in English and Comparative Literature, No. 117 (New York, 1934), *passim*. Sadleir is noticeably biased in favor of Bulwer, while Thrall is perhaps too eager to justify *Fraser's*, and particularly its editor, William Maginn.

24. Volume 4, two unnumbered pages preceding p. 641. (*Fraser's* pagination from the end of one month to the beginning of the next is erratic and sometimes, as in this case, duplicates the page numbers in two separate issues.) Colburn was Bulwer's publisher at the time. "*Liston* Bulwer" is a tag which recurs in *Fraser's* over the next ten years. The humor lies in the incongruous association of the genteel novelist with John Liston, a frustrated tragic actor turned popular comedian who played bumpkins, clowns, and comic servants. A review of Bulwer's *Ernest Maltravers* by Thackeray in 1838 (*Fraser's*, 17, 85–89) extends the comparison by noting that Bulwer, "like Liston or Cruikshank, and other comic artists, persists that his real vein is the sublime" (p. 85).

25. Volume 5, 107–113. For the question of authorship see Sadleir, p. 253; and Thrall, p. 304.

26. *Bulwer: A Panorama*, p. 253.

27. The three most important recent authorities are of the opinion that Thackeray did not write *Elizabeth Brownrigge*: Thrall, pp. 62–64; Hollingsworth, *The Newgate Novel*, pp. 95 and 244n.83; and Gordon Ray, whose biography *Thackeray: The Uses of Adversity* (New York, 1955) silently disdains mention of the parody. Thrall and Hollingsworth concur in attributing it to Maginn.

28. Volume 6, 144. (*Elizabeth Brownrigge* appeared in *Fraser's* in Aug. and Sept., 1832, pp. 67–88 and 131–148. Page references are to this publication.)

29. Ed. Standish Meacham (Chicago, 1970), pp. 211–212.

30. The phrase is from the 1845 dedication to *Zanoni* (Boston, 1932), p. vii.

31. In "The New Timon, and the Poets" (signed "ALCIBIADES"), *Punch*, 10 (1846); rpt. in Sir Charles Tennyson's "Tennyson and 'The New Timon,'" *The Nineteenth Century and After*, 109 (1931), 756–764. The lines from which the present chapter takes its title read: "A lion, you, that made a noise, / and shook a mane en papillotes."

32. James and Horace Smith, *Rejected Addresses* (facsim. New York, 1977), p. 111.

33. Page 136. Page references are to *Punch*, 12 (1847), 136–137, 146–147, and 155.

34. The similarity was first pointed out by Anthea Trodd, "Michael Angelo Titmarsh and the Knebworth Apollo," *Costerus*, n.s. 2 (1974), 60.

35. Page 48.

36. *Monthly Chronicle*, 1 (1838), 48.

37. *Dickens, Reade and Collins*, pp. 170–171.

38. (London, 1849), pp. xi and xii.

39. Bulwer had written, in the Dedicatory Epistle to *The Last of the Barons* in 1843: "This fiction is probably the last with which I shall trespass upon the public." Saint Botolph ed. (Boston, 1898), p. xxiii.

40. *Thackeray: The Uses of Adversity* (New York, 1955), I, 393; *The Newgate Novel*, p. 217; and "Michael Angelo Titmarsh," pp. 70–74.

41. Misnumbered in the 1832 edition as 4.10.

Chapter 5

1. The manuscript letter is one of three in his hand disputing the same matter, affixed to a copy of James Inglis's *Phrenological Observations on the Skull of Eugene Aram* (London, 1838) in the library of the University of Illinois. This copy originally belonged to the recipient of the letters attached to it: Effingham Wilson, Walker's cousin, who was a friend of Jeremy Bentham and well known in his time as a London publisher and bookseller. Wilson's inscription on the reverse of the pamphlet's front cover asserts his promised right to the possession of Aram's skull, an issue which so preoccupied him throughout much of his life that it was even mentioned in his obituary (*Bookseller*, July 1, 1868, p. 459). Each of Walker's letters denying his claim becomes increasingly terse and less cordial. Walker kept the skull only until Wilson's death, soon after which he perversely donated it to the Museum of the Royal College of Surgeons in London, where it is still on exhibit. Walker's letter of Dec. 9, 1869, offering the skull to the museum, remarks particularly that "a second cousin of mine, used often to teaze me to give it to him"– quoted in Jessie Dobson, "Eugene Aram," *Annals, Royal College of Surgeons, England*, 10 (1952), 273.

2. *The Diary of Joseph Farington*, ed. Kenneth Garlick and Angus Macintyre (New Haven, 1979), V. 1,603.

3. Page iii.

4. The pamphlet is listed in an Aram bibliography in Speight's *Nidderdale*, p. 250.

5. *Trial and Life*, p. 48n.

6. *Eugene Aram*, p. v.

7. *Memoirs*, p. 3.

8. *Memoirs*, pp. 3 and 32.

9. Volume 102 (1832), 448. The Sept., 1837, account is reprinted in *N&Q*, ser. 6, xi (1885), 131.

10. Arthur H. Norway, *Highways and Byways in Yorkshire* (London, 1890), p. 390.

11. By J. M. Richardson, quoted in a review of Escott's *Edward Bulwer, N&Q*, ser. 11, i, (1910), 280.

12. Quoted in Jessie Dobson, p. 272.

13. Series 1, ii (1850), 361. See also ser. 1, ii (1850), 310, and x (1854), 361.

14. Series 6, xi (1885), 47, 131–132, and 254.

15. *Trial and Life*, p. 3.

16. "The Decay of Murder," *Cornhill*, 20 (1869), 724. The real Clark was, of course, a young newlywed of twenty-three.

17. Series 11, ii (1910), 105 and 319.

18. "Eugene Aram: Phrenology," p. 25.

19. See Watson, pp. 176–177, *"Extract from the Morning Chronicle for 25th August, 1838, reporting a meeting of the British Association."* Effingham Wilson's marginalia in the University of Illinois copy of the Inglis pamphlet contradict several of Inglis's details relevant to the successive ownership of the skull, although John Walker's letter to the Royal College of Surgeons seems to support Inglis on those same points. Regardless, it is now almost certain that the skull which the phrenologists examined and which today forms a part of the Hunterian Museum collection (No. 446 [ex. 337]) at the Royal College of Surgeons is the same that Hutchinson salvaged from the gibbet. At some time in its more recent history, however, perhaps during the bombing of the museum in 1941, the skull appears to have suffered damage, for Dobson's article in the RCS *Annals* of April, 1952, describes and pictures it as missing "the facial parts, save for a small part of the left maxilla and nasal bone, and the mandible" (p. 273), whereas Inglis's engravings represent the facial bones intact.

20. Quoted in Inglis, pp. 24 and 21–22. Inglis conveniently underplays such contradictory points in the cited testimony of other practitioners, explaining that "Phrenologists differ not in the developements they take, but often in the characters they form from such developements" (p. 24).

21. James Roose-Evans, *London Theatre from the Globe to the National* (Oxford, 1977), p. 77.

22. Allardyce Nicoll, *British Drama*, 6th ed. rev. (London, 1978), p. 158.

23. (London, 1965), p. 122.

24. *N&Q*, [continuous ser.], clxxxvii (1944), 182.

25. February 9, 1832, p. 3, col. 2. A commentator for the *Sunday Times*, which was usually less discriminating than its daily namesake, turned in a blandly favorable report for the issue of Feb. 12, p. 3, col. 4.

26. See J. R. Stephens, "Jack Sheppard and the Licensers: The Case against Newgate Plays," *Nineteenth Century Theatre Research*, 1 (1973), 1–13.

27. On Purkess, see Montague Summers, *A Gothic Bibliography* (London, [1941]), p. 132. The four acting editions were Cumberland's Minor Theatre (later called French's Acting Edition)—five separate printings 1832–187?; Richardson's New Minor Drama—three separate printings in 1832; Dicks' Standard Plays—one printing in 1883(?); and Lacy's Acting Edition—one printing in 1850(?). Later in the century, new plays were intentionally withheld from print as a protective measure, since it was a punishable offense for a rival company to stage an uncopyrighted drama that had never been published.

28. [Advertisement], *Times*, Feb. 13, 1832, p. 2, col. 4.

29. [Advertisement], *Times*, May 14, 1832, p. 4, col. 5. *Eugene Aram* was revived briefly at Sadler's Wells in 1836.

30. Frank Rahill, *The World of Melodrama* (University Park, Pa., 1967), p. xv.

31. *The Scenic Art: Notes on Acting and the Drama: 1872–1901*, ed. Allan Wade (New York, 1957), pp. 160 and 220.

32. *The Drama of Yesterday & To-day* (London, 1899), II, 69.

33. "Eugene Aram at the Lyceum," *Times*, April 21, 1873, p. 8, col. 4.

34. In later revivals of the play, their path was lit by the feeble rays of what was once the real Aram's lantern. The lantern belonged to Sir Henry Irving, to whom it was given by a Mr. Aldam Heaton of Bingley. Heaton had acquired it

upon the death, in 1882, of its previous owner, his friend Dante Gabriel Rossetti. After Irving's death, in 1905, the lantern was bought by Messrs. Henry Sotheran & Company, London. See Harry Speight, *Upper Nidderdale* (London, 1906), pp. 76 and 326; an illustration of the lantern appears on p. 326.

35. "Mr. Wills's New Drama," *Sunday Times*, April 27, 1873, p. 3, col. 1.

36. Madeleine Bingham, *Henry Irving and the Victorian Theatre* (London, 1978), p. 141.

37. Volume 62 (April, 1873), 402.

38. [Frances Cashel Hoey], "Eugene Aram," *Temple Bar*, 38 (June, 1873), 394–397).

39. [Joseph Knight], *Athenaeum*, April 26, 1873, pp. 543–544.

40. "*Eugene Aram* at the Lyceum," *Saturday Review*, 35 (April, 1873), 550–551.

41. *The Scenic Art*, p. 106.

42. *Henry Irving* (New York, 1930), pp. 60, 67–68, and 74.

43. *Henry Irving*, p. 64.

44. [Review of *Daddleton's Difficulties* (second piece to Wills's *Eugene Aram*)], *Sunday Times*, May 18, 1873, p. 3, col. 3.

45. "Theatricals" column, *Sunday Times*, May 4, 1873, p. 3, col. 2.

46. [Review of *The Ku-Klux-Klan*], *Sunday Times*, May 18, 1873, p. 3, col. 3.

47. Erroll Sherson, *London's Lost Theatres of the Nineteenth Century* (London, 1925), p. 10.

48. [Advertisement], *Sunday Times*, May 11, 1873, p. 4, col. 2.

49. A. E. Wilson, *East End Entertainment* (London, 1954), p. 170.

50. *Crime and the Drama, or Dark Deeds Dramatized* (London, 1927), p. 34.

51. Malcolm Morley, *Margate and its Theatres, 1730–1965* (London, 1966), p. 125 and *passim*.

52. Newton, p. 35.

53. January 25, 1902, p. 10, col. 5.

54. Page 4, col. 2.

55. [H. A. K.], "Plays and Players," *Sunday Times*, Jan. 19, 1902, p. 6, col. 1.

56. January 25, 1902, p. 124.

57. "Mr. Martin Harvey as Eugene Aram," *Illustrated London News*, 120 (Jan. 25, 1902), p. 118.

58. *The Oxford Companion to the Theatre*, ed. Phyllis Hartnoll, 3rd ed. (London, 1967).

59. *Bertie Wooster Sees It Through* (London, 1946), p. 55; *So Much Blood* (New York, 1976), *passim*.

60. Curtis Dahl, "Edward Bulwer-Lytton," in *Victorian Fiction: A Guide to Research*, ed. Lionel Stevenson (Cambridge, Mass., 1964), p. 33.

61. In evidence of the very worst that Aram could inspire, they are here reproduced:

> "*St Robert's* cave good pilgrims mark—
> *Another* claims it for his own,
> The murder site of Daniel Clarke,
> T'was there he breathed his dying groan.

But, in the days of Socialism,
Theft will be virtue, murder law,
And faith, merged in materialism,
With Moses' ten commandments thaw!

For, with the covetous content!
Stealing and murder no more barred,
Each thief will have his monument,
Each murderer his *State* reward!

Then not the *murderer's*, or the *saint's*,
This cave with Socialism will be,
But his—the *murderer*, fiction paints—
Aram, the greatest of the three!"

Knaresborough Castle: With Introduction on the Feudal System, Reform of the House of Lords, Socialism, the Referendum, and Cabinet Reform (Bristol, 1915), pp. 184–185.

Chapter 6

1. The letter, to a Dr. Philipps, is reproduced in the *Gentleman's Magazine*, 59 (1789), 905, under the heading, "Original Letters of Eminent Persons on Welsh History."

2. Library Ed. (Philadelphia, 1828), II, 492.

3. *Critical Review*, 8 (1759), p. 238. The same article praises Aram as "a man of profound learning."

4. John Nichols, ed., *Illustrations of the Literary History of the Eighteenth Century* (London, 1817–1848), VII, 464–465. Maj. Charles Vallancey was a military engineer who, while stationed in Ireland, had become an ardent student of the Irish language and antiquities.

5. Volume 60, 219.

6. Volume 60, 324.

7. See Richard D. Altick, *The English Common Reader* (Chicago, 1957), chapter 2, "The Eighteenth Century"; and G. M. Trevelyan, *English Social History*, 3rd ed. (London, 1946), pp. 264–265.

8. See Leon Radzinowicz, *A History of English Criminal Law* (New York, 1948–57), I, 708–709.

9. Andrew Kippis, ed., 2nd ed. (London, 1777), I, 234–235.

10. *Enquiry Concerning Political Justice*, ed. K. Codell Carter, p. 35.

11. From a letter of April 22, 1894, to Susan Hayes Ward of the *Independent*, which had bought his first poem. *Selected Letters of Robert Frost*, ed. Lawrance Thompson (New York, 1964), pp. 20–21.

12. E. G. Bell, *Introductions to the Prose Romances, Plays, and Comedies of Edward Bulwer, Lord Lytton* (Chicago, 1914), p. 92.

13. *History of English Criminal Law*, I, 467–486.

14. The best and most recent biography of Wainewright is Charles Norman's *The Genteel Murderer* (New York, 1956).

15. John Selby Watson's life is recorded in the *Dictionary of National Biography*.

16. A. Duncan Smith, *Trial of Eugène Marie Chantrelle*, 2nd ed. (Edinburgh, 1928), p. 18.

17. May 19, 1871, p. 5, col. 1.

18. January 5, 1871, p. 8, col. 1.

19. *New York Times*, May 19, 1871, p. 5, col. 1.

20. Rulloff's explanation of his hypothesis (as quoted in the *New York Times*, Jan. 23, 1871, p. 1, col. 6) is from a letter he wrote to the *Binghamton Democratic Leader* on Jan. 16, 1871, five days after his conviction for murder. The letter declares his innocence and begs a hearing for his language theory, lest it be lost to the world by his execution.

21. In 1865 Jefferson College, the parent institution of Jefferson Medical College in Philadelphia, merged with Washington College of Washington, Pennsylvania, to become Washington and Jefferson College. At the time of Rulloff's association it was a very small school with only a handful of faculty and fewer than two hundred students. It had a reputation for instilling high principles, and although it was nondenominational, many of its graduates were destined for the ministry. See James Pyle Wickersham, *A History of Education in Pennsylvania* (Lancaster, Pa., 1886), pp. 400–403.

22. *New York Times*, April 3, 1871, p. 5, col. 2. The *Times* designation appears to have been a misnomer for the University of North Carolina in Chapel Hill, which title that institution has held since its establishment in the last decade of the eighteenth century. None of the most detailed histories of education in North Carolina or of the state university itself admits the existence of a separate "Chapel Hill College." See especially Kemp P. Battle, *History of the University of North Carolina* (Raleigh, N.C., 1907) and Charles Lee Smith, *The History of Education in North Carolina* (Washington, D.C.: GPO, 1888).

23. *New York Times*, April 23, 1871, p. 1, col. 3.

24. May 23, 1871, p. 4, col. 7.

25. *New York Times*, May 13, 1871, p. 8, col. 1.

26. Page 5, col. 4.

27. On the poor scholar, a category which rose to special prominence during the Victorian era, see Reed, pp. 94–104. For the criminal tradition in fiction, see Frank Wadleigh Chandler, *The Literature of Roguery* (Boston, 1907; rpt. New York, 1958).

28. (London, 1849), p. 282.

29. See Richard A. Zipser, *Edward Bulwer-Lytton and Germany* (Berne and Frankfurt, 1974).

30. [William Maginn], "A Good Tale Badly Told," *Fraser's Magazine*, 5 (February, 1832), 107–113.

31. The *DNB*, in an article of 1887, calls *Paul Ferroll* a "novel of great power and considerable imagination" and indicates (ironically, it now seems) that Mrs. Clive's fame rests upon it chiefly.

32. Tauchnitz Ed. of British Authors (Leipzig, 1856), p. 261. Subsequent references are to this edition.

33. August 18, 1855, pp. 947–948.

34. Volume I (Jan. 12, 1856), 192–193.

35. (New York, 1862), p. 235.

36. Volume 10 (Dec. 29, 1860), 838–839. The *Athenaeum* did not notice

Mrs. Clive's new book.

37. *Orley Farm* (New York, 1950), p. 565.

38. *Barnaby Rudge*, New Oxford Illustrated Ed. (London, 1954), p. 497.

39. *Martin Chuzzlewit*, New Oxford Illustrated Ed. (London, 1951), p. 774.

40. Jack Lindsay partly attributes to *Eugene Aram* a tragic irony in *The Mystery of Edwin Drood* (1870): Aram learns too late that he has inherited a small fortune which, had he known of it, would have made Clark's murder unnecessary—in much the same way that John Jasper, after apparently murdering Edwin Drood, discovers the prior termination of Drood's engagement, which had motivated the crime. *Charles Dickens: A Biographical and Critical Study* (London, 1950), p. 449. Another commentator suggests that Little Nell of *The Old Curiosity Shop* (1841) may "owe something to *Eugene Aram*"—presumably the deathbed scene of Houseman's little daughter. Park Honan, Introduction to *Falkland* (London, 1967), p. xiv.

41. See Richard D. Altick, "Education, Print, and Paper in *Our Mutual Friend*," in *Nineteenth-Century Literary Perspectives*, ed. Clyde de L. Ryals (Durham, N.C., 1974); and Philip Collins, *Dickens and Education* (London, 1963), *passim*.

42. *Our Mutual Friend*, New Oxford Illustrated Ed. (London, 1952), p. 518. Subsequent references are to this edition.

43. *The Godfather* (New York, 1969), p. 365.

44. *Crime and Punishment*, Norton Critical Ed., ed. George Gibian, tr. Jessie Coulson (New York, 1964), p. 219. Subsequent references are to this edition.

45. Malcolm V. Jones cites a 1971 article by a Russian scholar, B. G. Reizov, that "traces the ideological and literary antecedents of Raskolnikov back more than half a century" and finds in Bulwer's Eugene Aram, among others, "analogues of Raskolnikov's belief that crime may be justified"—*Dostoyevsky: The Novel of Discord* (London, 1976), p. 77. Jones notes as well that in Part 2, chapter VI, Razumikhin calls Raskolnikov, significantly, a "translation from a foreign language" (p. 209, n. 45). Others who have observed the Aram parallel in Dostoyevsky's work are Frank Chandler, II, 375, and Keith Hollingsworth, *The Newgate Novel*, p. 89. It is Régis Messac who argues the possibility of direct influence, in his article, "Bulwer Lytton et Dostoïevski: de Paul Clifford à Raskolnikof," *Revue de Littérature Comparée*, 1926, pp. 638–653.

46. See Edmund Wilson, *The Wound and the Bow* (New York, 1947), p. 1; Donald Fanger, *Dostoevsky and Romantic Realism* (Cambridge, Mass., 1965), *passim*; and N. M. Lary, *Dostoevsky and Dickens* (London, 1973), *passim*.

47. "Traditional Symbolism in *Crime and Punishment*," *PMLA*, 70 (1955), 979.

48. See Joseph Frank, "The World of Raskolnikov," *Encounter*, June, 1966, pp. 30–35.

49. *The Newgate Novel*, p. 89. As Raskolnikov does not confess at any length to the authorities, Hollingsworth had in mind, no doubt, his confession to Sonya in Part V, chapter 4, and to Dunya in Part VI, chapter 7.

50. "Bulwer Lytton et Dostoïevski," p. 649.

BIBLIOGRAPHY

Altick, Richard D. "Education, Print, and Paper in *Our Mutual Friend*." In *Nineteenth-Century Literary Perspectives*. Ed. Clyde de L. Ryals. Durham, N.C., 1974.

———. *The English Common Reader, a Social History of the Mass Reading Public, 1800–1900*. Chicago, 1957.

———. *The Shows of London*. Cambridge, Mass., 1978.

———. *Victorian Studies in Scarlet: Murders and Manners in the Age of Victoria*. New York, 1970.

Archives of Richard Bentley & Son 1829–1898. Microfilm Publication. Cambridge, Eng.: Chadwyck-Healey, 1976.

Baine, Rodney M. *Thomas Holcroft and the Revolutionary Novel*. Athens, Ga., 1965.

Barzun, Jacques, and Wendell Hertig Taylor. *A Catalogue of Crime*. New York, 1971.

Battle, Kemp P. *History of the University of North Carolina*. 2 vols. Raleigh, N.C., 1907.

Bell, E. G. *Introduction to the Prose Romances, Plays, and Comedies of Edward Bulwer, Lord Lytton*. Chicago, 1914.

Bingham, Madeleine. *Henry Irving and the Victorian Theatre*. London, 1978.

Biographia Britannica. 7 vols. London: W. Innys, 1747–66.

Biographia Britannica. Ed. Andrew Kippis. 2nd ed. 5 vols. London: Strahan & Bathurst, 1778–93.

"The Blood of the Innocent Calleth Loudly for Vengeance, Exemplified in the Discovery of the Murder of Daniel Clark, Fourteen Years After it was Perpetrated by Eugene Aram." London, 1809.

Booth, Michael R. *English Melodrama*. London, 1965.

Braddon, M. E. "Lord Lytton." *Belgravia*, 20 (1873), 73–88.

Brereton, Austin. *The Life of Henry Irving*. London, 1908; rpt., 2 vols. in 1, New York, 1969.

Brett, Simon. *So Much Blood*. New York, 1976.

Bristow, W., ed. "The Genuine Account of the Life and Trial of Eugene Aram, School-Master, for the Murder of Daniel Clark...." London: W. Bristow, [1759].

Brown, John. "Thackeray," *The North British Review*, 40 (1864), 210–265.

Bulwer, Edward. "Confessions and Observations of a Water-Patient, in a Letter to the Editor [Wm. Harrison Ainsworth] of the 'New Nonthly [*sic*] Magazine.'" *New Monthly Magazine*, n.s. 75 (1845), 1–16.

———. *England and the English*. Ed. Standish Meacham. Chicago, 1970.

———. *Eugene Aram. A tale. By the Author of "Pelham," "Devereux,"* &c. 3 vols. London: Colburn and Bentley, 1832.

———. *Eugene Aram. A tale*. London: Chapman and Hall, 1849.

———. "Eugene Aram, A Tragedy." *New Monthly Magazine*, n.s. 38 (1833), 401–416. Rpt. in *Eugene Aram. A tale*. London: Chapman and Hall, 1849, pp. 277–296.

———. *Falkland*. Ed. Herbert Van Thal. First Novel Library ed. London, 1967.

———. "Monos and Daimonos. A Legend." *New Monthly Magazine*, n.s. 28 (1830), 387–392.

———. "On Art in Fiction." *Monthly Chronicle: A National Journal of Politics, Literature, Science, & Art*, 1 (1838), 42–51 and 138–149.

———. "On the Faults of Recent Poets: Poems by Alfred Tennyson." Review. *New Monthly Magazine*, n.s. 37 (1833), 69–74.

———. *Pelham, or the Adventures of a Gentleman*. Ed. Jerome J. McGann. Lincoln, Neb., 1972.

———. Unpublished Letter. National Library of Scotland. MS. Blackwoods Correspondence 4086/165.

———. *Works*. Saint Botolph ed. 27 vols. Boston: Little, Brown, 1896–98.

———. *Zanoni*. Boston, 1932.

Burton, John. *Monasticon Eboracense: and The Ecclesiastical History of Yorkshire*. York, 1758.

Carlyle, Thomas. *Sartor Resartus, Book III. Fraser's Magazine*, 10 (1834), 182–193.

Cazamian, Louis. *The Social Novel in England, 1830–1850*. First published 1903. Tr. Martin Fido. London, 1973.

Chandler, Frank Wadleigh. *The Literature of Roguery*. 2 vols. Boston, 1907; rpt. New York, 1958.

Christensen, Allan C. "Edward Bulwer-Lytton of Knebworth, 25 May

1803–18 January 1873." *Nineteenth-Century Fiction*, 28 (1973), 85–86.

————. *Edward Bulwer-Lytton: The Fiction of New Regions*. Athens, Ga., 1976.

Clive, Caroline. *Paul Ferroll. A Tale. By the Author of "IX. Poems by V."* Tauchnitz Ed. of British Authors. Leipzig, 1856.

————. *Why Paul Ferroll Killed His Wife. By the Author of "Paul Ferroll."* New York, 1862.

Clubbe, John. *Victorian Forerunner: The Later Career of Thomas Hood*. Durham, N.C., 1968.

Cole, William, ed. *Story Poems, New and Old*. Cleveland, Ohio, 1957.

Collins, Arthur. *The Peerage of England*. London, 1735.

Collins, Philip. *Dickens and Crime*. London, 1962.

————. *Dickens and Education*. London, 1963.

————. "'Sikes and Nancy,' Dickens's Last Reading." *Times Literary Supplement*, June 11, 1971, pp. 681–682.

Craig, [Edward] Gordon. *Henry Irving*. New York, 1930.

Critical Review, 9 (1759), 229–238. [Rpt. of Bristow pamphlet with concluding note praising Aram.]

Cruse, Amy. *The Victorians and Their Reading*. Boston, n.d.

Dalziel, Margaret. *Popular Fiction 100 Years Ago: An Unexplored Tract of Literary History*. London, 1957.

Dent, Edward J. *A Theatre for Everybody: The Story of the Old Vic and Sadler's Wells*. London, 1945.

DeQuincey, Thomas. "William Godwin." In *Essays on the Poets, and Other English Writers*. Boston, 1865, pp. 207–218.

Dickens, Charles. *Barnaby Rudge: A Tale of the Riots of 'Eighty*. New Oxford Illus. Ed. London, 1954.

————. *The Life and Adventures of Martin Chuzzlewit*. New Oxford Illus. Ed. London, 1951.

————. *Our Mutual Friend*. New Oxford Illus. Ed. London, 1952.

Dickinson, William. *Antiquities Historical, Architectural, Chorographical, and Itinerary, in Nottinghamshire and the Adjacent Counties*. 2 vols. London, 1801.

Disher, M[aurice] Wilson. *Melodrama: Plots That Thrilled*. London, 1954.

Dobson, Austin. *Fanny Burney*. English Men of Letters Series. London, 1903.

Dobson, Jessie. "Eugene Aram." *Annals, Royal College of Surgeons, England*, 10 (1952), 267–275.

Dostoevsky, Feodor. *Crime and Punishment*. Ed. George Gibian. Tr. Jessie Coulson. Norton Critical Ed. New York, 1964.

Douglas, Lord Alfred. *Oscar Wilde: A Summing-Up.* London, 1940.

Eigner, Edwin M. "Raphael in Oxford Street: Bulwer's Accommodation to the Realists." In *The Nineteenth Century Writer and His Audience.* Lawrence, Kans., 1969, pp. 61–74.

Ekwall, Eilert. *The Concise Oxford Dictionary of English Place Names.* 4th ed. Oxford, 1960.

Eliot, George. *Felix Holt, The Radical.* Ed. Peter Coveney. Penguin English Library ed. Harmondsworth, Middlesex, 1972.

Ellis, S. M. *William Harrison Ainsworth and His Friends.* 2 vols. London, 1911.

Escott, T. H. S. *Edward Bulwer, First Baron Lytton of Knebworth, A Social, Personal, and Political Monograph.* London, 1910.

"Eugene Aram: Phrenology." *Literary Gazette*, Jan. 21, 1832, p. 25. [Letter, signed "CIVIS".]

Fanger, Donald. *Dostoevsky and Romantic Realism: A Study of Dostoevsky in Relation to Balzac, Dickens, and Gogol.* Cambridge, Mass., 1965.

Farington, Joseph. *The Diary of Joseph Farington.* 10 vols. Ed. Kenneth Garlick and Angus Macintyre. New Haven, 1979.

Farrer, William, ed. *Early Yorkshire Charters.* 12 vols. Edinburgh, 1914–65.

Flagg, Jared B. *The Life and Times of Washington Allston.* New York, 1982.

Fletcher, J. S. *Picturesque History of Yorkshire.* 6 vols. London, [1904].

Flower, Sibylla J. "Charles Dickens and Edward Bulwer-Lytton." *Dickensian*, 69 (1973), 79–89.

Foster, Joseph, ed. *Alumni Oxonienses: The Members of the University of Oxford* [1500–1714]. 4 vols. London, [1891–92].

———. *The Register of Admissions to Gray's Inn, 1521–1889.* London, 1889.

Frank, Joseph. "The World of Raskolnikov." *Encounter*, June, 1966, pp. 30–35.

Frost, Robert. *Selected Letters.* Ed. Lawrance Thompson. New York, 1964.

Fryer, Michael. *The Trial and Life of Eugene Aram; several of his letters and poems; and his plan and specimens of an Anglo-Celtic Lexicon, etc.* Richmond, Eng.: M. Bell, 1832.

Gentleman's Magazine, 102 (1832), 448. [Reminiscence of the historical Eugene Aram.]

The Genuine and Authentic Account of the Murder of Daniel Clarke, Shoemaker, on the 8th of February, 1744-5. . . . York, [1759]. [The York Pamphlet.]

Gibian, George. "Traditional Symbolism in *Crime and Punishment*." *PMLA*, 70 (1955), 979–996.

Godwin, William. *Caleb Williams*. Ed. David McCracken. London, 1970.

——. *Enquiry Concerning Political Justice*. Ed. K. Codell Carter. Oxford, 1971.

——. *Enquiry Concerning Political Justice*. Ed. F. E. L. Priestley. Toronto, 1946.

Griffiths, Maj. Arthur. *Mysteries of Police and Crime*. 3 vols. London, [1901].

Hargrove, Ely, ed. *The Genuine Account of the Trial of Eugene Aram, for the Murder of Daniel Clark, Late of Knaresbrough*....10th ed. Knaresborough, 1810.

Hazlitt, William. *The Complete Works*. 21 vols. Ed. P. P. Howe. London, 1933.

Hearn, Lafcadio. *Interpretations of Literature*. 2 vols. 1915; rpt. Port Washington, N.Y., 1965.

Heppenstall, Rayner. "The Children of Gomer." *Times Literary Supplement*, Oct. 17, 1958, p. 600.

[Heraud, John Abraham, and William Maginn.] "*The Dominie's Legacy*: Fashionable Novels." *Fraser's Magazine*, 1 (1830), 318–335.

Hibbert, Christopher. *The Road to Tyburn: The Story of Jack Sheppard and the Eighteenth-Century London Underworld*. New York, 1957.

Hoey, Frances Cashel. "Eugene Aram." *Temple Bar*, 38 (June 1873), 393–398. [Review of Wills's *Eugene Aram*.]

Holcroft, Thomas. *Memoirs of Bryan Perdue: A Novel*. 3 vols. London, 1805.

Hollingsworth, Keith. "Bulwer's *Paul Clifford* Again." *Modern Language Notes*, 66 (1951), 288. [Corrects his note in *MLN*, 63 (1948), 489–491.]

——. *The Newgate Novel 1830–1847: Bulwer, Ainsworth, Dickens and Thackeray*. Detroit, 1963.

——. "Who Suggested the Plan for Bulwer's *Paul Clifford?*" *Modern Language Notes*, 63 (1948), 489–491. [Argues Thomas Campbell rather than William Godwin.]

Hood, Thomas. *The Letters of Thomas Hood*. Ed. Peter F. Morgan. Toronto, 1973.

——. *Selected Poems of Thomas Hood*. Ed. John Clubbe. Cambridge, Mass., 1970.

——. *Works*. Ed. Frances Broderip (née Hood) and T. Hood, Jr. 7 vols. London, 1862–63.

Hunt, Leigh. "*Eugene Aram* — Mr. Bulwer's New Novel." *Tatler*, 4 (1832),

13–14. Rpt. in *Leigh Hunt's Literary Criticism*. Ed. Lawrence Huston Houtchens and Carolyn Washburn Houtchens. New York, 1956, pp. 394–400.

Inglis, James. *Phrenological Observations on the Skull of Eugene Aram, With a Prefixed Sketch of His Life and Character*. London, 1838.

Irving, Laurence. *Henry Irving, the Actor and His World*. New York, 1951.

James, Elizabeth. "The Publication of Collected Editions of Bulwer Lytton's Novels." *Publishing History*, 3 (1978), 46–60.

James, Henry. *The Scenic Art: Notes on Acting & the Drama: 1872–1901*. Ed. Allan Wade. New York, 1957.

Jeffrey, Lloyd N. *Thomas Hood*. Twayne's English Authors Series. New York, 1972.

Jensen, Gillian Fellows. *Scandinavian Settlement Names in Yorkshire*. Navnestudier udgivet af Institut for Navneforskning, Nr. 11. Copenhagen, 1972.

Jerrold, Walter. *Thomas Hood: His Life and Times*. London, 1907.

Jones, Malcolm V. *Dostoyevsky: The Novel of Discord*. London, 1976.

Jones, Rowland. *The Origin of Language and Nations, Hieroglyfically, Etymologically, and Topografically Defined and Fixed, After the Method of an English, Celtic, Greek, and Latin English Lexicon. . . .*, 1764; facsim. Menston, Yorks.: Scolar Press, 1972.

K., H. A. "Plays and Players." Review of *After All*. *Sunday Times*, Jan. 19, 1902, p. 6, col. 1.

Knight, Joseph. Review of Wills's *Eugene Aram*. *Athenaeum*, April 26, 1873, pp. 543–544.

Knipe, William. *Criminal Chronology of York Castle*. York, 1867.

Lang, Andrew, ed. *The Life and Letters of John Gibson Lockhart*. 2 vols. London, 1897.

Lary, N. M. *Dostoevsky and Dickens: A Study of Literary Influence*. London, 1973.

Lewis, Michael. *England's Sea-Officers: The Story of the Naval Profession*. London, 1948.

Lindsay, Jack. *Charles Dickens: A Biographical and Critical Study*. London, 1950.

Lively, Cheryl. "Truth in Writing: The Standard of Realism for the Novel in *Fraser's Magazine* 1830–1850." *Victorian Periodicals Newsletter*, 6 (1973), 3–10.

"Living Literary Characters, No. V—Edward Lytton Bulwer." *New Monthly Magazine*, n.s. 31 (1831), 437–450.

Lloyd, Michael. "Bulwer-Lytton and the Idealizing Principle." *English*

Miscellany, 7 (1956), 25–39.

Lytton, Edward Robert Bulwer, earl of Lytton. *The Life, Letters, and Literary Remains of Edward Bulwer, Lord Lytton*. 2 vols. London, 1883.

Lytton, Victor Alexander George Robert, 2nd earl of Lytton. *The Life of Edward Bulwer, First Lord Lytton*. 2 vols. London, 1913.

Mackenzie, Shelton. "Memoir of William Maginn, LL.D." In *Miscellaneous Writings of the Late Dr. Maginn*. 5 vols. New York, 1857, V, ix–cx.

[Maginn, William.] *Elizabeth Brownrigge: A Tale*. *Fraser's Magazine*, 6 (1832), 67–88 and 131–148.

[Maginn, William.] "A Good Tale Badly Told." Review of Bulwer's *Eugene Aram*. *Fraser's Magazine*, 5 (Feb., 1832), 107–113.

The Malefactor's Register; or, the Newgate and Tyburn Calendar. . . . 5 vols. London: Alexander Hogg, [1779].

Meadley, George Wilson. *Memoirs of William Paley, D.D.* 2nd ed. Edinburgh, 1810.

Mee, Arthur, ed. *Yorkshire: West Riding*. The King's England Series. London, 1941.

Melville, Lewis [pseud.]. *Some Aspects of Thackeray*. Boston, 1913.

Messac, Régis. "Bulwer Lytton et Dostoïevski: de Paul Clifford à Raskolnikof." *Revue de Littérature Comparée*, 1926, pp. 638–653.

———. *Le "Detective Novel" et l'Influence de la Pensée Scientifique*. Paris, 1929.

"Modern Novelists: Sir Edward Bulwer-Lytton." *Westminster Review*, 83 (1865), 468–503.

Monasticon Anglicanum. 3 vols. London, 1655–73.

Monro, D. H. *Godwin's Moral Philosophy: An Interpretation of William Godwin*. London, 1953.

Morley, Malcolm. *Margate and Its Theatres, 1730–1965*. London, 1966.

Newton, H[enry] Chance. *Crime and the Drama, or Dark Deeds Dramatized*. London, 1927.

Nichols, John, ed. *Illustrations of the Literary History of the Eighteenth Century. Consisting of Authentic Memoirs and Original Letters of Eminent Persons, and intended as a sequel to The Literary Anecdotes*. 8 vols. London, 1817–48.

———. *Literary Anecdotes of the Eighteenth Century*. 9 vols. London, 1812–15.

Nicoll, Allardyce. *British Drama*. 6th ed. rev. London, 1978.

Norman, Charles. *The Genteel Murderer*. New York, 1956. [Biography of

Wainewright.]

Norway, Arthur H. *Highways and Byways in Yorkshire*. London, 1890.

Notes and Queries, ser. 1, ii (1850), 310 and 361; ser. 1, x (1854), 361; ser. 6, xi (1885), 47, 131–132, and 254; ser. 11, i (1910), 280; ser. 11, ii (1910), 105 and 319; and [continuous ser.], clxxxvii (1944), 182.

Noyes, Russell, ed. *English Romantic Poetry and Prose*. New York, 1956.

"Obituary: Mr. Effingham Wilson." *Bookseller*, July 1, 1868, pp. 459–460.

Ousby, Ian. *Bloodhounds of Heaven: The Detective in English Fiction from Godwin to Doyle*. Cambridge, Mass., 1976.

The Oxford Companion to the Theatre. Ed. Phyllis Hartnoll. 3rd ed. London, 1967.

Parsons, James. *Remains of Japhet*. 1767; facsim. Menston, Yorks., 1968.

Paul, C[harles] Kegan. *William Godwin: His Friends and Contemporaries*. 2 vols. London, 1876.

Pegge, Samuel. Letter to Philipps. In "Original Letters of Eminent Persons on Welsh History." *Gentleman's Magazine*, 59 (1789), 905.

Phillips, Walter C. *Dickens, Reade and Collins, Sensation Novelists: A Study in the Conditions and Theories of Novel Writing in Victorian England*. New York, 1919.

Pollock, Lady [Juliet (Creed)]. "The Judgement of Paris." *Temple Bar*, 40 (1875), 391–400.

Puzo, Mario. *The Godfather*. New York, 1969.

Radzinowicz, Leon. *A History of English Criminal Law and Its Administration from 1750*. 4 vols. New York, 1948–57.

Rahill, Frank. *The World of Melodrama*. University Park, Pa., 1967.

Ray, Gordon N. *Thackeray: The Uses of Adversity*. 2 vols. New York, 1955.

Records of the Borough of Nottingham. 7 vols. Nottingham, 1882–1947.

Reed, John R. *Victorian Conventions*. Athens, Ohio, 1975.

Reid, J[ohn] C[owie]. *Thomas Hood*. London, 1963.

"The remarkable trial of Eugene Aram, of Knaresborough, in the county of York, schoolmaster, for the murder of Daniel Clark, shoemaker, committed on the 8th day of February, 1744–5." *The Annual Register, or a View of the History, Politicks, and Literature, of the Year 1759*. 2nd ed. London, 1760.

Renier, Anne. *Friendship's Offering: An Essay on the Annuals and Gift Books of the 19th Century*. London, 1964.

Renton, Richard. *John Forster and His Friendships*. New York, 1913.

REVIEWS, ANONYMOUS AND UNATTRIBUTED:

After All. Athenaeum, Jan. 25, 1902, p. 124.

Daddleton's Difficulties, second piece to Wills's *Eugene Aram*. *Sunday Times*, May 18, 1873, p. 3, col. 3.

Eugene Aram. A tale. Athenaeum, Jan. 7, 1832, pp. 3–5.

Eugene Aram. A tale. Edinburgh Review, 55 (1832), 208–219.

Eugene Aram. A tale. Examiner, no. 1251 (Jan. 22, 1832), 51–52.

Eugene Aram. A tale. Monthly Review, Feb. 1832, p. 302.

Eugene Aram. A tale. Spectator, 5 (1832), 16–19.

"*Eugene Aram* at the Lyceum." *Saturday Review*, 35 (April 1873), 550–551. [Wills's *Eugene Aram*.]

"Eugene Aram at the Lyceum." *Times*, April 21, 1873, p. 8, cols. 4–5. [Wills's *Eugene Aram*.]

The Gem, a Literary Annual, ed. Thomas Hood. *Literary Gazette*, Oct. 18, 1828, pp. 661–663.

The Ku-Klux-Klan, second piece to revival of Moncrieff's *Eugene Aram*. *Sunday Times*, May 18, 1873, p. 3, col. 3.

Moncrieff's *Eugene Aram*. *Times*, Feb. 9, 1832, p. 3, col. 2.

"Mr Bulwer's Eugene Aram." *Spectator*, 5 (1832), 16–19.

"Mr. Martin Harvey as Eugene Aram." *Illustrated London News*, 120 (1902), 118.

"Mr. Wills's New Drama." *Sunday Times*, April 27, 1873, p. 3, cols. 1–2.

Paul Ferroll. Athenaeum, Aug. 18, 1855, pp. 947–948.

Paul Ferroll. Saturday Review, 1 (1856), 192–193.

Why Paul Ferroll Killed His Wife. Saturday Review, 10 (1860), 838–839.

Wills's *Eugene Aram*. *Illustrated London News*, 62 (1873), 402.

Robertson, John. "Sir Lytton Bulwer." *Westminster Review*, 39 (1843), 33–69.

Robinson, Henry Crabb. *Henry Crabb Robinson: On Books and Their Writers*. Ed. Edith J. Morley. 3 vols. London, 1938; rpt. New York, 1967.

Roose-Evans, James. *London Theatre from the Globe to the National*. Oxford, 1977.

Rosa, Matthew Whiting. *The Silver-Fork School: Novels of Fashion Preceding* Vanity Fair. New York, 1936.

Rothstein, Eric. "Allusion and Analogy in the Romance of *Caleb Williams*." *University of Toronto Quarterly*, 37 (Oct., 1967), 18–30.

Sadleir, Michael. *Bulwer: A Panorama: Edward and Rosina, 1803–1836*. Boston, 1931.

Scatcherd, Norrisson. *Memoirs of the Celebrated Eugene Aram: With the "Gleanings" After Eugene Aram . . . .* 2nd ed. Harrogate, 1871.

Scholes, Percy. *The Great Doctor Burney*. 2 vols. London, 1948.

Scott, Clement. *The Drama of Yesterday & To-day*. 2 vols. London, 1899.

Scott, Sir Walter. Review of Godwin's *Fleetwood. Edinburgh Review*, 6 (1805), 182–193.

Shepperson, Archibald Bolling. *The Novel in Motley*. Cambridge, Mass., 1936.

Sherson, Erroll. *London's Lost Theatres of the Nineteenth Century*. London, 1925.

Smith, A. Duncan. *Trial of Eugène Marie Chantrelle*. 2nd ed. Edinburgh, 1928.

Smith, Charles Lee. *The History of Education in North Carolina*. Contributions to Am. Educational History, no. 3. Bureau of Education Circular of Information, no. 2. Washington, D.C.: GPO, 1888.

Smith, James and Horace. *Rejected Addresses: or the New Theatrum Poetarum*. London, 1812; facsim. *Rejected Addresses and Horace in London*. New York, 1977.

Smollett, Tobias. *The History of England, From the Revolution in 1688 to the Death of George II*. Library Ed. 2 vols. Philadelphia, 1828.

Speight, Harry. *Nidderdale and the Garden of the Nidd: a Yorkshire Rhineland. Being a complete account, historical, scientific, and descriptive of the beautiful valley of the Nidd*. London, 1894.

_____. *Upper Nidderdale, with the forest of Knaresborough, being a record of the history, antiquities, scenery, old homes, families, &c. of that romantic district*. London, 1906.

Stephen, Leslie. "Art and Morality." *The Cornhill Magazine*, 32 (1875), 91–101.

_____. "The Decay of Murder." *Cornhill*, 20 (1869), 722–733.

_____. "The Late Lord Lytton as a Novelist." *Cornhill*, 27 (1873), 345–354. Rpt. in *Men, Books, and Mountains: Essays by Leslie Stephen*. Ed. Samson O. A. Ullman. Minneapolis, 1956, pp. 112–127.

_____. *Studies of a Biographer*. 4 vols. New York, 1899–1902.

Stephens, J. R. "*Jack Sheppard* and the Licensers: The Case Against Newgate Plays." *Nineteenth Century Theatre Research*, 1 (1973), 1–13.

Stevenson, Burton Egbert, comp. *The Home Book of Verse, American and English*. 2 vols. 9th ed. New York, 1953.

Stevenson, Lionel, ed. *Victorian Fiction: A Guide to Research*. Cambridge, Mass., 1964.

Stoker, Bram. *Personal Reminiscences of Henry Irving*. 2 vols. New York, 1906.

Stottler, James F. "A Victorian Stage Adapter at Work: W. G. Wills 'Rehabilitates' the Classics." *Victorian Studies*, 16, no. 4 (1973), 401–432.

Summers, Montague. *A Gothic Bibliography*. London, [1941].

Symons, Julian. *Mortal Consequences: A History — From the Detective Story to the Crime Novel*. New York, 1972.

Talfourd, Sir Thomas Noon. *Memoirs of Charles Lamb*. Ed. Percy Fitzgerald. London, 1892.

Tennyson, Alfred Lord. "The New Timon, and the Poets." *Punch*, 10 (1846), 103.

Tennyson, Sir Charles. "Tennyson and 'the New Timon.'" *The Nineteenth Century and After*, 109 (1931), 756–764.

Thackeray, William Makepeace. *The Complete Works*. 25 vols. London, 1903.

_____. "*Ernest Maltravers*." Review. *Fraser's Magazine*, 17 (1838), 85–89.

_____. "George de Barnwell." *Punch*, 12 (1847), 136–137, 146–147, 155.

_____. "Going to See a Man Hanged." *Fraser's Magazine*, 22 (1840), 150–158.

_____. *The Letters and Private Papers of William Makepeace Thackeray*. Ed. Gordon N. Ray. 4 vols. Cambridge, Mass., 1945–46.

Thoroton, Robert. *Thoroton's History of Nottinghamshire: Republished, with Large Additions, by John Throsby*. 3 vols. Nottingham, 1790–97.

Thrall, Miriam M. H. *Rebellious Fraser's: Nol Yorke's Magazine in the Days of Maginn, Thackeray, and Carlyle*. Columbia Univ. Studies in English and Comparative Literature, no. 117. New York, 1934.

Trevelyan, G. M. *English Social History*. 3rd ed. London, 1946.

Trodd, Anthea. "Michael Angelo Titmarsh and the Knebworth Apollo." *Costerus*, n.s. 2 (1974), 59–81.

Trollope, Anthony. *Orley Farm*. New York, 1950.

Twyford, Capt. A. W. *York and York Castle: An Appendix to the 'Records of York Castle.'* London, [1883].

Victoria Regina. *The Girlhood of Queen Victoria: A Selection from Her Majesty's Diaries Between the Years 1832 and 1840*. Ed. Reginald Baliol Brett, 2nd viscount Esher. 2 vols. London, 1912.

Walton, James. "'Mad Feary Father': *Caleb Williams* and the Novel Form." In *Romantic Reassessment*. Salzburg Studies in English Literature, No. 47. Salzburg, 1975, pp. 1–61.

Waters, Sampson. *Knaresborough Castle: With Introduction on the Feudal System, Reform of the House of Lords, Socialism, the Referendum, and Cabinet Reform, by Sampson Waters, B.A., Christ*

Church, Oxford, Harrovian, Barrister-at-Law. Bristol, 1915.

Watson, Eric R. *Eugene Aram: His Life and Trial*. Notable English Trials Series. Edinburgh, 1913.

Watts, James C. *Great Novelists: Scott, Thackeray, Dickens, Lytton*. London, 1880.

Webb, John. *Historical Essay Endeavoring a Probability that the Language of the Empire of China is the Primitive Language*. London, 1669.

Weintraub, Stanley. *Beardsley: A Biography*. New York, 1967.

Whiteford, Robert Naylor. *Motives in English Fiction*. New York, 1918.

Wickersham, James Pyle, *A History of Education in Pennsylvania, Private and Public, Elementary and Higher, from the time the Swedes settled on the Delaware to the Present Day*. Lancaster, Pa., 1886.

Wiles, Roy McKeen. *Freshest Advices: Early Provincial Newspapers in England*. Columbus, Ohio, 1965.

Willis, Nathaniel Parker. *Pencillings by the Way*. Letter CXIX, 1835. Rpt. in *Library of Literary Criticism*. 8 vols. Ed. Charles Moulton. New York, 1966.

Wilson, A[lbert] E[dward]. *East End Entertainment*. London, 1954.

Wilson, Edmund. *The Wound and the Bow: Seven Studies in Literature*. New York, 1947.

Wodehouse, P. G. *Bertie Wooster Sees It Through*. London, 1946.

Wood, A[lfred] C[ecil]. *A History of Nottinghamshire*. Nottingham, 1947.

Woodcock, George. *William Godwin: A Biographical Study*. London, 1946.

Zipser, Richard A. *Edward Bulwer-Lytton and Germany*. Berne and Frankfurt, 1974.

INDEX